Twentieth Century Drifter

T0097726

© 2012 by Diane Diekman
All rights reserved
∞ This book is printed on acid-free paper.

The Library of Congress cataloged the cloth edition as follows:
Diekman, Diane.
Twentieth century drifter : the life of Marty Robbins / Diane Diekman.
p.   cm. — (Music in American life)
Includes bibliographical references and index.
ISBN 978-0-252-03632-3 (hardcover : alk. paper)
1. Robbins, Marty. 2. Country musicians—United States—Biography.
3. Automobile racing drivers—United States—Biography. I. Title.
ML420.R663D54   2012
782.421642092—dc23   2011031779
[B]

Paperback ISBN 978-0-252-08125-5

Dedicated to

my sister and research assistant
Lorraine "Kayo" Diekman Paver

and

in memory of
Barbara J. Pruett (1942–2010) and
Bill D. Johnson (1939–2009)

Contents

Preface

The idea of Marty Robbins as my second biography subject came to me while doing research for *Live Fast, Love Hard: The Faron Young Story*. I was watching an episode of *The Marty Robbins Spotlight*, with Faron as Marty's guest. Marty has always been one of my favorite singers, and I liked his connections to NASCAR and the U.S. Navy. I asked myself the same question I'd asked about Faron: Would I ever tire of hearing his music or talking about him? I remember painting our farmhouse while "Tonight Carmen" played on the transistor radio my parents gave me at my high school graduation. It's still my favorite Marty Robbins song. My only meeting with Marty occurred at the Grand Ole Opry in 1972, when we posed together for a photo on the steps of the Ryman Auditorium.

Marty possessed the innate ability to sing any style of music, from traditional country to rockabilly or western ballads to popular standards. Throughout his career, he experimented with varying styles to bring his music to larger and more diverse audiences. He is still unparalleled as a writer of story songs, especially western ballads, but also dark stories like "The Chair," about capital punishment. He repeatedly said love songs were his favorite to sing, followed by western ballads; he only stopped recording those styles when fans stopped buying them.

Deep insecurities, both personal and financial, plagued Marty his entire life. He never outgrew his father's rejection or his poverty-stricken childhood. He discovered as a child that being the class clown covered up those insecurities, and he later developed an outsized stage persona to overcome his shyness.

Faron and Marty possessed similar backgrounds, and both craved attention. But while Faron would rather have negative attention than none at all, Marty required approval. He was a perfectionist who spoke properly, dressed sharply, and constantly worked on his music. Stage performances had to sound like the records, because he only gave his audience the best. He set tough standards for himself and demanded the same of others.

Marty showed the typical attitudes of his generation, believing the music industry was no place for a woman and referring to his office staff as "my little secretaries." He encouraged his son in a singing career but refused to allow his wife and daughter to attend his shows—although he did eventually hire his daughter to work in the office.

When I began my interviews, the comments about Marty were so over-whelmingly positive that I started searching for flaws. No one is perfect, after all, and I wanted to give a balanced view. Indications of stubbornness and a hot temper, especially in his earlier years, were all I could find. He seemed to be universally loved, admired, and respected.

My research didn't turn up any promiscuity. But considering Marty's need for attention, the culture of the entertainment business, the availability of doting women, and the time away from home, it seems highly improbable he would have resisted temptation. He had the power to insist on confidentiality and the loyal followers to give it. In a belated attempt to address the issue, I asked Jack Pruett for comment and was told, "You know good and well I wouldn't answer that question. I'll let you use your own judgment." Okie Jones said, "Well, I better not touch that. Let's just leave it like that."

The only book I found about Marty was Barbara Pruett's bibliography, *Marty Robbins: Fast Cars and Country Music*. I purchased a copy and wrote in it, "Merry Christmas to me, 2005." Several years later, Barbara contacted me and we met for coffee. She said she'd put together her collection of resource material with the hope it would be used for a Robbins biography. She wanted to read my completed manuscript but was in the hospital when I finished it. I couldn't contact her, and she died without us speaking again. Knowing the amount of research a biography requires, I'm not sure I would have tackled this without Barbara's book as a starting point.

Bill Johnson, one of the first band members I located, had gone to the Nashville library after Marty's death and copied every newspaper article that mentioned Marty. He sent me his complete file, along with lists compiled by Donnie Jennings from Oklahoma. Bill and I had numerous telephone conver-sations, and I looked forward to meeting him. Unfortunately, he died a few months before I organized a reunion of The Marty Robbins Band in Nashville.

Of forty-seven band members identified in my research, I spoke with twenty-five of the twenty-eight still living.

Ralph Emery gave me thirty hours of audio tape of *The Ralph Emery Show* with Marty as his guest on WSM radio. This wonderful resource allowed me to include Marty's voice throughout the book.

My sister, Lorraine "Kayo" Paver, served as my research assistant, traveling companion, and index maker. I relied on her willingness to make telephone calls and her ability to keep conversations flowing.

I am indebted to the Internet Writing Workshop members who critiqued and improved the book chapters as I wrote them. My special thanks go to Gary Presley, who critiqued individual chapters and then read the entire manuscript to help me condense it.

Tad Ringo is my editor, and I enjoy my continuing association with the University of Illinois Press. During five years of working on Marty's biography, I obtained interviews or other information from almost one hundred people. Bill Hulme, Jo Wenger, Dominique Anglares, Sue Middagh, and Sherwin Linton are among those who sent me documents. John Rumble and Mick Buck provided assistance at the Country Music Hall of Fame, and Skip Jackson took Kayo and me to the Fairgrounds Speedway. Kayo and I had several enjoyable visits with Marty's son, Ronny, and I conducted a telephone interview with Marty's daughter, Janet.

If I've neglected someone who should be thanked, I apologize for any oversight. I'm grateful for all assistance in completing this project.

I'm a listener and a dancer, not a musician, and I don't feel personally qualified to analyze or give an aesthetic judgment on Marty's music. My goal is to bring the story of his life and music to people who remember him and to those who might discover this legendary artist. I hope readers will want to find his songs and listen to them, either again or for the first time.

Marty was a drifter, in the sense of always seeking something and never finding it. That "something" was security. His drifter mentality kept him aloof, searching for acceptance and approval but never getting too close to or trustful of others. He was always the little boy wandering the desert, longing for a stable home and a father who loved him. We can still hear the drifter today, singing and searching in the timeless songs of Marty Robbins.

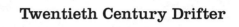

Twentieth Century Drifter

In the Hall of Fame

It was October 11, 1982, and Marty Robbins sat in the audience at the Grand Ole Opry House near Nashville, Tennessee, during the Country Music Association's nationally televised awards show. He believed in dressing up for awards shows, and his pinstriped swallowtail coat with vest, ruffled white shirt and black bow-tie fit that description. A red handkerchief peeked from his breast pocket, and his large round eyeglasses held photochromic lenses. A country music star for thirty years, he was one of five nominees in the "active performer" category for the Country Music Hall of Fame. With this being his first time as a finalist, he didn't expect to hear his name called.

Eddy Arnold, elected sixteen years earlier, stood on the stage. He had been chosen to reveal the newest member, and he announced, "Marty Robbins, come up here."

Throwing back his head in surprise, Robbins grinned and stood. As he started toward the stage, he paused to turn and wave to the audience. Arnold whipped the red cover from an easel, revealing a large bronze plaque, and said, "Welcome to the Hall of Fame, Marty."

At the microphone, Robbins glanced at the engraved bronze likeness and joked, "Well, I don't know—somebody's looking at me." Appearing genuinely happy, he said, "I never had any idea that this would happen, because I really feel there are other people that deserve it, y'know, before I should get it, but I have a feeling, y'know, possibly, that it might not happen again, so I'm gonna take it tonight." He told the audience, "And I thank everybody that had anything to do with it."[1]

Eight weeks later he was dead. His fourth heart attack took his life on December 8, 1982, at age fifty-seven. The first heart attack occurred during a NASCAR race in 1968 and went undiagnosed. A major heart attack in August 1969 led to triple bypass surgery the following January. His third heart attack came eleven years later. Each time he had returned to an active schedule of singing and racing.

"I certainly thought he deserved the Hall of Fame honor and was happy that he received it," says "Whispering" Bill Anderson. "When he died such a short time later, I was especially glad that he knew in this lifetime how much he was admired and appreciated."[2]

Longtime Grand Ole Opry star Charlie Louvin calls "the passing of Marty Robbins" the Opry's greatest loss. "There've been others, naturally," he says, "but I think Marty was the biggest loss the Opry has taken."[3]

During his three decades of recording, Marty Robbins placed ninety-four songs on *Billboard*'s country music charts, four of them after his death. Sixteen reached number one, including his first charted song ("I'll Go On Alone") in early 1953. He received two Grammy awards for songs he wrote and recorded, "El Paso" and "My Woman, My Woman, My Wife." The Academy of Country Music honored him with its Man of the Decade Award in 1970.

"No artist in the history of country music has had a more stylistically diverse career than Marty Robbins," states one music guide.[4] His Hawaiian songs, rockabilly hits, teen ballads, gunfighter ballads, pop standards, and straight country songs showcased his versatility. He hosted television shows and starred in movies about country music, cowboys, and stock car racing. When the Grand Ole Opry moved from the Ryman Auditorium to the new Opry House at Nashville's Opryland in 1974, Robbins was the last performer at the old location and one of the first at the new.

"He knew how to work that Opry crowd," a fan recalls. "He would sing a song, and the show was supposed to be over at midnight, and he'd run over to the side of the stage—and people would be going nuts—and he would take his hand and move the clock back, like a quarter to twelve, and he kept on singing."[5]

In addition to music and the Old West, Robbins loved stock car racing. From a hobby at Nashville's Fairgrounds Speedway, he moved into the NASCAR circuit. "He started out being a singer driving a race car, but he became a race car driver who could sing," NASCAR's Bobby Allison says. "He could drive," comments NASCAR driver/owner James Hylton. "There's no doubt about it, if he'd put full time into racing like he did his singing, he could have been a winner."[6]

His best NASCAR finish was fifth place in the 1974 Motorstate 400 at the Michigan International Speedway. "Marty felt like he didn't want to take the money from those guys by beating them," says NASCAR legend Cotton Owens. "He was running fourth and actually backed off to let a car pass him there at the end, because he didn't want to take the money from that guy."[7]

A 1973 magazine article described Robbins at a race as follows: "The boots he wears, with two-inch stacked heels, just boost him up to about 5-feet 9-inches. He's short and wiry, hard-muscled . . . his hair's getting longer now, mussed and matted and sun-bleached to a color that's almost strawberry roan; the mustache barely slips around the corners of his mouth. . . . His eyes, even hidden behind the bronze-tinted glasses, are open and honest."[8]

Robbins combined singing and racing interests when he wrote and recorded a ballad called "Twentieth Century Drifter." It honored the dedicated race car drivers who barely earn enough money to feed their families but keep dreaming of an eventual win. It also captured a yearning of Robbins himself. When asked in 1981 if he had everything he'd always wanted, the country music superstar replied, "No, no. I want security. I don't have it yet."[9]

Such an answer might surprise anyone unfamiliar with the history of Martin David Robinson, the son of a hardworking frontier mother and abusive alcoholic father. After a childhood of moving from shack to tent to shack in the Arizona desert, he spent his early teens in trouble with the law. Then came World War II combat in the South Pacific, followed by an assortment of short-term jobs before being hired as a singer and guitar player in 1947. The shy young man walked onstage singing because he was too nervous to talk. His only words during those early performances were, "My next song is . . ." and "Thank you."[10]

He changed his name to Marty Robbins, developed a stage presence, and established himself as an entertainer, songwriter, and NASCAR driver. Although still searching for security, he was adored by thousands of fans around the world.

[2]

Child of the Arizona Desert

Martin David Robinson was born at 9:55 PM on Saturday, September 26, 1925, five minutes before his twin sister, Mamie Ellen. They joined the family of Jack and Emma Robinson and five children. Lillie, seven at the time, remembers their Grandma Heckle had come to spend a few days, a visit that pleased her because of enjoyable times they spent together. Grandma woke the children on Sunday morning and told them of a surprise in their mother's room. Lillie recalls, "Mamma was still in bed, which was unusual. On a cot were two tiny babies, each with a fist in its mouth. Grandma said the doctor had come during the night and brought two little twin babies." When Lillie asked which was the boy, Grandma Heckle proudly pointed, and Lillie covered the baby's face with the blanket. She didn't want another brother. Three were enough.

She says she didn't know she was "covering the face of a future great country and western singer and composer."[1] With his father's charm and his mother's work ethic and integrity, the boy would someday be Marty Robbins.

Emma, born in 1890, was a daughter of Texas Bob and Anna Heckle. Raised on the Arizona frontier, she and her twelve siblings learned to ride and rope, while sharing chores and struggling to make a living. At nineteen, Emma married Dan Cavaness because she was pregnant and her father insisted on a wedding. Two years later Cavaness returned to his family ranch, leaving Emma with a toddler, Robert (nicknamed Pat), and an infant, Anna Mae.

Jack Joe Maczinski, born of Polish immigrants in 1890, left his home state of Michigan to avoid the World War I draft. He moved to Arizona and changed his name to Robinson. In February 1917, he met Emma Heckle Cavaness, divorced and working at a boarding house in Phoenix. An attractive man with brown hair and mustache, Jack matched curly-headed Emma in height, approximately five-eight. They married three months later.[2] Lillie was born in 1918, followed by Johnny in 1920 and George in 1922.

The Robinson family lived a nomadic existence. Jack's attempts to provide for his growing family were hampered by his alcoholism, his temper, and his thievery. His skills were carpentry, mechanics, and smooth talk. Emma's relatives often found jobs for him or offered his family a place to stay. But he would get in an argument or steal something, and they would move again.

"This must have been humiliating to my mother," Mamie says, "who had the pride of a generation that, even though they grew up in the hills, took care of their own. Dad, being an Easterner with a totally different background—and I think of a larcenous nature—was not blessed or burdened with this virtue. That Mom's family tolerated him at all was a miracle, and probably due to pity and love for Mom and her brood."[3]

Martin and Mamie were born in a shack on the desert eight miles north of Glendale, a town established three decades earlier when the Arizona Canal project brought water to the desert. Jack had dismantled an abandoned shack and hauled the pieces in his old pickup to an unclaimed spot near a bridge along the main road to Glendale. Then called Lateral Eighteen of the Arizona Canal, the road was later renamed 59th Avenue. Pregnant Emma and teenaged Pat helped build one main room to serve as the parents' bedroom and dining room. They added a smaller room for the children's bedroom and a lean-to for the kitchen. Jack constructed beds from discarded lumber and old bed springs he found in deserted houses.[4] "He wasn't always particular whether a place was deserted or not, especially if something was in sight and he could haul it," Lillie remembers.

One day Jack drove home in a stolen car, chained it to the house, and hid himself in a mesquite thicket upon seeing a sheriff's car arriving. When the deputies found the car and left to get an arrest warrant, Jack escaped in the stolen car. He told Emma he would send for the family. Eventually he did, and Emma's brother moved her and the children to join Jack at a ranch on the Agua Fria River, east of Prescott.

They later moved to Humboldt where Jack got a job at a smelter. Around spring 1929, Lillie recalls, "A car drove into the yard and, as usual, Daddy ran and climbed under the house." The men looking for him left when told he was gone, and Jack escaped that night in his car. Emma ran out of money and food during the next few weeks, but she refused to ask for help. When Lillie confessed to her teacher she had no lunch and had not eaten breakfast, the teacher fed the Robinson children. That evening, visitors brought a supply of groceries. Although Emma gave Lillie one of her worst spankings, Lillie considered it worth the price.

A few days later the children came home to find their mother in the midst of packing, a not uncommon scene in their young lives. Jack arrived after dark in a Ford Model T with headlights turned off and drove behind the house to load their belongings.[5]

The twins were almost four years old, and Mamie vaguely remembers stopping for several days along Black Canyon Highway when the truck broke down. They took shelter under a huge tree with dense branches hanging down to form a room. Emma set up a stove and placed cots and lanterns all around.

"I was enjoying everything about this playhouse," Mamie says, "so I was real surprised when the 'roof' leaked and everything and everyone began to get a soaking." Jack stretched a tarp over the back of the truck, and the family huddled there until the rain stopped.[6]

Their next home was near Cave Creek Dam, where Emma's brother-in-law helped Jack get hired at White's Mine. Emma and her sister cooked for the miners. Following a confrontation between the two men, Jack took his family back to the house where Martin and Mamie had been born; later, they moved to Phoenix when he found a new job.

Emma took in washing and ironing to help feed the family. Lillie, Johnny, and George attended Longfellow school in Phoenix. The children enjoyed living along the railroad tracks and getting acquainted with the hobos, who cooked over a campfire and made delicious soup. "There were many days the family would not have eaten had it not been for the hobos," Lillie recalls. "Some of them were always bringing something for the family, maybe a sack of onions or day-old bread."[7]

When the Robinsons left that house, they moved to an empty lot in the same school district. At 1701 East Madison Street, Jack constructed a shelter consisting of a tent for sleeping quarters and a spot for cooking. Using tin and lumber scrounged from the city dump and wherever else he could find it, he added a room that became the kitchen and the parents' bedroom. The twins slept with Emma, and Jack had his own bed. Their "house of advertising" was covered with soft drink signs—Coca Cola, Whistle Soda, Delaware Punch, and others. With no hobos to bring food, they sometimes had little to eat.

Emma managed to retain a sense of humor in spite of work and stress. Lillie remembers coming home from school one day and sitting on the kitchen stool while her mother made supper. She described what she'd learned in English class, and Emma asked her what part of speech "but" was. Lillie replied, "A conjunction." Emma told her, "Get your conjunction off my stool and set the table for supper."[8]

Jack supported his family by operating a garbage-hauling route. The 1930 U.S. census lists him as a business owner and a truck driver in the garbage industry. He brought home vegetables plucked from the garbage, and generous customers on the route often provided toys and clothing. Emma used her old Singer treadle sewing machine to remake items into clothing for her children. Jack built an additional room onto the front of their dirt-floor shack, and he designed an oil heater that burned used oil collected from service stations.[9]

When twins Harley and Charley were born in June 1930, a neighbor lady acted as midwife. The Robinsons could not afford doctors, and their only way of receiving assistance for medical emergencies was to contact county health authorities.[10]

Martin began playing a harmonica at age four. "He was always making some kind of music," Mamie says. "Just sitting at the table he'd take a knife or fork and hit on everything and try different sounds." One of his uncles encouraged him, often playing the fiddle for Martin to accompany with his harmonica. Emma had an old wind-up Victrola record player, and she enjoyed listening to records while she fixed dinner. One of her favorites was a Jimmie Rodgers tune, "All Around the Water Tank (Waiting for a Train)." Martin sang along, to his mother's great pride.[11]

The family attended Open Door Mission Church, a large tent with sawdust spread over the ground, located at the corner of 17th and Washington Streets. Mamie remembers five-year-old Martin being coaxed to sing and play his harmonica. The offer of a nickel or dime would overcome his shyness, and he then enjoyed the attention he received. "I was always in his shadow," Mamie says, "but that suited me just fine. Whatever good happened to him made me just as happy as it did him. We were always together, making our own conversation and good times." Their eldest sister, Ann, taught their Sunday School class, and she frequently had her five students sing for the congregation. One day she was teaching them a new song, and Martin said, "Ah, Sis, you just tell us the words and we'll do the singing." At age five Martin was awarded a Bible for singing in church.[12]

Christmas celebrations would have been few, according to Lillie, if not for the Masonic Lodge. Masons brought presents and groceries. When Jack worked at the smelter in Humboldt, he bought Christmas presents at the company store, on credit, before losing his job. A man from the store came after Christmas to take the toys back. One year the children searched the desert until they found a creosote bush shaped like a pine tree. Emma helped them decorate it. "We did all we could to make this scraggy desert plant look festive," Mamie recalls. "It wasn't long till we had the spirit of the season."[13]

Marty once told an interviewer, "I had a little iron truck when I was about six years old. I played with it all the time, see. About two weeks before Christmas, it disappeared. Christmas morning I opened up this package and here's a little green truck, looked just like the red one." He said he received the same toy wrecker five years in a row, painted a different color and looking new every year. In Mamie's version, Emma had the children fix and wrap their old toys themselves. Emma then wrote names on the packages and placed them under the tree on Christmas Eve. The surprise was seeing which package each child would open.[14]

Jack uprooted his family again in the summer of 1931 when he became caretaker of a hog ranch. They moved into an abandoned two-room shack near Cactus, twelve miles north of Phoenix. Emma slept with the twins in the kitchen/living room and the older children shared the bedroom. Her husband built himself a small room away from the house.[15] Jack still operated his Phoenix garbage route. Before the garbage went to the hogs, the family retrieved useable food.

This was a relatively prosperous time for the Robinsons, with cows and chickens to provide milk and eggs. Emma made delicious stew with rabbits she shot. "Mamma was the hunter," Lillie recalls, "and had an old twelve gauge shotgun. When she aimed at something she always got it. If she didn't, there might not be a meal for the family. No one could cook rabbit like Mamma could."[16]

Martin and Mamie entered first grade in the autumn of 1931 and spent two years at Sunnyside School, a two-room structure housing grades one through eight. They rode the bus with their three siblings. "There was my older sister, two older brothers, and my twin sister," Marty said in an interview. "I remember times when we did not have lunch, and people would get together and bring a lunch for us to have. So I know what it is to be poor."[17]

The twins handled their shyness in opposite ways. Mamie cried and begged to sit close to Martin. When he got tired of her clinging, she was moved next to Lillie. Martin compensated for his shyness by becoming class clown. Hiding his fears, he quickly made friends and was well liked. During a school play, he dressed as a package and sang a verse. "This was right up his alley and he gave it all he had," Mamie recalls. "Martin looked for attention, and thrived on it."[18]

Even his busy mother succumbed to his charms. Both Mamie and Lillie remember Martin as Emma's favorite child. "The feeling was mutual," Mamie says, "and he never lost that love or ever stopped wanting to do as much as he could for her. I never remember a time when she got mad at him, criticized or abused him in any way, verbally or physically. She must have known he was special in some way." Mamie believes Emma's support gave Martin courage to go forward, even when feeling self-conscious and awkward. Being spoiled by his mother made him "a bit obnoxious to others at times, but she seemed unaware of it," Mamie says. "He was her only topic of conversation, even before he became a success. It seemed to me he was always allowed to do exactly what he wanted to do."[19]

Music was one thing Martin had in common with his father. Jack played a harmonica, danced Polish jigs, and sang German songs when in a good mood. But Jack's good moods seldom lasted long. On nights he didn't return from his garbage route at the expected time the family waited in fear, wondering whether he would come home a bad drunk or a good drunk. After putting the children to bed Emma sat by a window, watching until she saw headlights. Then she would get into bed and everyone would pretend to be asleep. If the house was cold, Jack might get the boys out of bed to go fetch firewood. Or he might send Emma outside to chop wood, even if a stack sat nearby.[20]

"Dad was a stern, impatient person and would not hesitate to take the belt to any one of us he thought deserved it," Mamie explains. "He was not fair in any sense of the word. So a whipping mostly depended on his mood at the time—or whoever was closest to him." She adds, "I never got over my fear of his temper tantrums, when he would throw hammers or whatever else he had in his hand." When drinking, he was either very happy or very violent, and the family never knew which mood to expect.[21]

After two years in Cactus—the longest they had lived anywhere—the Robinsons moved back to Glendale. Lillie says they moved so she could attend high school. Marty blamed his father's drinking: "We could have been wealthy, I believe, because at one time we had a section of land in Arizona and could have bought all the land we wanted for a dollar an acre, and my father was capable of buying it. We had a hog ranch, my father had three trucks, and had the franchise from the garbage route in Phoenix, Arizona, hauling garbage, feeding it to the pigs—and he started drinking. And that was the end of that."[22]

Their new home, a mile from the twins' birthplace, was much like all other shacks in which they'd lived. Martin and Mamie spent their days playing in the desert, grateful to be away from the endless bickering at home. The eight-year-old twins worried about their mother, after realizing she should not have to tolerate their father's drinking and cruelty. "We would talk about growing up and marrying each other and taking care of Mom," Mamie says. "She seemed old to us, and we were afraid she was going to die."[23]

Emma lost an important source of support when her parents died in late 1931. They had both been ill, and Texas Bob died two months after Anna. For a time, Emma's sister Ellen lived near the Robinsons. "We were fortunate in having our cousins nearby to play with and their home to give us a refuge when needed," Mamie says. "Many times we had to walk to their place to stay out of reach of a drunken, mean and dangerous father." She felt safe with her relatives, saying, "Uncle Mart would play his fiddle for us all and it was like a party, except we knew Mom was back there with him and there was nothing we could do about it." Emma kept Harley and Charley by her side, which made Jack less likely to bother her. Mamie says, "It was amazing that he could be so happy and fun loving sometimes, and turn into a raging fool at other times. During his drunken periods, he would fly off at anyone close at hand. So we tried hard to stay out of his way."[24]

Martin and Mamie enrolled in the third grade at Peoria Elementary School on September 14, 1933. "As before, new clothes arrived from somewhere," Mamie remembers. "Sometimes clothes may have come from the county, because we always had new ones at the start of the school year even when we had no money to buy them." Clothes didn't stay new for long, though, when each child possessed only one set. Lillie's high school dresses were furnished by the welfare department, where dresses of different-colored fabric were sewn from the same pattern. The style of her dress marked her as being on welfare.[25]

When Emma was hospitalized with double pneumonia, Lillie dropped out of school to care for three-year-old Harley and Charley. Johnny, George, and the older twins still attended school. "I know what it is like to be laughed at because your shoe doesn't have a sole in it and because your pants have a hole in them," Marty told an interviewer in 1981. "Not only by other kids but I know what it's like to be ridiculed by a teacher. That used to hurt me so much." He said, "I never really cared too much for school. I guess because we moved around so much when I was little; I'd lose friends and go to new schools. We were poor. We never had nice clothes. Even then, as young as I was, I could still be embarrassed by having torn clothes."[26]

Classmate Earl Romine remembers Martin as "this mischievous little guy always teasing his sister." He recalls sitting against the outside of the school building, eating one of his mother's homemade fried pies, when "this little guy" walked up and said, "I'd like to have a bite of that pie." Romine offered to bring a bite the next day, and he brought Martin a whole pie.[27]

Martin excelled in sports. He could run fast and throw straight. In spite of his small size, he was always chosen first for football and baseball teams and usually won his wrestling challenges. Fighting with his older brothers toughened him. He would provoke Johnny and George by throwing rocks at them, and they would chase him into the desert. Mamie says, "He made an elusive target as he disappeared into thickets of mesquite and *palo verde,* and was seldom hit by the barrage of stones and sticks thrown at him."[28]

The teacher's attempts at discipline did not stop Martin's clowning in school. "I cried a lot when she would spank his hand with a ruler," Mamie recalls. "It was not so hard to understand her impatience with him, though." The teacher put Scotch tape over Martin's mouth because he talked too much. "She knew she wasn't going to call on him for answers," Mamie says. "His total lack of concentration for anything academic kept him in constant trouble in the classroom." But when it came time for school plays, the teacher always gave him a lead role.

Throughout their elementary school years Martin antagonized teachers and students while Mamie defended him to others and begged him to change his ways. She explains, "One of his stunts was to walk behind the teacher mimicking her walk and expressions until she turned around and saw him. Then there would follow the inevitable paddle. This . . . always brought laughs from other students that seemed to make the punishment worthwhile to him."

His devilish streak could be balanced by a kinder, more thoughtful nature. Mamie remembers seeing him walk toward a lonely-looking little Mexican girl eating her lunch. Because Mamie was so used to being pestered by Martin, she feared he would snatch the girl's lunch. But he merely sat down beside her, took out his harmonica, and played a song.[29]

[3]

A Drifter

One summer Saturday afternoon in 1937, Martin walked into the Glendale movie theater and saw Gene Autry in the middle of the *Yodelin' Kid from Pine Ridge*. The singing cowboy climbed into a wagon, a guitar mysteriously appeared, and Autry said, "Well, I'm not much at making speeches. I guess I'll just have to sing for you."[1]

Eleven-year-old Martin found a hero. He wanted to be a singing cowboy like Gene Autry. Every Saturday from then on, he was at the theater when it opened. "I was down there sitting in front," he recalled. "I would sit so close to the screen that I would get powder burns when them guns would go off. I tell you, I'd get sand kicked in my face; tumbleweeds rolled across me."[2]

He worked to earn money for movies. "[Mr. Harris] would let me pick cotton for him in the evenings after school, in the late spring," Marty reminisced. "Then he would let me clean ditch, which was a man's job and there I was, only eleven years old. I wouldn't get but about twenty-five cents a day. But it only cost ten cents to get in the movie, and the biggest bottle of pop you could get was a nickel, and you could get a big sack of popcorn for five cents also. So I would have a nickel left." He stayed until the theater closed at 10:00 PM and then walked home from Glendale to Peoria. "But I wasn't afraid," he stated. "Because I had just seen Gene Autry, and I was Gene Autry that night." The first five miles were along a dark country road and the remaining half was desert. "The desert's full of rattlesnakes, centipedes, scorpions, sidewinders," he said, "but it didn't bother me. I was Gene Autry. They didn't dare come out of the bushes after me."[3]

Years later, his autobiographical song "Gene Autry, My Hero" stated, "When as a kid from our shack on the desert I'd roam, my daddy would whip me cuz I'd never be around home. But Mom understood . . . when I'd say Gene Autry and I had been rounding up outlaws all day."[4]

Again, without explanation, Jack Robinson uprooted his family. Although still in the Peoria school district, their new home consisted of a pair of tents connected by a tarp-covered breezeway. Emma and the two sets of twins slept in one, and the other contained the kitchen. Johnny and George slept on cots outside, and Jack built himself a small shed nearby.[5] "When it gets down in the twenties in Arizona," Marty said years later, "it's very cold. And we didn't have nothing to put over us but a big piece of canvas. A lot of people had it tough, but I don't think anybody had it any tougher than I did."

"My dad didn't care too much about me," Marty explained to an interviewer. "He had his favorites, and I wasn't one of them. I was kind of a mean kid. I was like him." One of the younger twins was Jack's favorite son. Martin and the little boy were fighting one day, and the younger twin called for their father. "My dad had a bad temper," Marty stated. "I ran away and I wouldn't come back. He chased me and threw a hammer at me like a tomahawk. I picked it up and threw it back as hard as I could and hit him in the chest with it. He never bothered me after that."[6]

For two summers Martin went with his older brother Johnny to herd angora goats in the Bradshaw Mountains north of Phoenix. The pair lived in a little rock house in the bottom of a big canyon. "I could outrun the fastest goat and out-climb any of them when I was little," he reminisced. "I was only eleven years old. I could throw a sailing rock maybe one hundred twenty yards and I could hit within ten feet of what I was throwing at. So I could turn that lead goat—I wouldn't even have to run; I could throw that rock up there and get him." The goat corral was a natural fence of ocotillo, a thorny desert plant with wicked barbs, closed by a gate placed at the open end. They locked three hundred goats inside at night, and they also lured wild mustangs into the corral with hay. After filling his pants with sacks of oats to cushion his fall, Martin would climb atop a chute the boys had built. "He'd run them through that chute and I'd just dive down on them," he said. "I'd get a handful of mane and I'd lock on as tight as I could and stay as long as I could. We'd break them enough so they could be sold from three to fifteen dollars apiece."[7]

In January 1938 Emma Robinson finally divorced her abusive husband. She moved her children into town to a house that had belonged to her mother. Marty described the house as "a little two-room shack down by the railroad tracks." Glendale residents called the area "the barrio." The track was a special one-mile line built to connect the beet sugar factory east of Glendale with the main railroad running through town. Glendale Avenue served as a dividing line, with most Anglos to the north and the Spanish and poor whites—such as the Robinsons—living on the south side.[8] All children attended Unit One School (now called Landmark Elementary), located on the corner of 58th and Myrtle Avenues. Martin and Mamie completed elementary school there.

The location held one memorable benefit for the future songwriter. Martin would listen late at night to Mexicans singing alongside the railroad tracks. "They'd get drunk on Saturday nights," he reminisced, "and you could just hear them singing—three, four, five, six of them at a time. It was real beautiful, and I could just lay there and listen to it all night long. I really learned to love Mexican music. So it's easy for me to write that kind of a tune."[9]

Two classmates would someday have their names immortalized in Marty Robbins ballads. One was fifth-grader Fidelina Martinez, who became Feleena in "El Paso." The other was Martin's close friend Jimmy Martinez, whose name provided the title for a song about a Mexican soldier killed at the Alamo. Martin and Jimmy both enjoyed boxing, and Jimmy eventually became a Golden Gloves boxer.[10] Martin boxed in forty amateur fights during their teen years together.

Emma received $11 a month in government relief to care for herself and five children. "So I had to work," Marty stated. "All the money I made was not for me, y'know. I had to help my mother as much as I could." Emma washed clothes for neighbors, and Martin did odd jobs to help support the family. For a while he sold newspapers, buying them for three cents apiece and selling them for five. The day he decided to quit he bought a few new copies and grabbed a stack of day-old newspapers. "I'd just scream out the headlines and keep the new ones on top," he said. "I got rid of every one of those damned old papers! Sold them all."[11]

"Martin's progress on guitar was one of the few bright spots in our day-to-day lives," Mamie says. "We no longer had the desert to play in, or cows and a garden to provide food. We became more aware too of how poor we were. In the desert the people we knew were much the same as us. Here we could see other kids were better dressed than us." The Robinson children sometimes could not afford shoes. "Under the circumstances, perhaps it's not surprising that Martin was sometimes tempted to just take what he wanted," she says. "He could be a thieving little devil, for little things. Perhaps it was the thrill of doing it that motivated him, more so than what he took."[12]

To get spending money, Martin rigged a series of telephone booths by stuffing napkins inside the change returns. For ten months, he made his rounds, collecting coins from each telephone. Many of Glendale's stores offered payoff pinball machines. Martin and his friends poked holes in the sides with ice picks and covered the holes with chewing gum. "We'd be back there, like we were really playing, keeping our eyes open," he said. "We had eight or ten machines that we had rigged up like this. We were careful; we'd only get about a dollar a night from each machine. We were only fourteen. But they were beginning to catch up with us. . . . The police were always talking to me about something."[13]

"Shack whapping" provided one form of entertainment. Whenever a freeze hit the groves, the teens filled a pickup with soft oranges and drove around town, throwing at houses. "Down in the section of town where I lived, most of the homes have shutters," Marty recalled. "They'd have windows but no glass; it was a big shutter you'd slide back and forth. We'd find one of those, and we'd throw one of these oranges in there."[14]

At one point Martin almost went to reform school for beating up an older teen who accused him and a friend of being thieves. "We were pretty mean," he said, "and we fought dirty. We sent him to the hospital." To hide Martin, Emma shipped him to a friend's farm fifteen miles out in the country.[15]

Mamie taught Martin how to dance while in high school. They practiced in private because he didn't want anyone to see him make a mistake. But he quickly learned the steps, and they developed their own routines. "We got so good, and I was so proud," Mamie says. "It was the only thing I ever taught him how to do. You see, he could do everything. He could skate, he could ride a bicycle first, he could swim. I couldn't swim because he would try to drown me every time I got in the water. The boys would come over and hold me down. When I'd try to skate he'd push me down." Her thrill at being his dance partner ended when he started dancing with other girls.[16]

During summers he worked on a ranch. Once he took a job harvesting carrots and worked from 6:00 until 8:30 the first morning. When he reached the end of the half-mile-long row, he saw a forty-foot-wide irrigation canal. He took off his clothes, put them in a carrot lug, and floated with the lug six miles down the canal to Glendale. "I didn't want no more of the carrots," he said. "I didn't even go back for my pay."[17]

He seldom attended classes, preferring to spend his days in a pool hall. He also worked odd jobs and occasionally hopped a freight train to Prescott. "I could not pass freshman English; I could not understand it," he said. "I needed three years of it, and I couldn't even get through one year." With World War II raging in Europe and Asia, he wanted to join the Navy, but Emma wouldn't let him.[18] By Martin's seventeenth birthday, the Germans had been halted in North Africa, and the battle of Midway stopped Japan's advance in the Pacific.

Martin was in school the day Gene Autry came to Glendale High School to give a free performance in late 1942. Autry had joined the Army Air Corps and was assigned to Luke Field. "I'll never forget that," Marty stated. "I didn't get to meet him, but I got to see him."[19]

Eventually, as always, Martin got his way with his mother. He dropped out of school and enlisted in the U.S. Navy on May 5, 1943. Mamie visited him in San Diego after he completed basic training, and he went home for a thirty-day leave before heading off to combat. The day after his eighteenth birthday, Seaman Second Class (S2c) Martin David Robinson and twenty-nine other men checked aboard USS *Crescent City* (APA 21), anchored at Noumea, New Caledonia, east of Australia.[20] The attack transport had participated in the invasion of Guadalcanal and was part of the task force preparing to hit Bougainville. The Solomon Islands ran parallel to Australia's northeast coast, with Guadalcanal at the bottom and Bougainville at the top of the island chain.

As the *Crescent City* practiced for its upcoming role, so did Martin. He was assigned as ramp operator on the four-man crew of a fifty-foot LCM (landing craft, mechanized). With diesel engines and a draft of three feet, the LCM carried one hundred Marines and traveled ten miles per hour. Using a small hand windlass, Martin dropped the ramp upon reaching the beach and then raised it to return to the ship. Marines entered the LCM by climbing a rope net down the side of the ship. The boat crew held the bottom of the "ladder" taut as the boat rose and fell with the sea. Training for Martin's crew included techniques for lowering and hoisting their boat, methods of loading the boat, using signals and beach markings, maintaining and operating their two .50 caliber machine guns, and performing first aid.[21]

In mid-October, the *Crescent City* steamed to Guadalcanal and loaded troops of the 9th Marine Regiment, 3rd Marine Division. Twelve transport ships of the Third Amphibious Force approached the south side of Bougainville Island early on November 1, and destroyers started shelling Cape Torokina's beach on Empress Augusta Bay at 6:00. "Commenced debarking passengers," the *Crescent City* watch officer wrote in the ship's log.[22]

"I was in the first wave and the third wave," Marty told an interviewer. "The first time we took in troops. The third time we took in a halftrack. The landing craft I was on weighed twenty-four tons, I think, and the surf picked it up with that halftrack in it and left it high and dry on the beach. Pow! Right out of the sea. So we had to get off. We didn't have any way to get back out to the ship, so we were left on the island with the Marines. We were supposed to go back for another load. I think the ship I was on had thirty-two boats and lost thirty. The surf was loaded with them."[23]

The landing was interrupted for almost two hours when dive-bombers from the large Japanese airbase at Rabaul attacked the ship. The *Crescent City* "completed disembarking all passengers" at 10:21. S2c Robinson and forty-three other sailors had been officially transferred that morning "to Boat Pool #11 with records, accounts, bag and baggage."[24] Remaining on the island with the Marines, they were administratively assigned to Advanced Naval Base, Unit No. 7, Guadalcanal.

Marty reminisced, "I'd seen movies about World War One, y'see, and some World War Two pictures. I'd seen dogfights, and bombs and things like that, y'know, and it was exciting, because I hadn't quite figured out that it was dangerous. Even though it was war, it was fun, y'know, watching them. I remember getting to shoot at airplanes; I really had a good time. Until I realized it was dangerous."[25]

Seven of twenty-nine sailors who came with Martin from San Diego also transferred to Boat Pool #11. One who didn't was Pedro Rodriguez. It's likely the two went through basic training together and were friends. With the military penchant for alphabetical arrangements, they probably bunked together and sat together in class. Martin would have felt a kinship with the Hispanic youth from New Mexico. During the morning's amphibious landings, Rodriguez "received gunshot wound in left chest, posterior. Fatal—received aboard dead."[26]

One reason for a beachhead at Empress Augusta Bay was to build an airfield only two hundred miles from Rabaul. As soon as Marines seized a perimeter, Seabees (sailors in a Navy construction battalion) fired up their bulldozers to clear trees and mud. Martin drove a bulldozer to assist the Seabees. On the seventh day after the invasion, a Japanese counterattack attempted to prevent American ships from bringing in fresh supplies and troops. Seabees had built a one-truck-width trail into the jungle and a truck sat on the trail. When Japanese planes began strafing, everybody ran for a foxhole. "There was only one foxhole left," Marty remembered, "and it was full of water. I said I'm not gonna get in that water. So I was looking out toward the beach, under the truck, y'know, and here come this br-br-br-br, a row of bullets right down by the truck. As soon as they let up, I ran and jumped in that water, just so my nose would be above the water. I didn't want anybody shooting at me."[27]

Martin advanced from Seaman Second Class to Seaman First Class on March 1, 1944, and Boat Pool #11 was redesignated Boat Repair Unit Navy 158 the same month. The new Seaman First Class wrote a letter to his hometown newspaper to "thank you a million times for sending me the *Glendale Herald.*" Martin said, "All of us out here realize there is a great job to be done, and it may take a long time to do it, so keep *The Herald* coming to us boys overseas and help us win our fight against homesickness." His P.S. stated, "I guess I could stand a few of Mrs. Clardy's English courses."[28]

Martin spent fifteen months on Bougainville with the Marines and Army. While the war effort "had gone plumb almost to the Philippines," he said, "we were still down fighting in the Solomons." When Japanese planes strafed the island, Martin and his crew would jump in their LCM and head out into the bay. They considered it the safest place as they took potshots at planes flying over them. It became a form of entertainment.[29]

Boxing came into his life again when Martin joined a boxing team on Bougainville and won more than half of his thirty-six Navy fights. At 129 pounds he boxed in the lightweight category. He considered himself "a pretty fair fighter." The Navy boxing team consisted of amateurs who were excused from work on Friday afternoons to train for Friday night fights. Their opponents were frequently professional fighters drafted into the Army and given time during the week to practice. On one particular night, the Navy team won only two of forty bouts. Martin was one of the winners.

"The only reason I was boxing in the first place was because I got that half day off and we got an egg for breakfast," he reminisced. "Once a week, a fresh egg." The Navy boat pool was at the bottom of the military pecking order on the island. "We got what the infantry didn't want—that's what we got to eat," he said.

Martin's worst defeat occurred on a night he had a touch of malaria and fought a husky New Jersey man who appeared to be 140 pounds instead of 129 pounds. "I couldn't stay away from the ropes," he said. "I was running backwards; I was doing everything to stay away from that guy. I managed to stay away for three rounds."

No opponent ever knocked him out, and he beat the only one who knocked him down—a professional fighter from Iowa. When they weighed in, the soldier told Martin, "Watch out for my left. I'll tell you right now, watch out for my left." Once in the ring, he immediately hit Martin's nose with his right. "I had just turned eighteen," Marty recalled, "and this guy was probably close to thirty years old—and made me so mad that he lied to me, an inexperienced kid; tell me a lie so he could hit me in the nose." As they punched each other, the Iowan hit Martin on the ear with a left hook and knocked him to his knees. Martin heard sweet music playing in his head but managed to rise to his feet. He then knocked his opponent under the bottom rope. The referee, an Army chaplain, counted, "Oooone, twoooo, c'mon, c'mon, get up, get up, threee, fooour, c'mon, can you make it, can you make it?" He kept counting until the soldier managed to stand. Martin was declared the winner, but without a knockout. He later said, "I learned enough in the amateur rank to know I didn't want any part of professional boxing. It hurts to get hit in the nose. My nose shows it, too."[30]

Martin commemorated his nineteenth birthday by sending Emma a photo of himself on his "island home." A September 1944 article in the *Glendale Herald* said it was a custom of Martin and Mamie "to have their pictures taken together each birthday, but this year the Pacific was between them." The article referred to Emma as "another Glendale mother who, with three sons in service, watches for the postman's call."[31]

In February 1945, Boat Repair Unit Navy 158 was consolidated with several boat pools into Boat Pool #15, Navy 3205, on the island of Manus in the Admiralty Islands of New Guinea. Martin spent almost six months in the twelve-hundred-man unit. A shipmate remembers him as "easy-going and liked music." The shipmate says, "He had a guitar and he'd sit around and play that thing almost every night. I thought he was great."[32]

At the end of July, Martin returned to the United States for a thirty-day leave. His ship was six days out of San Francisco when the war ended. While he visited his mother's home in Glendale, the newly married Mamie hosted a birthday dinner, which she held early because Martin returned to duty on September 25, the day before their twentieth birthday. An article in the local newspaper exclaimed, "It is with pleasure that the publishers of *The Herald* learn that Martin has received this paper every week since he has been gone."[33]

On February 25, 1946, Martin received his honorable discharge from the U.S. Navy in San Diego. He returned to Glendale and $20 per week as a military veteran in the "52–20 club." When his year of government support ended, he looked for work, holding eight different jobs in six months. "Just enough to get a paycheck," he said, "and then I'd kinda slack off work and rest for a while. I'd work two weeks, and then I'd rest for four weeks."[34]

One job was as an ice man. "I only weighed one hundred thirty-four pounds," he said. "I used to carry a hundred pound piece of ice up two flights of stairs. Every Tuesday and every Thursday, I carried it. Two different places. A hundred pounds of ice." He worked as a mechanic's helper in a garage, an electrician's helper, and one day as a milkman's helper. He worked on a well-drilling rig and did first class carpenter work—receiving carpenter's helper wages. He carried bricks for bricklayers and mixed mortar. "I only got fired from the last one," he said. "I quit all the others. I'd only work long enough for a payday." His longest job lasted thirty days, while he waited for the monthly paycheck.[35]

The eighth job was driving a brick truck between Phoenix and Glendale. He loaded and unloaded the two-ton truck himself. He wore out one side of a pair of gloves loading the truck and the other side unloading it. "Do that two loads a day, making a buck an hour, and spent two dollars a day on gloves," he said. "I'd throw about twenty blocks up there, and then I'd jump up on that truck and stack them, and I'd jump down and throw twenty more up. And that went on, y'know, thirty days, and I said I just don't think this is for me. I said there's got to be another way to make a living."[36]

[4]

Music and Marizona

During the job-hopping months after his discharge, Martin told people he was looking for a better position in life. "What I was really looking for was a way to get out of work and still make a living," he admitted later. "I knew I was lazy, but I didn't want people to know it."

When not at work, he drank heavily. "I had a little problem with policemen at times, and with anybody, really," he said about his behavior while drinking. "I was a happy-type person, but it could change in a second if somebody said the wrong thing."

One night Martin was sitting alone in a bar, feeling sorry for himself after being turned down for a date. Then a song on the jukebox caught his attention—

Eddy Arnold's "Many Tears Ago." Martin memorized the lyrics, replaying the song while he drank. "I had never heard anybody sing with that much feeling, and sing so pretty," said the man who had been raised on big band music. "That was the first real country song I liked, and that started me on country music." He added, "Eddy Arnold made me like country music."[1]

He also loved western music, which he considered "American folk music from the western part of the United States," as opposed to country music. Ever since those Saturdays spent watching Gene Autry on the movie screen, Martin wanted to be a cowboy singer. But his uncles and brothers believed singing was no job for a man. "They thought you've got to do a hard day's work in order to be worth your salt," he explained. "I had different ideas. If I had salt in my body, I was keeping it; I wasn't gonna sweat it out."[2]

Working his brick truck route, Martin stopped for lunch at a little open air market along the highway between Glendale and Phoenix. "I heard this guy singing two days in a row," he recalled, "and I made a point to stop there a third day, and he was singing again, and I asked these people does he sing every day, and they said yeah."[3] The radio was tuned to KOY in Phoenix, and Martin thought the singer "was pretty bad. One time, he got right in the middle of his song and he forgot the words and didn't know what to do. And I thought, man, this guy has got to be making a living doing this."

On Monday he told his boss he had a dentist appointment in Phoenix, and with his two major possessions—a guitar and a motorcycle—he headed for the radio station. Not knowing whom he was supposed to see, he asked for the owner. The receptionist sent him to the program director. When he said he wanted to be a cowboy singer at the radio station, Sheldon Gibbs answered, "We have a cowboy singer." Martin countered, "Yeah, and he's not very good either." "Can you do better?" "Yes, sir, I think I can," and Martin sang "Strawberry Roan." Gibbs fired the other singer and hired Martin. The first song he sang on the air was "I Love You for Sentimental Reasons," a recent hit by Nat King Cole.[4]

Martin initially called himself Jack Robinson because, he said, "I didn't want my mother or my brothers or sisters to know. They knew I didn't like to *work*, y'know, but I didn't want them to think I was lazy, because my brothers worked pretty hard." He felt ashamed he had chosen a lazy man's job—only someone who couldn't do a full day's work would play music. "To get paid for doing something you liked . . . I didn't see how it could be right."[5] Why he used his father's name is unknown. After his parents divorced, he had no contact with Jack and wanted none.

Sometime in 1947, singer Frankie Starr hired Martin to fill in as guitar player at Vern and Don's, a club on East Van Buren Street in Phoenix.[6] "He asked me one night when I was listening to him sing at the radio station, if I wanted to work that night," Marty recalled. "I couldn't play very well at all, but I could play better than Frankie, so he thought I was pretty good. He gave me $10 for three hours work. And that was a lot of money to me. I had only been making a dollar an hour driving that brick truck. So I went back over to him and said, 'Frankie, this is too much; you gave me too much money, didn't you?' He said, 'No, that's union scale.'" Martin became a regular member of the band. "That was great," he said. "Getting paid that much for doing something I loved."[7]

Starr described Martin as dressed in an old pair of Levi jeans with his wallet about to drop out of a hole in the back pocket. A white T-shirt and pair of penny loafers completed his usual outfit. Martin's dress might have reflected his insecurities, while his clowning around tried to disguise his self-consciousness. He remembered what Mamie's girlfriend said when he was seventeen: "Martin is so unattractive he's attractive."[8] Breaking his nose while boxing in the Navy made him even more self-conscious, and he probably didn't notice his perfect teeth and dazzling smile.

One night Starr was sick, and the owner asked if Martin could sing. The idea of singing in front of a live audience petrified the introverted youth. "I couldn't look up at the people," he said, "because I thought they were all making fun of me." He was so embarrassed he held his head down as he sang. Eddy Arnold's "Many Tears Ago" was the first song performed by the future Marty Robbins on stage.[9]

Watching Starr meet people and interact with the audience provided Martin with a valuable lesson. "There are tricks to getting people to come back and see you a second time, and I learned from watching him," he said years later. "I learned early how to treat an audience."[10] It would be years, however, before he perfected those skills himself.

In addition to working with Starr at Vern and Don's, Martin joined him on KTYL in Mesa, Arizona. "We had a big window, and cars would drive up to the studio and look in at the show," Starr explains. "We started singing 'When My Blue Moon Turns to Gold Again,' and when Marty was singing, I looked cross-eyed at him, and it broke him up. He started laughing, and he'd look at me and I'd laugh and he started looking cross-eyed and we laughed the whole show. I guess our sponsors didn't appreciate that."[11]

At some point during 1947–48, still ashamed to admit what he was doing, Martin discussed the matter with a boyhood friend named Harry Tolmachoff. "Why don't you shorten your name to Marty Robbins," Tolmachoff suggested, "and nobody will know. It will make a nice name, too." Martin agreed. With dreams of a record contract, he thought Marty Robbins would look better on a record than Martin David Robinson.[12] He immediately began using the stage name and soon adopted it completely, although he never legally changed his name.

In 1948 Marty moved from Mesa's KTYL to KPHO in Phoenix, where his half-hour show aired weekday mornings at 7:30. Because his nightclub work kept him out until after 1:00 AM, he would barely get to sleep before time to go to the radio station. "I wouldn't get to sleep until three or four," he said, "because I'm excited after a show, and I don't go to sleep. I gotta lay there and think about it." After awhile, he was allowed to tape the show in the afternoon.[13]

He tried to show his mother he could make more money as a musician than driving a truck and hauling bricks. Even though she always enjoyed having him sing for her, Emma thought her son should get a real job. He told her he liked performing and wanted to try it for a while. Finally, his earnings from his nightclub and radio shows convinced his mother he could support himself with music.[14]

Many singers at that time issued songbooks to make extra money and publicize themselves. Frankie Starr arranged with a Los Angeles publisher to print a songbook with his and Marty's songs, as well as photos of both of them. In June 1949 he paid for a demo session in Phoenix on which Marty sang four of his own songs, all heartbreak ballads. The acetates were to be transcribed by the publishing company and printed in the songbook. Although never released, and not made for release, these acetates are now preserved as the first recordings of a singer who would become a legend. The songbook never got printed because, according to Starr, Marty refused to pay his half of the cost. Marty did, however, give Starr ownership rights to the songs.[15]

Radio station pay might have been enough for a bachelor but not for a married man. By this time, Marty needed money to support a family. He'd met Marizona Baldwin in summer 1946, shortly after his Navy discharge, when he and a buddy walked into Upton's Ice Cream Parlor on Glendale's main street. Martin was immediately captivated by the teenaged clerk at the soda fountain, and he checked his pockets to see if he had enough money to make a purchase.

When he asked her name, and she said Marizona, he thought she'd misunderstood the question. He asked again, "What's your name?" She answered again, "Marizona." Thinking she was telling him she was from Arizona, he said, "I'm from Texas, ma'am."

"I didn't know what to say," he remembered. "Because I'd never had a car and I didn't have a job, I couldn't ask her out." As the two young men drank their soda pop and watched the slender girl with light brown hair and wide smile working behind the counter, Martin told his friend, "Leon, I think I'll marry that girl."[16]

"It must have been love at first sight," Marizona says. "I was fifteen and he was twenty. . . . He drove up on a motorcycle while I was working in the malt shop. I worked until midnight, and he asked if he could walk me home. That's how it started."[17]

Marizona Baldwin, whose unique name combined the state of Arizona with the county of Maricopa, came from a family of seven children. Like the Robinsons and other penniless Depression-era families, they wore hand-me-down clothes. The teenager had a dream: "I'd go out every night and wish on a star for a cowboy singer. And pretty clothes. . . . It was important I got pretty clothes along with that cowboy."[18]

Three months later, Martin finally asked her for a date, and they went to a high school football game. After Marizona moved from her parents' house to live with a friend, Martin asked if the friend would mind if he brought his guitar over and sang for them. Marizona says, "He knew all those old songs I loved so much. All those cowboy songs, so it was precious."[19]

The young couple planned to surprise Mamie by going to her town and getting married on the twins' twenty-third birthday, a Sunday. But Martin had to work that day, and they arrived in Parker for their wedding on Monday, September 27, 1948. They honeymooned in a cabin across the river in Earp, California. Mamie and her husband provided some financial assistance. Mamie expressed the typical family attitude by saying, "He wouldn't work. All he wanted to do was music, and at that time nobody ever thought he would be a star."[20]

The newlyweds moved into a little one-room trailer behind Emma's house. Martin kept assuring his bride he would be on the Grand Ole Opry and he would make records. "On a good week he probably brought in about $14," Marizona recalls. "And I thought it was a pipe dream. . . . The first I ever heard him on radio, he was so timid and so bashful . . . I didn't think he'd ever get beyond that."

On July 16, 1949, Marizona gave birth to Ronald Carson Robinson. They named the baby after Carson Robison, one of Marty's favorite country-western singers. Robison had a current hit with "Life Gets Tee-Jus, Don't It."

Ronny was three months old when Marty and Marizona scraped together enough money for a trip to California. They went to Capitol Records in Hollywood, seeking a recording contract. This may have been the same trip Frankie Starr referred to when he said he took Marty to Capitol Records. All the way to California, Marty sang Eddy Arnold's "What Is Life without Love." He wanted to learn how to do a high falsetto and so practiced breaking his voice. "He almost drove me crazy going over there and back," Starr says, "trying to hit that high part. But I'll tell you one thing, when he learned it, he learned it good, because he did have a beautiful falsetto."[21]

The record label wasn't interested. "So we came back and lived on field corn from the field next door to our house," Marizona says, "and then went by my mother's very conveniently at separate times. Or his mother would make a stew for us. He'd get odd jobs now and then." Still, Marty would repeat, "I'm gonna be on the Grand Ole Opry, and I'm gonna make records." And, according to Marizona, he would add, "If I pray and it's something God wants me to have, and I have faith for it, I'll get it."[22]

Mamie remembers visiting them once when all they'd eaten for days was cream of wheat. "I felt so sad," she says, "but I thought he'd never do any better."[23]

Sporadic gigs and time-consuming travel didn't bring in a steady income for a man with a family. To supplement earnings from his Phoenix radio shows and nightclub appearances, he purchased a car and accepted whatever singing jobs he could find in the surrounding area. "When I first started, I used to have to do imitations of just about everybody, 'cuz I didn't have any hits and I had to sing other people's songs," he said. "I used to imitate Hank Snow, Ernest Tubb, Gene Autry, Tex Ritter, Bing Crosby, Al Jolson, Johnny Ray, Perry Como, and Gabby Hayes." He sang old western songs and those of Roy Acuff and Eddy Arnold.[24]

Coming home after a show, Marty usually had difficulty settling down. "He'd want me to get up and eat ice cream with bananas in it at three o'clock in the morning," Marizona recalls. He would put her favorite songs on the record player, and she would tell him, "I've got a little baby that's gonna be squalling at six o'clock."[25]

Often he went out with friends late at night. Bill Hickman, who worked the evening shift at a service station, says the group would go to whatever bar Martin was working at in the Glendale-Phoenix area, and wait for him to finish singing. Then they would take off in Hickman's convertible to go "cat-n-doggin.'" Glendale's streets were decorated with sour orange trees and the young men would pick the fruit off the trees to use as ammunition for throwing at stray cats and dogs. Lack of money made this their entertainment. "We had a lot of fun," Hickman recalls. "The cops around town knew what we were doing, but they never bothered us too much, because we never caused anyone any trouble."

"Martin didn't have any money," Hickman says, "and he would come around the station where I worked. He was working on an old body to try to fix himself up a hot rod." Hickman doesn't remember Marty being much of a drinker, but he does remember his story of going home one night drunk and arguing with Marizona. She said, "I'm getting tired of you coming home drunk—I know you don't work this late." She wanted him to promise he'd stop. When he came home late again, she was hiding behind the door with a shoe in her hand. Martin was laughing when he later told Hickman, "I was trying to cover my head, and she was whacking me with that damn shoe."[26]

"I drank as many as twenty-four bottles of beer between nine and one at night," Marty once told an interviewer. "People are always buying you drinks when you play those clubs." One night after drinking beer all evening, he went to a party where he drank whiskey until 4:00 AM. Heading home to Glendale, he drove along a four-lane highway bordered by oleander trees. "All of a sudden I wake up on the wrong side of the highway," he recalled, "going about ninety miles and the trees are brushing the windshield." He steered the car back into his lane, and the next thing he remembered was running a red light in Glendale. A police car chased him to his mother's house, and he ran inside. "He gave me a ticket for reckless driving," Marty stated. "He could've hauled me off to jail. I learned something in life from that. I was so lucky during those years that they never shipped me off to jail."[27]

Such behavior reinforced the reason some Glendale residents remember him as a troublemaker. Hometown acquaintances may have remained too long fixated on his youthful misbehavior, but Marty matured to become universally loved and admired. "I had a lot of confidence," he said years later, "but I didn't know how I was going to get on record, or become a recording star, but I never worried about it. Because I had found what I wanted and I didn't see how I could fail. So I knew it had to happen, that there could be no other way."[28]

$$[5]$$

On Columbia Records

Although Martin David Robinson became Marty Robbins, with his birth name used for legal matters, Marizona would forever remain Marizona Robinson. The young couple struggled with both their relationship and their finances as 1950 approached. Marty spent little time at home, working gigs wherever he could find them, and Marizona took care of the house and baby. During this period Marty's songwriting focused on heartache, usually pining for a lost love. Years later, he would say, "I like to be by myself because I like the feeling of being lonely. When I get to feeling that way, then I can write a song. But if I'm happy, I can't write a song."[1] He must have felt unhappy a lot. Some songs were autobiographical: "You seem to forget you're not perfect; you show me my faults every day. . . . We're never apart, yet I'm second in your heart, and it looks like I'm just in your way."

"I had become a Christian," Marizona says, "and he felt threatened by it." He wrote a song titled "I'll Go On Alone" and left for an out-of-town gig. "With you believing like you do, you say I live so wrong," the lyrics said. "But I can't change the way I live, I've lived that way too long."

Upon his return, he gave Marizona another song, "It's Your Heart's Turn to Break." The self-accusing lyrics said, "You didn't try to understand when she was feeling blue, your every wish was her command, she lived her life for you." Marty told Marizona, "Honey, I'll never do anything like that to hurt you again," and he gave her five dollars to put in the offering plate at church. "So I knew he was truly repentant," she says. Marizona adored her singing cowboy, gladly providing Marty with the attention he craved throughout his life. "He'd sit on the end of the bed with his guitar and sing," she recalls. "It would be one or two o'clock in the morning and it's special because those are songs we learned as children."[2]

Mamie once went to see her twin brother sing in a nightclub, and he told her to go home to her husband. She felt Marty "could be domineering" with Marizona, as he had always treated Mamie. "With her long dresses and hair pulled back, I thought she had a Holy Roller look," Mamie says. "I wonder now whether part of her attraction for him was that he felt she was somebody he could keep in the background."[3]

Marty took over as headliner at Vern and Don's in late 1949 when Frankie Starr left Phoenix for Texas. Fred Kare from Chicago purchased the club on East Van Buren Street and renamed it Fred Kare's Bar and Supper Club. Two musicians who joined the band at Starr's invitation stayed with Marty—Floyd Lanning on lead guitar and Jimmy Farmer on steel guitar. Known as the K-Bar Boys, the trio worked there for three years. "It wouldn't hold more than one hundred people," Marty said. "But every night, it was packed. They'd stand in line outside waiting for somebody to come out so they could go in." Lanning sang Eddy Arnold songs, and Marty learned other popular songs of the day. Whenever he got a chance to sing "It's a Sin," he did it exactly like Eddy Arnold's number one record.[4]

Sometime in 1950, Marty moved his family from Glendale to 2940 West Pima in Phoenix. Their new location lessened his travel time to KPHO and Kare's. Marizona regularly attended Westside Assembly of God on 29th Avenue, and when Marty wasn't working out of town, he went to church with her and Ronny. A teenaged church member, Betty Sexton, enjoyed visiting the Robbins house. "We would go down to their house, and he'd get the guitar out and play and sing for us," she says. "He'd written a couple of religious songs he'd sing, his big bare foot patting on the floor."[5]

Television came to Arizona when KPHO-TV began broadcasting from Hotel Westward Ho in downtown Phoenix. It was the only station between San Diego and El Paso. One day in 1950 the KPHO program director asked Marty if he would like to do some television; the visual side of the station had nothing to play for fifteen minutes and needed to fill the slot. "I said, no, sir, because it made me nervous," Marty recalled. "Almost sick to my stomach." The program director asked, "Do you like your radio job?" "Yes, sir." "If you want to keep your radio job, you'll do fifteen minutes of television."

Wearing his simple outfit of cowboy shirt and Levis, Marty went in front of the KPHO-TV camera. He'd written the names of songs on a piece of paper and put it in his shirt pocket. He couldn't remember the songs he planned to sing, so he would pull the paper out of his pocket and say, "For my next song, I would like to sing . . ." The show was a success. "I guess maybe the people were feeling sorry for me," he reminisced, "because I was shy and embarrassed looking."

The station received so many cards and letters the program director required him to do a fifteen-minute show every week by himself. "A couple of times I threw up before the show," he said. "Then I'd get through the show, and I'd be so relieved and I'd sleep so good that night! But then next morning I couldn't sleep again, knowing I had to go through that same thing the next Friday."[6]

Late one night in December, Marty came home, drunk, and found eighteen-month-old Ronny deathly sick and Marizona exhausted. Marty held the toddler in his arms and prayed for his son's life. "I thought he was gonna die, y'know, he was so hot," Marty remembered. "So hot, and his heart was—you could hear it, and it was hurting me because it was hitting so hard I could feel it. And I thought he couldn't stand it. And so I prayed, and I promised God I would never ever again touch alcohol if he wouldn't take my son away. And at that very second I could feel my son get well." Ronny quit crying and fell into a peaceful sleep.[7]

Years later, a magazine reporter quoted Marty as saying, "I wasn't just a hell-raiser. I was a mean drunk. I wanted to fight everything that moved. . . . Well, when Ronny got sick it sobered me up and I made a deal with the Lord." Marty objected to the magazine headline, "Marty Robbins Made a Deal With

God." In 1978, he said he hadn't touched alcohol since the night he promised to stop drinking, and "I never will touch it again. You make a promise to anybody you do your best to keep it, naturally, but when you make a promise to Him, it's pretty important that you keep it. But I didn't make a deal with God. 'Cuz I'm too small to make a deal with Him."[8]

While Marty was working a two-week gig in Yuma, Arizona, his car threw a rod. When ready to return home, he didn't have money to replace the broken rod. He decided to "take one more rod off so it won't bother anything. But I didn't take the right one off, and it wasn't balanced." The car shook so badly he abandoned it fifty miles out of Yuma. He and a fellow musician hitchhiked to Phoenix and borrowed his mother-in-law's automobile, retrieved his car, and towed it to a garage in Glendale.

Days later, Phoenix policemen knocked on the door of Marty's house at 5:00 AM. "And I mean they took me," he remembered. "Didn't say nothing, just said 'C'mon.' I said, 'Well, what for?' He said, 'Just c'mon.'" Marty spent the night in the Phoenix jail and was taken to Yuma the next day. During the three-hour drive, he chatted with the policemen and learned the reason for his arrest. A Yuma liquor store had been robbed, and a witness gave Marty's license plate number. He asked when the robbery occurred, they told him, and he said his car had been in a garage; it must be a case of someone reporting the wrong plate number. While he spent that night in jail in Yuma, authorities checked his story and confirmed his car had been in the garage.

When he appeared in court, the judge authorized his release, along with $5 and a bus ticket back to Phoenix. The judge must have known what Marty was thinking, because he asked, "You don't have any thoughts of suing us for false arrest, do you?" Marty responded, "No, sir, I sure don't." Afraid they'd put him back in jail, he just wanted to go home.[9]

In the spring of 1951, Grand Ole Opry star Jimmy Dickens came to Phoenix with a package show to play a local venue called Madison Square Garden. KPHO manager Harry Stone, former general manager of Nashville's WSM Radio, invited Dickens to appear on an afternoon TV show to advertise that evening's performance. "It was Marty Robbins and Jimmy Farmer, just the two of them," Dickens recalls, "on a fifteen-minute television show." There was no audience in the studio and only a small space in front of the camera as Marty sang and played rhythm guitar. "He just stood there and listened," Marty remembered. "He told me he thought I was good. He said, 'I'm going to speak to the people in Los Angeles when I see them.'" And he did. Dickens remembers telling "Uncle Art" Satherley that "someone should come down and listen to him, because I was very, very much impressed with his singing."[10]

"He liked me real well and he's the one that got me on record," Marty stated. "I don't like to say discovered; I've never been discovered." Art Satherley, A&R (artists and repertoire) representative for "hillbilly and race music," took Dickens's advice and went to Phoenix.[11] Marty's one-year renewable contract with Columbia Records, dated May 25, 1951, listed him as "Martin Robinson (Professionally known as MARTY ROBBINS)," with Harry Stone of Radio Station KPHO as point of contact.

Stone, with Nashville connections, arranged Marty's Grand Ole Opry debut a month later, on June 30. Marty appeared on the Prince Albert portion, a half-hour show broadcast over the NBC network, and host Red Foley's introduction included, "Just recently he signed a brand-new recording contract and his records will be out before you know it." When Marty walked onstage, Foley commented, "Marty, a nice looking bunch of people here, huh?" Marty responded, "There's a lot of them." Foley asked if he had anything to say before his song, and Marty told him, "I'd like to sing this song for all the people back in Arizona." The first of his two songs that evening was his own "Ain't You Ashamed?"[12]

Fred Kare brought Marty to Nashville in his big Chrysler, and the car so impressed Marty that he said he would buy one if he ever made enough money. Kare transported Marty to numerous engagements across the South and Southwest, as well as to his first recording session, held in Los Angeles on November 14, 1951.[13]

Satherley had sent him about twenty songs and asked him to pick four to record. "But I wrote songs and I said to myself, my songs are better than these, so I didn't bother to learn them," Marty stated. "None of them fit me or fit my style." When he and his band arrived with Fred Kare for the recording session, Marty was asked about his progress in learning the songs. He said he didn't like any of them, and four of his own were better. The session leader demanded co-writer credit before allowing them to be recorded. Marty refused. He told Lanning and Farmer, "Okay, get your things. We're going home." The session leader quickly conceded, "Oh, uh, wait a minute. You can record them."[14]

On March 24, 1952, "Love Me or Leave Me Alone" and "Tomorrow You'll Be Gone" were released as Marty's first single. The other two songs recorded on that session, "I Wish Somebody Loved Me" and "Crying 'Cause I Love You," were released as the second single in June.

Although no songs charted, they did get radio play. Peggy Ann Munson in Brunswick, Georgia, liked Marty's singing well enough to organize "The Dixie

Land Chapter of the Marty Robbins Fan Club" in May.[15] She would remain Marty's fan club president for more than two decades.

One evening while traveling to a nightclub, Marty tuned his car radio to WCKY in Cincinnati and heard a song he liked. Gradually, he recognized the song as one he'd written, and then he realized it was his recording. "It scared me so much I nearly had a wreck," he recalled. "I stopped on the side of the road, it thrilled me so much to hear myself on the radio; I'll never forget that." Another thrill was finding "Love Me or Leave Me Alone" on the jukebox at a restaurant he frequented. "I would play it about three times while I was in there," he said. "When I'd leave I would put a quarter in and punch it five times."[16]

Charlie Walker, a Texas music promoter and disc jockey who owned a honky-tonk, booked Marty for $75, after being told the new artist had one record that was doing well. The Old Barn, six miles east of San Antonio on Highway 90, could hold over seven hundred people. Marty was so timid he wouldn't talk to the audience, and Walker encouraged him to take breaks instead of singing for the entire four hours. "Yeah, but I don't know what to say to them," Marty replied.[17]

Marty's second Columbia session took place at Jim Beck's studio in Dallas, Texas, on June 3. The location was chosen by Don Law, who replaced Satherley as Marty's producer, possibly to develop a more modern sound. The first session, with what a music analyst called "a distinctive old-timey flavor," had not matched the character of other Columbia recordings of the period. Marty's story of troubles with Marizona, "I'll Go On Alone," was the first song recorded in Dallas. Released October 10, 1952, and backed with another of his songs from the session, "You're Breaking My Heart (While You're Holding My Hand)," it hit *Billboard*'s Country Singles Chart on December 20 and stayed eighteen weeks, with two weeks at number one. Marty credited disc jockey Fred Wamble for helping put the song on the bestseller list. Wamble's coverage on WBAM Radio's Deep South Jamboree in Montgomery, Alabama, gave Marty's music much wider exposure.[18]

Nashville competition came from Webb Pierce, whose first three singles to chart on *Billboard* had gone to number one. Pierce covered "I'll Go On Alone" and had a double-sided hit, with both sides peaking at number four.[19]

Two Texans who later became well known in the country music industry remember first hearing Marty sing "I'll Go On Alone" on the radio in 1952. One was ten-year-old Eddie Kilroy. The other was seventeen-year-old Johnny Bush, who says, "When I heard that voice, it was so special; he sang so great. He had a voice unlike anything I'd ever heard in country music. It took Texas by storm that anyone could sing like that." They waited for an edition of *Country Song Roundup* to provide pictures and stories of this new artist. More than half a century later, Bush states, "If anybody tells you they're a Marty Robbins fan, I guess I would be at the top of the list."[20]

When scheduled for his first tour, seven days in California in September 1952, Marty left KPHO. As a recording artist, he wanted to go on the road because that's where he expected to make money.[21] He didn't realize it would be more work than money.

Marty's famous inability to sleep at night originated that year during a two-week tour in Texas and Louisiana. "I was doing all the driving by myself," he said, "and making six-hundred-mile jumps every night, drinking coffee and taking NoDoz tablets." He would play a club from nine until one and then drive five or six hundred miles to get to the next gig. "I remember the last jump I made was from Shreveport to Phoenix, nonstop, and I was wide awake when I got there and wide awake four days later. I lay down and closed my eyes and they'd pop plumb open." He added, "And I haven't slept since then."[22]

Don Law scheduled Marty's third session, again in Dallas, on November 26. In addition to the usual heartbreak songs, Marty recorded Cindy Walker's "Lorelei," a Hawaiian song of lost love. Of twenty-nine songs in Marty's first seven Columbia sessions, twenty-two were about heartbreak. Marty wrote all of them, as well as three of seven Hawaiian and gospel songs.

Near the end of 1952, Marty received an offer to join the Grand Ole Opry. Harry Stone had contacted Fred Rose, who owned Acuff-Rose Music Publishing with Roy Acuff in Nashville. Rose, quick to recognize songwriting talent, flew to Phoenix to meet Marty. "Him being the writer that he was," Marty later said, "I always felt that was the greatest compliment I've ever had, y'know, since I've been in the business, is to have him fly out there to sign me up as a writer." At the time, Marty did not realize how unusual the experience was, that a major publishing house president would travel more than three thousand miles round trip to sign an unknown.[23]

"We moved to Nashville," Marizona says, "and I'm telling you, it was hard on me. I loved Phoenix." Her friend Betty Sexton believes Marizona would have been happy anywhere, as long as she could be with her singing cowboy. "She was going with HIM," Sexton explains, "and they were going to make a living out there. They were a wonderful couple."[24]

Marty and Marizona packed their car and, with three-year-old Ronny, headed east.

[6]

Mr. Teardrop

When Marty renewed his Columbia contract on December 12, 1952, he listed his
address as 1887 Loney Drive in Nashville. He and Marizona purchased the house
the following year. "You couldn't see a mile down the road," Marty said about
his early impression of the South. "[Roads] were crooked, trees everywhere.
I felt trapped down here. I almost went back to Arizona. I couldn't handle the
cold weather down here; I couldn't take the humidity."[1]

He first appeared on the Grand Ole Opry as a member on January 24, 1953.
Too shy to look at the audience, he stared at the floor and never looked up.
WSM Radio gave him his own show, Monday through Friday, from 5:45 to 6 AM,
sponsored by Martha White flour. "I Couldn't Keep From Crying," recorded

during the most recent Dallas session, became Marty's second *Billboard* chart song, debuting in March 1953 and reaching a peak of number five. More than a year would pass before another of his songs charted.[2]

Because Marty didn't have a band, one was assigned. "I don't know who decided that," rhythm guitarist Ray Edenton says about finding sidemen for Marty to use in Nashville and on out-of-town shows. Initially, they were Edenton, Floyd "Lightnin'" Chance on bass, Don Slayman on fiddle, and Jack Evins on steel guitar. There was no lead guitar. Chance was a comedian, with considerable frontman experience, and Jack Stapp assigned him to the band to "carry the ball" for Marty. "All Marty could do was sing," Chance said in an oral history. "He'd be standing singing his heart out and the show died completely." They all worked with other entertainers and filled in when Marty needed them. Evins, who played steel for Ray Price, agreed to help Marty until Jim Farmer arrived from Phoenix. Lum York, a former Hank Williams band member, was freelancing in Nashville, and he occasionally took his upright bass and comedy act on the road with Marty when Chance wasn't available.[3]

"It was like starting all over," Marty recalled. "In Phoenix on radio and television shows, I learned to talk to audiences a little bit. But when I moved to Nashville, I met stars and I was absolutely tongue-tied. It took me three or four years to get over that."[4]

"He just wasn't suited for that Martha White circuit we worked," Edenton states. "That was strictly a bluegrass circuit." Their road shows were out-and-back dates within two hundred miles of Nashville. "We had a lot of fun on the road, working with him," Edenton reminisces. "I don't have many stories about Marty; he was too straight. He didn't drink, he didn't smoke, he didn't run around." But Marty did like to make the rounds of clubs, and he took Edenton, a partying bachelor, with him. "We'd go around all night long," Edenton says, "and he'd buy me drinks to stay with him. We had a big time, and we'd stay up all night and get in just in time to do the radio show in the morning."[5]

One night at a drive-in theater in Sparta, Tennessee, their guitars lost tune in the moist night air. Evins carried his steel guitar on his shoulder as they all climbed a ladder to get to the platform under the movie screen. "People didn't applaud at a drive-in theater," Evins explains. "They blew their horns. You couldn't see them, sitting in their cars. I remember how weird that feeling was. You couldn't see anybody; it was awful." Before the show, Marty told Lightnin' Chance, "If I get stuck now, you come to my rescue." Chance replied, "Don't worry, Little Chief, I'll take care of you." Chance usually did most of the talking. "Marty was *very* shy," Evins recalls. "He wasn't much of a spokesman. He depended on others to fill in for him, because he'd get stuck. He'd get up there and start talking and he'd run out of things to say." That night he sang two or three songs, and the crowd responded with honking horns. After saying, "It's a pleasure to be with all you people up here," Marty stammered and couldn't remember the name of the town. Finally he turned sideways and spoke into the microphone, "Lightnin,' dang it, say something!"[6]

Acuff-Rose, Marty's publishing company, scheduled an interview for him with Ralph Emery, a twenty-year-old disc jockey at WAGG Radio in nearby Franklin. The scheduler told Emery, "He's kind of shy; he won't talk much." Although the meeting began a friendship that lasted until Marty's death, Emery remembers only that "his hair was incredibly curly, and he was not outgoing."[7]

"When I first got to Nashville, I didn't get much road work," Marty stated. "In fact, it got to the point where I was ready to go back to Arizona, because I wasn't doing very good. Jim Denny, who booked all artists on the Opry, [would] book me, say, one night in Washington, D.C., and I had to drive there and back and carry four people, so I wasn't making any money." In early 1953, Denny called Charlie Walker at The Old Barn in San Antonio and asked if he'd like to book Marty again. "Yeah, how much do you want?" "$300." Walker protested that the charge had been $75 a few months earlier. Denny replied, "But he's a member of the Opry now." Marty went alone to Texas. "There wasn't too many of them carried bands," Walker says. "It cost too much money. You carry musicians if you need them, and if you don't, you go by yourself."[8]

Marty recorded four of his heartbreak songs at his first Nashville session, held at Castle Studio in March 1953. He wanted Jim Farmer on steel guitar, and his friend drove from Phoenix for the event. Farmer didn't stay in Nashville, because the musician's union refused to admit out-of-town steel players. Marty liked the Roy Wiggins-type steel guitar sound on Eddy Arnold records. "The tuning I had wasn't set up for that," Evins states. "I could do it but it wasn't the best tuning for that type of steel guitar. But I did it evidently to his satisfaction, and we got by with it."[9]

Because Evins was committed to his primary job with Ray Price, and Farmer returned to Phoenix, Marty searched for another steel player. He found Joe Vincent, newly discharged from the Army and working at WLAC Radio with Big Jeff Bess and His Radio Playboys. "Marty came up one morning looking for a steel guitar player," Vincent remembers, "and wanted to know if I could play like Roy Wiggins. And Jeff says, 'Yes, he can.' I didn't know whether I could or not." Marty sang a few Eddy Arnold songs and then asked, "Are you in the union?" When Vincent said no, Marty told him, "Meet me down at the union hall at ten o'clock, and we'll get you in the union." Marty paid Vincent's union dues and told him they were leaving that night for Dallas for a recording session. Vincent packed his bag, and Marty picked him up. "I thought, well, ain't this something," Vincent reminisces. "Got up one morning at home, ate me a bowl of cornflakes, go to meet Big Jeff in the morning, and darn if I ain't on the way to Texas this evening."[10]

They did three sessions there in 1953. "I felt more at ease with the Dallas musicians than I did in Nashville," Marty once said. One song he recorded on his first Dallas session represented his frustrations about trying so hard—and unsuccessfully—for a hit. He wrote "At the End of a Long Lonely Day" while feeling sorry for himself. "Tomorrow means another day to cry; it makes no difference whether I live or die," the lyrics moaned. "It sounds like I was writing to somebody, but I was just writing to the people," he explained. "I felt like I was being neglected, y'know, by the people."[11]

When they worked Dallas nightclubs, Vincent provided Roy Wiggins-style steel guitar, and local musicians completed the band. The pair also traveled periodically to Austin to work the Skyline Club. On one Texas trip they checked into a motel, sharing one room with double beds, and saw a sign warning them to have proper ventilation because of natural gas heat. Vincent, who held a fear of suffocating from gas, was so tired he fell across his bed. When he tried to move and couldn't, he thought he was dying from gas poisoning. He didn't realize he was merely too tired to move. "I was so glad when I woke up the next morning," he says, "so glad to see Marty there."[12]

In the fall of 1953, Marty and three sidemen (Chance, Edenton, and Vincent) performed at the high school auditorium in Savannah, Tennessee. A senior named Earl White was running through the basement to get to the show, when someone called his name, and White turned to see one of his friends sitting on a bench with Marty and the band. Noticing White, a 230-pound football player, Lightnin' Chance said, "Well, look at old Seldom Fed." Marty loved the term and took it as a nickname for his son. "That's what he always called me, growing up," Ronny says.[13]

Marty bought a 1953 Chrysler New Yorker soon after moving to Nashville. He'd kept his promise to himself to buy one as soon as he could afford it. Bill

Hickman remembers him coming home to Glendale and showing up at the gas station with his new car. "All the rest of us drove Fords," Hickman says. "Chrysler used to be a pretty expensive car." The Nashville musicians had never ridden in a car with power steering and air conditioning. "Lightnin' and I were used to driving," Edenton says. "Some of these show dates were so far, you had to drive eighty or ninety miles an hour to get there—on old bad roads. Marty wouldn't let us drive over fifty-five. He drove like a bat out of hell, but he wouldn't let us drive over fifty-five; he said we scared him. We made him and Joe Vincent do all the driving." Marty would "raise cain because we wouldn't drive. We'd get up under the wheel, and the first thing we did was run up to eighty miles an hour, and he'd make us stop."[14]

Vincent left in late 1954, after Marty worked a show with Faron Young, who did not yet have a band. Hubert Long, Young's personal manager and owner of a talent agency, invited Vincent to "come to work with us." Not knowing which direction to go, Vincent said, "Well, okay." The timing worked for everyone because Marty finally convinced the union to admit Farmer, who moved to Nashville. Vincent remembers Marty as a "let's-have-some-fun-boys kind of guy. He was a lively person, a good-hearted guy, good to work with, but liked to pull a lot of pranks. I really did like him. He was a wonderful person." Vincent recalls driving to Dallas, feeling half asleep, with Marty in the backseat. All of a sudden he'd be shocked awake by hearing a boomp-boomp-boomp noise that sounded like a flat tire. But it would be Marty beating on a tray pulled out from the seatback.[15]

Frankie Starr and his wife, June, moved to Nashville from Phoenix in 1954, and Starr recorded a tape of himself and Marty singing together and reminiscing about working in Phoenix. Marizona and Ronny were also present, and at one point Marty called to Ronny to sing a song. When the five-year-old refused, his dad told him, "Ronny, come here and sing a little song. Or I'll get the clippers after you. I'll get those hand clippers, not the electric clippers." Since Ronny apparently didn't want his hair cut, he came to the microphone to sing "Jesus Loves Me." He hummed the key and then Marty accompanied him on guitar. "That's fine, Ronny," Marty reassured his son.[16]

Marty appeared on a package show with Hank Snow at a theater in Miami, Florida, doing three shows a day. "I didn't have any kind of hits, so I was allowed fifteen minutes," he told a reporter years later. "The people didn't know my songs, so I went out and sang and didn't get much of a hand." He asked Snow's band members for some jokes to tell. "I started telling more jokes than singing, and doing much better as a comedian," he explained. As well as practicing a format that would serve him well in later years, he honed his skill at imitating other performers—Ernest Tubb, Gene Autry, Tex Ritter, and Al Jolson.[17]

Marty's final two Dallas recording sessions occurred in 1954, as did two others in Nashville. He wrote thirteen of sixteen songs recorded. The first Nashville session was documented as "Ray & Roy." Marty, calling himself Roy, provided harmony for Ray Edenton singing lead on four songs. Producer Don Law filed the tapes without releasing any songs. The second Nashville session, on December 7, finally produced a hit. Elvis Presley's version of "That's All Right" had been released several months earlier and didn't make the charts. Don Law agreed to let Marty cover the song, and Marty wanted his rhythm guitarist to play lead. "I played horrible lead guitar," says Edenton. "But I did it, on all those rockabilly things."[18] The song entered *Billboard's* chart in February 1955 and stayed eleven weeks, peaking at number seven. After recording country heartbreakers, gospel songs, and Hawaiian music for three years, Marty found a new musical style in the rockabilly craze. His versatility would continue to expand throughout his career.

In May 1955, Marty and Marizona paid $25,000 for their second house, 807 Redwood Drive in Brentwood, a suburb on Nashville's southern edge. The long brick rambler, set back from the street on a large lawn, seemed more fitting for a singing star than the little wood-sided Loney house in a crowded neighborhood. About his personal life, Marty told a magazine interviewer, "When I'm not too busy, I like to get out on the open road on my motorcycle. I also enjoy boxing, am a rabid hot rod fan and like to work out with the Opry baseball team." He described himself as five foot ten, 175 pounds, and with "sandy hair and brown eyes."[19]

Marty appeared with Elvis Presley in Beaumont, Texas, and Mobile, Alabama, in June. Their two days in Beaumont had been advertised heavily for two weeks, and five sold-out performances raised $10,000 for the local police department. The Maddox Brothers and Rose opened the show, and Presley came on just before headliner Marty. After the first night, according to Rose Maddox, Marty switched places. Nobody could follow Elvis. "I'd stand there in amazement at these girls," Maddox says, "screaming and fighting and drooling over that man." Marty and Presley also shared the spotlight a month later in Fort Myers, Florida.[20] Those shows and the success of "That's All Right" must have helped Marty choose his next single. His version of Chuck Berry's "Maybellene," recorded as "Maybelline" at his August recording session, charted in October and reached the top ten.

"I played rhythm, until he did one of these songs that had me playing lead on record; then I'd play lead," Edenton explains. "Marty played pretty good rhythm. Back in those days bands weren't near as big as they are now. We all doubled." By then they were touring greater distances than the local Martha White circuit of two years earlier. Sometime in 1955 Marty played Sioux Falls, South Dakota, with a band consisting of Ray Edenton, Don Slayman, Lightnin' Chance, and Jim Farmer. On October 28 he headlined a show at Fair Park Coliseum in Lubbock, Texas, with Buddy Holly as opening act.[21]

Marty's two 1955 recording sessions were the last ones Edenton did with him for sixteen years. Edenton, already becoming one of the famed A-Team sessionmen on Music Row, recalls, "He called me in to do the session on 'Singing the Blues.' I played lead electric guitar."[22] Recorded in November, the song would become a surprise hit when released ten months later.

Because of his many heartbreak songs, Marty became known as "the boy with the teardrop in his voice," a title he credited to Jolly Joe Nixon, a Fort Worth disc jockey. The term first appeared in print as a magazine quote in late 1953. "At the time I *was* a boy," Marty told an interviewer years later. "I was just a young man, but it always embarrassed me when somebody'd say 'Mr. Teardrop.' It used to be rumored that every time I would sing a song I would cry. I might get more emotion into a song maybe than some people do, but I don't cry. I was asked many times in the early part of my career, 'Do you really cry on your recording sessions?' No, I don't really cry on my recording sessions."[23]

By late 1955 Marty felt far enough along with his career to hire a manager and a permanent band. He chose Eddie Crandall as manager, and no one seems to know who decided on "Marty Robbins and the Teardrops." Hillous Butrum, Earl White, Joe Wright, and Jim Farmer were the original Teardrops. As Wright describes their positions, "Hillous played rhythm guitar, and he could play bass, too. Earl played fiddle, rhythm, and bass. When Earl played fiddle, Hillous played bass. Jim Farmer and I were the only ones in the group that didn't swap around. Jim played steel and I played lead guitar. Hillous and Earl played whatever they had to at the moment." Farmer, Marty's friend from Phoenix, had been working with him since late 1954. Next came Butrum, who says, "I was an original Drifting Cowboy [with Hank Williams], then an original Rainbow Ranch Boy [with Hank Snow], then an original Teardrop with Marty Robbins."[24]

White had moved to Nashville after graduating from Savannah High School. He and Joe Wright, also a recent high school graduate, performed as the Kountry Kats every Saturday afternoon on a WSIX-TV show for nonunion musicians. Hillous Butrum told White that Marty Robbins planned to start "a regular group" and would White like to be part of it? "When I got over my fainting spell," White recalls, "I said of course. I was still eighteen years old, and not only wet behind the ears, but green."[25]

White then called Wright and said, "Marty Robbins is putting together a band, and he just hired me. I told him about you, and he wants to hear you play." Wright played for Marty at the Friday Night Frolic in December 1955, and Marty said, "If you can get in the union, I start rehearsal on a network television show Monday." Wright joined the union on Monday morning, and they started rehearsing that afternoon for a Purina network television show. Wright's mother paid White's union dues.[26]

Following a Saturday night Opry in January 1956, Marty and his Teardrops left Nashville on a two-week tour and drove to Riverside, California, with a stop in Phoenix to visit Marty's family. They drove Marty's black-and-white 1955 Chrysler Imperial and pulled a little teardrop-shaped trailer with "Marty Robbins and the Teardrops" painted on the side. "Five of us in an ol' Chrysler," Joe Wright says. "With a hump in the back, and I had to sleep on the floorboard with my head on the hump."

Returning briefly to Nashville, they next went to Newark, New Jersey, arriving in time for a Sunday matinee on February 5. Following the evening show, they drove three thousand miles, straight across the country, to Bremerton, Washington, for another show and then south to Portland, Oregon. "I think we were gone sixteen days and we slept nine nights in a bed," Wright says.

They almost didn't find a room in Portland because all hotels were booked for rodeo week. Someone at the radio station called around town and finally found them a little motel with one available room. When they arrived to check in, the office door was locked. While waiting for a clerk, Marty entertained his companions. He had never outgrown his need for attention. Just as little Martin risked the teacher's wrath to draw his classmates' laughter, Marty took every opportunity to make his band laugh. "We'd do anything to break the boredom of those trips," Wright says. "Marty had a knack for getting caught at the wrong time." He didn't realize they were laughing at more than his antics. "He would priss across the porch one way, and he would lick his little finger and rub his eyebrow, and then priss back across," as Wright describes the scene. "When he prissed back across and turned to go the other way, the old woman from the motel walked out of the room right behind him. All she saw was this guy with blond wavy hair prissing across that porch and four men with him, and she drew her own conclusions." Once the band members stopped laughing, it took them half an hour to convince her to rent them the only room in town.[27]

Wright and Marty had a ritual every time they checked into a hotel. They would throw their suitcases on the bed and immediately meet in the hall to wrestle. "I was young and thought I was strong," Wright says, "and he was thirty-two and *was* strong. And he whipped me every time." White comments, "I believe the most I've ever seen Marty worried was one night when he and Joe Wright were wrestling in the hotel, and he chipped a tooth. He got really upset."[28]

When Marty's turn came to drive, his band members never knew what to expect. One night extreme bouncing woke the exhausted men, who saw Marty laughing uproariously as he chased jackrabbits across the Nebraska prairie. The Teardrops insisted he get back on the road.[29]

During his 1950s performances, Marty usually wore a business suit and tie, and sometimes western-tailored jackets with various degrees of design. His band dressed in white shirts and string ties and later in matching business-type suits or western attire. Marty was always concerned about appearance but not so concerned about a "moniker," as Faron Young referred to titles such as his own "Young Sheriff," or Ernest Tubb, the Texas Troubadour, or Hank Snow, the Singing Ranger. Although Marty acknowledged, "Some of my fans call me Mr. Teardrop," he didn't use the name. "I never had a name for my band," Marty said in 1982. "They used to call the band 'Marty Robbins and the Teardrops.' And it would embarrass me so much. I'd come into a little town and see window placards that said, 'Coming here October 16th, Marty Robbins and the Teardrops.' And I'd say oh, my God, take that out of there. I'm sure glad they finally got away from that."[30]

The name didn't embarrass Marty enough to keep from writing a song with that title. He loved the Inkspots, and he took an old Inkspots song, rewrote the words to include teardrops, and slightly changed the melody. "I wrote it for Johnny Raye," Marty said. "He wouldn't record it, so I did it myself."[31] He recorded "Mister Teardrop" on March 13, 1956, and it was released as the B side of rockabilly "Long Tall Sally," the follow-up to "Maybelline." Neither side charted.

In April, Marty recorded two duets with Lee Emerson, whom he'd met during a West Coast tour and then helped get a Columbia recording contract. Emerson moved to Nashville and began playing rhythm guitar with the Teardrops. Butrum and Emerson alternated fronting the show when there was no opening act. Although Marty never designated a band leader, the others looked up to Butrum because he had the most experience.[32]

Marty hosted the Opry's *Prince Albert* show, the portion sponsored by R.J. Reynolds Tobacco Company, on May 19. He'd been a guest numerous times in the past five years, and this was his first time to host the prestigious half-hour show carried nationwide on NBC Radio. When time came to recite the Prince Albert jingle, "Nature in her own pure way puts the flavor in P.A.," Marty said, "Nature in her own P.A. puts the flavor in its pure way." He came off the stage nearly crying, White remembers, fearful he would never be allowed on the show again. "He thought sure he was ruined for life," White says. "He thought his career was over. But, needless to say, it wasn't."

Eighteen-year-old White received Marty's help after mentioning he wanted a car instead of relying on the city bus. "Up at the old WSM studio," White recalls, "he sat down and wrote me a check for $200 for the first car I ever owned." Several weeks later, White repaid the debt with the paycheck he earned when Marty and the Teardrops filmed several *Stars of the Grand Ole Opry* shows.[33]

Al Gannaway of the Gannaway-VerHalen production company contracted with WSM Radio for two thirteen-week *Stars of the Grand Ole Opry* series in 1955 and 1956. Opry performers were told when and where to be for their segments.[34] Gannaway, seeing potential in several Opry stars, signed Faron Young, Webb Pierce, Carl Smith, and Marty to movie contracts with Republic Pictures.

In June and July 1956, they filmed outdoor scenes for three western movies at Kanab, Utah, and the remaining scenes at Corriganville near Los Angeles. *The Badge of Marshal Brennan* and *Raiders of Old California* were released to theaters in 1957, while *Buffalo Gun* reached the screen in 1961. In *The Badge of Marshal Brennan,* Marty played a Mexican outlaw named Felipe. The other Opry star in the movie was sheriff Carl Smith.

Marty's next film starred Faron Young and was originally called *Stampede* and then *Six Guns and a Gavel* before being released as *Raiders of Old California.* Marty played an outlaw shot by marshal Faron Young during an ambush. Young holstered his gun and rolled the outlaw into his arms to check his wound. Marty looked up and said, "I'm hurt, Marshal. I think I'm done." According to Young,

Marty winked when he was supposed to be dying. "So they had to cut," Young recalls. "I'll bet we did this thirty times. The worst part was when I finally get him to the local jail. I had to get Marty off the horse and put him on my back. . . . I get him over my shoulder, and I'm walkin' right at the camera, and Marty is goosin' me. I'm tryin' to keep a straight face. So we did this about ten takes, too." Young later commented that Marty spent half his time on the set rewriting scripts to make them more realistic, and the other half divided between acting and playing tricks.[35]

Buffalo Gun was filmed in July. Marty narrated the movie, which began with him saying, "That there's Webb Pierce, and that's Carl Smith, and that's me, Marty Robbins. Sure can't figure out why, but we're all in—" and the Jordanaires started singing "Buffalo Gun." After the song, the narrator picked up again: "This story begins in 1875. Me and Smith and Webb Pierce are on this cattle drive . . ." Pierce played a government agent who deputized the other two for assistance in finding stolen buffalo guns. Silliness outranked seriousness, as shown in the scene where Pierce rode up to Smith, who lost his horse after fighting an Indian. Pierce dismounted and said, "Things like this just don't happen in Nashville."[36]

On August 11, Webb Pierce and Marty joined Carl Smith on the Opry stage where they sang "Why Baby, Why" while wearing western costumes and guns. Their appearance fulfilled their promise to a *Country Music Reporter* columnist that they would return from making western movies in Hollywood "and wear their same western dress on the stage of the Grand Ole Opry."[37]

In addition to singing and acting, Marty moved into the business side of the music industry when he and Hillous Butrum started a publishing company in Nashville in mid-1956, co-located with Marty's office at 319 Seventh Avenue. They derived the title of Be-Are Music Publications, Inc. from Butrum-Robbins (B-R). Butrum became president and Marty vice president. Because Acuff-Rose held his songwriting contract, Marty could not place his own songs in the new company. He recorded his first two Be-Are songs, both written by Lee Emerson, in September.[38] Producer Don Law apparently didn't consider them of high enough quality for Columbia to issue.

This was about the time Jack Pruett replaced Joe Wright on lead guitar. "Marty told us when he hired us, if anyone ever upstaged him, we were fired, because he was the star," Wright explains. With rockabilly songs like "Maybelline" and "Long Tall Sally," Marty's show drew teenagers. "He would have twenty-five pretty women wanting his autograph after the show, and I'd have

150 little teenyboppers," Wright says. "I'd been an athlete and a gymnast in school, so when I'd do a ride on one of his songs, I'd do a backbend or splits or something. All those little girls ate it up." One day the Teardrops were riding down the road, and Marty smiled at Wright and said, "By the way, you're fired." He added, "This is your two-week notice." Wright thought Marty was joking, but when he arrived for the Friday Night Frolic two weeks later, Jack Pruett was there. "Him firing me actually turned out to be a favor to me," Wright maintains. "I then became the second highest paid musician in Nashville." He traded working the road for Nashville television shows and local appearances with other Opry acts. He also developed a friendship with Marty, becoming a late-night companion for wandering around town, the role Ray Edenton filled several years earlier.[39]

Jack Pruett was hired by Hillous Butrum, whom Marty sent in search of a replacement. Marty never needed to find another lead guitar player because Pruett stayed with him until the end. About Marty's opinion of the Teardrop name, Pruett says, "Somebody'd already hung that handle on him, and he was never happy about that. He never liked the idea of Teardrops."[40] No one seems to know who originated the idea or why Marty allowed the name to be used for so long. It did, however, appropriately describe his voice on his records.

According to Ralph Emery, then a deejay on WSIX Radio, Marty thought lack of WSM airplay was one reason for his lack of hits. He would visit Emery's show and complain that WSM's Eddie Hill didn't play his records. Marty retaliated in unique fashion. He drove to nearby Murfreesboro to get to a long-distance telephone line and called the influential Hill during his overnight radio show. Disguising his voice, Marty introduced himself as a truck driver who wanted to hear a Marty Robbins song. He returned to his car and listened gleefully as Hill played a song for an old pedal-pushing buddy.[41] This stunt became a Marty Robbins tradition and would later dupe Emery when he took over Hill's WSM show.

Marty's next release didn't need his help in getting airplay.

[7]

Singing the Blues in a White Sport Coat

"Marty Robbins did it this week—yes, he won the cherished *Billboard Magazine* Triple Crown with his fabulously successful 'Singing the Blues' record for Columbia," said a *Nashville Banner* article of November 22, 1956. The Triple Crown consisted of three *Billboard* Country Hit Parade charts—jukebox play, store sales, and radio play. Runner-up recordings were Ray Price's "Crazy Arms," Elvis Presley's "Don't Be Cruel," and Johnny Cash's "I Walk the Line."[1]

"Singing the Blues" had come to Marty's attention at WSM's Friday Night Frolic more than a year earlier, when young Melvin Endsley from Arkansas rolled up in his wheelchair and boldly announced, "I have four songs I want you to listen to. Can you stay after the show and hear them?" Marty answered,

"Sure, I'll be glad to." Endsley sang to the accompaniment of his friend's lead guitar and Marty's rhythm guitar. Marty said he liked the songs but not well enough to record them. "Well, I got one more," Endsley said. "You probably won't like it." Marty told him to sing it anyway.[2] He sang "I Never Felt More Like Singing the Blues."

Endsley, born in January 1934, contracted polio at age three. He was twelve when a nurse at Crippled Children's Hospital in Memphis gave him a guitar as a reward for singing at hospital events. He started writing songs, keeping them all in his head. In July 1954 he was holding his guitar and gazing out a window when the words "I never felt more like singing the blues" popped into his mind. He finished the song and sang it on the air the next day during an amateur program at a local radio station. The favorable reaction made him concerned someone would steal it, so he laboriously wrote words and musical notes and had it copyrighted. A year later he made the trip to Nashville to find someone interested in his fifty songs. Marty took Endsley to Wesley Rose, who signed him as a songwriter with Acuff-Rose Music Publishing. Rose provided a tape recorder for Endsley to transfer his songs from his head to tape.[3] Endsley would celebrate his twenty-third birthday with his song holding a month-long lock at the top of two major music charts.

Marty recorded "Singing the Blues" ten months before Don Law released it in September 1956 as the B side of one of Marty's compositions, "I Can't Quit (I've Gone Too Far)." At first, the two songs climbed the charts together. *Folk and Country Songs* magazine even asked readers to mail in a vote as to "which side will be the big one." In the end, "I Can't Quit" reached number seven. "Singing the Blues" spent thirteen weeks at number one and stayed on *Billboard's* country charts for seven months.[4] It became the first of Marty's recordings to cross over to the pop charts, staying there four months and peaking at number seventeen.

Also in September Marty recorded twelve songs intended for an album. Reminiscent of his early radio shows in Phoenix, he sat with his guitar in front of the microphone and sang a dozen traditional folk songs from as far back as the 1800s. Long-playing albums (LPs) weren't yet vehicles for choosing hit singles and no airplay was expected from them. After an artist had a large enough fan base the record company would order an album. Its purpose was to produce sales to existing fans, rather than showcasing the artist's songs. Columbia had packaged and issued Marty's previously recorded songs twice in 1956 on its

House Party series. *Carl, Lefty and Marty* held two songs apiece by the three named artists, and *Rock'n Rollin' Robbins* contained six rockabilly songs.[5]

Marty's September effort was never released. Columbia issued four songs on an extended-play (EP) 45-rpm record, *The Letter Edged in Black,* and sales apparently weren't high enough to follow with a full album. In mid-January 1957 he recorded twelve songs made popular by other artists, including his heroes Gene Autry and Eddy Arnold. *The Song of Robbins,* released in April 1957, became his first official album. In November *Billboard*'s Tenth Annual Disk Jockey Poll would name him Favorite Male Artist of C&W Jockeys and give *Song of Robbins, Marty Robbins* the number two spot in the category of Favorite C&W Albums.[6]

In the meantime "Singing the Blues," the biggest hit of Marty's entire career, might have been even bigger if not sabotaged by Columbia Records, his own record company. In New York City, Mitch Miller, head of Artists and Repertory for Columbia (and future host of television show *Sing Along With Mitch*), chose Guy Mitchell to record a cover version. It entered the pop charts before Marty's rendering crossed over, capturing most of the popular airplay. After displacing Elvis Presley's "Love Me Tender," Mitchell's cover spent nine weeks at number one, inside Marty's thirteen weeks. With pop music always attracting a larger audience than country music did, Mitchell sold approximately two million copies to Marty's half a million.[7] No one can know how much of a smash "Singing the Blues" would have been if Columbia had marketed Marty to both audiences instead of using the song to rejuvenate Mitchell's career.

And then Columbia did it again. Marty's second Endsley song, "Knee Deep In the Blues," was released in December while the two "Singing the Blues" recordings held their number one spots. His version of "Knee Deep In the Blues" hadn't yet charted when Mitchell's cover entered the pop charts in mid-January. That was enough for Marty. He arranged with Mitch Miller for a recording session at Columbia studio in New York City. (His recording of "Knee Deep In the Blues" entered the country charts in February and reached number three, while Mitchell had a number sixteen pop hit.)

The song Marty planned to record in New York City, "A White Sport Coat (And a Pink Carnation)," had come to him one night while driving across Ohio from one show date to another. He was sitting in the back seat and thinking about a song he'd written, "A Ring and a Promise." He couldn't record it because Sonny James had a current hit with the similar-sounding "Young Love" (a crossover number one for James on both country and pop charts).

"I was *so mad*," Marty said later, "because I thought somebody had heard my song and stolen my idea and melody." Looking out the window, he noticed a sign that said eleven miles to the next town. In that instant, the words "a white sport coat and a pink carnation" popped into his mind. The two songs he'd been thinking about had nothing to do with white sport coats or pink carnations, and he never could explain where the idea came from, except to acknowledge that pink, black, and white was then a popular color combination. "I grabbed a pencil—I always had a pencil and a writing pad handy," he said, "and I started writing. When I looked up, I'd finished, and we were at the city limits of the town. So it took me eleven miles to write the song."[8]

Joe Wright remembers Marty asking his opinion of the song—because Wright was still a teenager—and wondering who should record it. Wright said Marty should do it himself. "But I'm thirty-one years old," Marty said. "I'm not a teenager." Wright reminded him no one would be watching a record.[9]

When Marty arrived in the Big Apple in January, his recording of "Singing the Blues" was in its tenth week as *Billboard*'s number one country song. Jack Stapp, WSM program manager, worked with WSM's New York representatives to publicize one of the Opry's hottest stars. One trade article reported, "Marty was wined, dined, interviewed, photographed, pursued by newspapermen and women, autograph hunters and hand shakers." Miller produced the two-day pop-flavored recording session at the Columbia studio.[10] The band leader and arranger was Ray Conniff, who had performed that same role on Mitchell's "Singing the Blues" and who would soon begin his own recording career as an orchestra leader. Using New York City musicians, Marty recorded four songs, three of which he wrote, and began the teen-ballad phase of his career.

"I changed my style of writing because I wasn't doing any good writing the kinds of songs I wanted to write," he said. "I wasn't doing any good singing the songs I liked, really." To adapt to the market, he gave up the sentimental love songs he preferred. He did not consider "White Sport Coat" a country song.[11]

"Singing the Blues" earned Marty the title of "Best Country and Western Performer for 1956" in the third annual United Press Disk Jockey poll. Eddy Arnold was a close runner-up, followed by Elvis Presley, Sonny James, and Johnny Cash. Five hundred sixty deejays from all forty-eight states and Hawaii cast votes.[12]

Columbia Records presented Marty and labelmate Ray Price with its first annual "Golden Guitars" awards on April 6, 1957, during the network *Prince Albert* portion of the Opry. The award honored artists whose records sold more than 250,000 copies. "Both Price [with "Crazy Arms"] and Robbins far exceeded this figure with their master hits which spread-eagled the Country Hit Parade for the last half of 1956," stated a newspaper article.[13]

As the Elvis Presley phenomenon burgeoned, and teenaged fans became a driving force behind record sales, the onslaught of rock 'n' roll placed country music in a struggle for survival. In the words of Faron Young, "About 1957, rock 'n' roll hit. Elvis. Fabian. Bang-bang. Hell, a hillbilly couldn't get a job." Ralph Emery, after becoming host of WSM Radio's all-night *Opry Star Spotlight,* credited WSM with keeping country music alive in the mid-to-late 1950s. He called WSM "a fifty-thousand-watt life support system."[14]

Numerous country artists tried to appeal to the rapidly growing teenage audience, among them Faron Young and Marty Robbins. Striving for two markets placed entertainers in the position of choosing songs and production styles that attracted teenagers without alienating existing fans. Reactions from older fans ranged from rejection to "anything he sings is good" to tolerating current efforts and waiting for a return to "normal." Marty must have been excited to read in *Billboard* in March that "the flying success of c&w is highlighted by the success of the hybrids, and with the continuing help of these c&w-pop crossbreeds, the country pot is likely to keep boiling on all fronts for a healthy spell."[15] "A White Sport Coat (And a Pink Carnation)" entered the charts in April and became Marty's third number one recording and fifth biggest of his career. It also reached number two as a crossover pop hit.

Mitch Miller pleaded with him to accept a guest slot on the *Ed Sullivan Show.* "Marty, why don't you want to go on?" he asked. "People all over the country will see you. You'll have a hit song; it will be the biggest smash." Marty responded, "I don't want these teenagers to see I'm not a teenager." Finally, he returned to New York City in May to sing the song on Steve Allen's Sunday night NBC-TV show.[16] For two years, Marty usually wore a white sport coat on stage.

Miller occasionally sent demonstration tapes to help Marty choose songs. The demo singer's voice brought out Marty's sense of inferiority. "He made me feel bad all the time," Marty recalled. "That guy had a beautiful voice." Marty worried his renditions wouldn't be the same quality. As for the actual sessions, he considered his in New York City to be a forerunner of the Nashville Sound of the 1960s. He called the "White Sport Coat" guitar work the "same type that was used in Nashville later on. I think that has a lot to do with the Nashville Sound with the guitar."[17]

Expanding his musical style from rockabilly and straight country to teen pop required changes in the band, as did Marty's plan to work dance halls in Texas. Needing drums and a piano, he hired Buddy Harmon and Floyd Cramer. They didn't stay long because they started making more money as sidemen on record sessions. Louie Dunn replaced Harmon on drums. Grover "Shorty" Lavender occasionally joined the group on fiddle, with Earl White moving to bass for those shows. Then Marty, as did other singers at the time, decided to modernize the band and get rid of the fiddle. "I understood what he was doing," says White. "I enjoyed those times. We didn't make much money, but we made a lot of memories." White became an Opry staff musician, a slot he still holds more than half a century later.[18]

Reaching back to identify members of the band at any specific time during this period is difficult because sidemen such as Lester Wilburn and Shorty Lavender were used when available and needed. Some worked with several artists and some were proficient on several instruments. Jack Pruett on lead guitar, Jim Farmer on steel, and Louie Dunn on drums formed the core of the Teardrops, along with Hillous Butrum on rhythm.[19]

Musicians in the 1950s gathered at the Clarkston Hotel coffee shop in Nashville, just as they would congregate at Linebaugh's on Lower Broadway the following decade. The Clarkston Hotel on Seventh Avenue North sat between the National Life and Accident Insurance Company Building and the Cumberland Lodge Building. The first housed WSM Radio and its Friday Night Frolic, and the second contained Marty's office and those of other music-related businesses. Musicians scheduled to be on WSM's weekday *Noontime Neighbors* show usually met in the Clarkston coffee shop midmorning. Other musicians and entertainers might arrive at any time just to see who was there.[20]

Marty added to his business ventures with a booking agency owned by Emerson-Robbins, Inc. Lee Emerson served as president of Lee-Mart Agency, which opened the summer of 1957 in the Seventh Avenue location. George Jones and Johnny Horton were clients, along with Marty and several other singers. This short-lived agency folded a few months later, when Emerson formed a new company and they sold the contracts (including Marty's) to the Emerson-Shucher Agency.[21]

In his usual way of helping others in the business, Marty found a secretary one night at a club called the Rainbow Room. He watched a song-and-dance performance by Hal and Ginger Willis, who had recently moved to Nashville. "Marty drank 7-Up," Hal Willis recalls. "He'd come to see a show, and he'd shake hands with everybody, and he'd buy everybody a drink." Marty asked if they planned to stay in Nashville; they said they would if they could get enough work. "I need a secretary," Marty said. "I just opened up an office over in the Cumberland Lodge Building on Seventh Avenue." Ginger told him she would accept the job if it didn't interfere with her entertaining. They agreed Marty would leave work on her desk whenever she went on tour, and she would have a key to open the office upon her return.[22]

Beginning with "White Sport Coat," his first record with background vocals, Marty wanted his live shows to replicate his recordings. He found what he needed in Grand Island, Nebraska, when someone knocked on his dressing room door after a matinee performance that summer.

"Will you listen to my boys sing?" asked Louis Glaser, a farmer from nearby Spalding. Marty agreed. Glaser, who acted as agent and mentor for his three youngest sons, had brought Tom, Chuck and Jim (ages 23, 21, 19) to the show to see their musical hero and, hopefully, to meet him. They wore identical aqua-blue shirts, ready for an engagement that evening at a drive-in theater. "Dad came out front with a big smile on his face and the three of us followed him backstage," Jim Glaser recalls. "I don't remember which three or four songs we sang for Marty in his dressing room; I do remember he was obviously impressed with what he heard and promised if we'd come to Nashville in a few weeks, he would take us into a recording studio and make a record with us."[23]

Marty started a recording company to introduce the Glaser Brothers. He placed Robbins Records, his third business, in his new umbrella corporation, Marty Robbins Enterprises, Inc. The Glasers' first session occurred August 19, 1957, at the Owen Bradley Studios, with Marty as producer.[24] Louis and Marie Glaser and their sons drove to Nashville where Marty made good on his promise. The family returned to their Nebraska farm after Louis Glaser and Marty negotiated an agreement. When that year's farm work was finished, the Glaser Brothers would move to Nashville and become part of Marty's touring entourage.

Robbins Records issued its first release that autumn—a Chuck Glaser-penned song, "Five Penny Nickel," by the Glaser Brothers. The brothers appeared twice with Marty before their January 1958 move to Nashville. They drove to Phoenix, Arizona, to join him on a fair tour. He wanted them to open his shows and help with his new songs. The Glasers provided the "do-wap" sounds of the Ray Conniff Singers. "We were repeating what they had done," Jim Glaser says, "so Marty had the vocal backing on stage." When Marty appeared on *American Bandstand* on November 19, 1957, he persuaded producers to let his prodigies perform their new single.

Because Marty believed a group could not achieve the same success as a solo performer, they became Tompall (from Thomas Paul) and the Glaser Brothers.[25] (This was before the Statler Brothers, Oakridge Boys, and Alabama.) At the time, the Wilburn Brothers and Louvin Brothers were extremely popular but with limited hits, and the Everly Brothers were moving away from country music.

In parallel with recording singles in New York City, Marty recorded his second full album during two Nashville sessions in October 1957.[26] *Song of the Islands,* released the end of December, expressed his love of Hawaiian music. It showcased his versatility and demonstrated a focus on music over commercial success. He didn't write any of the songs, and none of them charted, but the album would forever be held as an innovative example of concept albums.

Hawaiian music gave Marty an opportunity to perfect the falsetto he loved and had been practicing for a decade. He'd tested the waters on an afternoon radio show in Nashville in 1953 when he sang "My Isle of Golden Dreams," a song he'd learned years earlier in the Hawaiian Islands. "Got a lot of mail," he recalled, "did it again, got a lot of mail again, so finally I recorded it." He described a falsetto as "when you don't sing in a natural voice. Hawaiians sing like they have more range because they use falsettos. Opera singers have quite a range, but they do not use falsettos; they have power." He considered a falsetto to be "kind of cheating a little bit." He said, "Instead of singing from deep down in the lungs, you sing from right in the throat area and out of the mouth."[27] A falsetto became one feature of his live performances, and audiences screamed whenever he stretched his neck and stood on tiptoe to reach the high notes.

Marty's singles from 1952 through 1957 had all been released both as heavy, breakable 78-rpm records and small 45-rpm records. The 78s were discontinued at the end of 1957 as the record business made its transition to 33-rpm albums.[28]

The year closed with "The Story of My Life" becoming Marty's fourth number one *Billboard* hit, as well as crossing over to number fifteen pop. His New York recording session in February 1958 produced a dual-hit phenomenon. Both sides of his next single entered the charts together in April. "Just Married" became his second consecutive number one record, and the flipside, "Stairway of Love," peaked at number two. Both appeared on pop charts. Marty wrote the follow-up single, "She Was Only Seventeen (And He Was One Year More)." This song, his last teen ballad hit, reached number four on country charts and twenty-seven on pop charts.[29]

His chart success did not keep him from being fired from the Grand Ole Opry on March 1, 1958. Early that day he'd had an argument with WSM general manager Robert Cooper. Marty urged the radio station to establish a staff country music orchestra as it had already done with pop musicians. He later explained, "I said during the discussion that if Jim Denny were still here, he'd have the Opry fully sponsored and would have a network television show."[30] That probably didn't go over too well with executives who had fired Denny eighteen months earlier for conflict of interest.

That evening Marty hosted the *Prince Albert* portion of the Grand Ole Opry and sang his current hit, "The Story of My Life." According to W. D. Kilpatrick, who replaced Denny as Opry manager, Marty was called into a conference after the show and told the Opry no longer needed him. "He indicated in a conference Saturday morning that he no longer needed Grand Ole Opry," Kilpatrick stated in an interview. "We simply cannot deal with prima donnas on this show." He added, "Robbins has displayed insubordination recently, which just could not be tolerated any longer." Marty's explanation was, "I said the right thing to the wrong person."[31]

WSM executives met with Marty the following Thursday and decided they had made a mistake. The station issued a statement saying "it was clearly conceded that Marty Robbins had not at any time said or indicated that he 'did not need the Grand Ole Opry.'" A newspaper article described Marty as representing "the younger element of the Opry. In contrast to the gaudy western costumes worn by some of the current stars and by most of the oldsters, he wore 'conservative' sports jackets and ties onstage. He also used vocal backgrounds in a lot of his stage presentations, a strictly modern touch."[32] Clearly, the *Opry* needed him.

"Grand Ole Opry star" was an important title in the 1950s, garnering higher performance rates on the road and better bookings. WSM's Artist Service Bureau controlled bookings until Jim Denny broke away with his own agency. Opry members were required to perform twenty-six nights every year, at a rate of $30 per performance—considerably less than playing to packed auditoriums across the nation. They had to arrange their travel schedules to be in Nashville on Saturday nights. Marty enjoyed being an Opry member and was willing to make that sacrifice.

Musicians received $15 for their first Opry show each evening and $7.50 for later shows. The more fifteen- or thirty-minute shows a sideman worked, the more he earned. "Money was not easy to come by and everyone helped everyone else make money," Joe Wright explains. A singer without a band might use one musician on the first show and another on the second, as Marty had done in his early days. One night after Wright left the Teardrops, he was at the Friday Night Frolic when Marty asked him to play piano. "Marty, I can't play piano," Wright protested. "You can chord," Marty said. "Come on and play rhythm." Wright remembers that performance as "easy $7.50 and the only time I ever made money playing piano."[33]

Marty switched his personal bookings from Emerson-Shucher to Jim Denny's Artist Bureau in May. He appointed Eddie Crandall, his personal manager, as vice president and general manager of Robbins Records in mid-June. The company was building a reputation as an independent label, and it must have been a thrill to read in trade magazines that "the indie label, headed by Marty Robbins, headquarters in Nashville."[34] Crandall pushed the Glasers' latest release, "Sweet Lies," a song written by Marty and performed by him on the Opry the night of his firing. Unfortunately, the single expected to give the company its boost did not chart.

A Nashville newspaper referred to Marty as "known in the industry as an artist who prefers to handle his own business affairs." Throughout his life, he was more comfortable with New York music industry executives than those in Nashville. "Whenever he'd have a problem with the record label," son Ronny explains, "he'd be on the phone to New York, calling somebody up there. And usually would get something done, which would tend to tick off the people down here." Joe Wright recalls Marty telling him, "I didn't like what they were doing here, Joe. I flew up to New York, and I went up to the top of the building there and talked to the president."[35] This attitude, and his unwillingness to socialize at Nashville industry events, may have been responsible for Marty obtaining less recognition than deserved.

Marty's last session with Mitch Miller and Ray Conniff, who were expanding their personal entertainment careers, produced "The Hanging Tree." Recorded in Hollywood in October 1958, it was the title song of a movie starring Gary Cooper.[36] "The Hanging Tree" appeared on the album, *Marty's Greatest Hits,* the following April. It marked the beginning of a new career phase—that of recording the western songs Marty loved.

[8]

Gunfighter Ballads and Trail Songs

In 1958 the center of Nashville's music industry began migrating from downtown to Sixteenth Avenue South, now known as Music Row. Marty, always a forward-looking businessman, moved his office from its downtown 319 Seventh Avenue North location to 713 Eighteenth Avenue South, an old house he and Marizona purchased in July. Other publishing companies and entertainers joined him on Music Row, with recording studios replacing WSM and the Grand Ole Opry as industry focal points. Marty later purchased two neighboring lots and the property housed Marty Robbins Enterprises, Inc. until years after Marty's death.

The foundation of Music Row had been laid in 1955 when brothers Owen and Harold Bradley purchased a house in a once-grand residential neighborhood and turned it into a recording studio. They quickly expanded into a Quonset hut built next to their original studio. Columbia moved Marty's sessions to the Bradley Film & Recording Studio at 804 Sixteenth Avenue South as soon as it opened. This coincided with the closing of Castle Recording Studio, which had provided services to Nashville artists for almost a decade in the downtown Tulane Hotel.[1] One other recording studio appeared in late 1957 when RCA Victor Records built a studio on Seventeenth Avenue.

Ginger Willis did not move to Marty's new location. "I was secretary for Marty for awhile," Jim Glaser says. "Since I could type, and didn't have anything to do during days we weren't on the road, I did the typing and wrote letters, and he paid me $25 a week. It's amazing to think that could even do anything, but money went so much further back then." An average Nashville house cost $8,500 in 1960.[2]

One job was keeping track of Marty's song publishing efforts. The album he recorded for Columbia in March, *Marty Robbins* (released in October), marked the end of his songwriter contract with Acuff-Rose. It also marked the end of Be-Are Music, with Butrum keeping most of those copyrights.[3] Marty then opened Marty's Music as his next publishing company.

A permanent frontman joined Marty's band in late summer 1958. Bobby Sykes had acquired his stage name several years earlier in Michigan when a program director didn't like his real name, Bishop Sykes, and told him, "From now on, you're Bobby." He sang on a Nashville television show until its cancellation. "One day at the Clarkston Hotel coffee shop," Sykes recalls, "I was going in and Marty was coming out. We said hello and passed by each other, and I heard, 'Hey, Bobby.' So I turned around, and Marty said, 'What are you doing now that the show's gone off the air?' I said, 'Nothing.' He said, 'You want a job? I've got an eighteen-day tour coming up. Why don't you take that tour with me?'" They agreed to discuss permanent employment at the end of the tour. Sykes stayed with Marty and their discussion never took place.[4]

When Chuck Glaser received his draft notice in late 1958, the brothers discussed finding a baritone to replace him. They thought of Joe Babcock, a friend from Nebraska. "In the summers, I'd work all day putting up hay," Babcock recalls, "and then I'd drive forty miles to the Glaser brothers, and we'd sing and pick half the night, then drive back over, and get up at five o'clock and put up hay again." His father owned the movie theater in North Loup, Nebraska, where the Glasers had held their evening performance after their audition for Marty. Babcock sold popcorn while the brothers sang before the movie started.

Tompall called Babcock, who had moved to Los Angeles in search of a music career, and said, "I traced you through your mother. She gave me this phone number. She told me how great you're doing." Actually, Babcock alternated between living in his car and staying with friends; he subsisted on $5 gigs in supermarket parking lots. "Could you possibly quit what you're doing for a couple years and come out here and sing with us—with Marty Robbins—on the Grand Ole Opry?" Babcock sold his car, caught a ride with a friend, and arrived in Nashville in January 1959. Tompall told him they would be playing the upcoming Friday Night Frolic and Babcock spent his last $60 on a suit. "I got to sing baritone on the Grand Ole Opry right away," Babcock recalls. "I thought that place would come down. Marty got five or six encores. That was quite something for a country boy from Nebraska, coming from being broke and down and out."[5]

Jim Glaser agrees. "That incredible jump from being a farm boy," he says, "taking care of chickens and cows and pigs, and then touring with Marty, who was already so well known. The Grand Ole Opry had been *so big* in our minds while we were growing up, and suddenly be a part of the business. And that was because he made it possible. It was just the most incredible notion."[6]

Marty postponed his scheduled western tour while waiting for Marizona to give birth. She spent most of January 29, 1959, in labor, and Marty and nine-year-old Ronny wandered from waiting room to waiting room throughout Baptist Hospital trying to get some sleep. In school the next day, Ronny bragged about his new baby sister and then fell asleep on the lunchroom table. Janet Karen was named for her maternal grandmother, Jeanette, and her parents liked the name Karen, which belonged to the little girl next door.[7]

When Marty and the Teardrops finally set out for the West Coast in February, they traveled in two station wagons from Nashville to Spokane, Washington, "packed in there like biscuits in a tray," says Babcock. They drove for two full days, pulling a trailer, on "those old roads in the dead of winter," as he recalls. "That was my inauguration into road life." After Spokane, they went to Seattle, then into Oregon, and down to San Francisco and Los Angeles. Tompall and the Glaser Brothers served a dual purpose: as Marty's opening act, with Jim on electric lead guitar and the other two playing rhythm, and providing background voices on Marty's latest hits.[8] The band during the tour consisted of Jack Pruett on lead guitar, Louie Dunn on drums, Jim Farmer on steel, Bobby Sykes on rhythm guitar, and Hillous Butrum on bass.

On February 21, while in Los Angeles, they appeared on *Town Hall Party*, a Saturday evening television show broadcast live from Compton Town Hall Dance Club. Marty looked comfortable on stage, smiling as if happy to be there and proud of his band. He hadn't yet adopted his later stage personality of clowning self-aggrandizement and audience interaction, but he had passed the period of being too shy to talk. He even consented to an onstage interview with singer-songwriter-guitarist Johnny Bond. They joked about meeting at Marty's 1951 recording session in Los Angeles. "It was my pleasure to pick the guitar on his very first record," Bond said. "He was young and he was nervous, and—" Marty interrupted with, "Boy, I sure was nervous."

When Bond asked about side businesses, Marty replied, "Just sort of to make it a little easier to get by, you mean? I have a publishing company." "Everybody's got a publishing company," Bond commented. "Don't you have a record company?" Marty said, "Yeah," and then chuckled. "I don't talk too much about that record company." By then he had already issued the ten singles recorded by Robbins Records (four of them belonging to the Glaser Brothers) and would soon fold the label.

"You've got a smasheroo out on the market right now from that Gary Cooper picture, *The Hanging Tree*," Bond stated. The movie had been released ten days earlier. Marty's version of the title song was already on *Billboard*'s pop chart and would reach number fifteen on the country chart. "Somebody else could probably have done a lot better job," Marty answered, "but—still, boy, I really like the song. I guess it's my favorite of all the songs I've ever done."[9]

He would soon find a new favorite song, one that lasted his lifetime—a song he wrote two years earlier. The song idea first occurred to Marty while driving his family home to Phoenix for Christmas in 1955. Seeing the city limits sign, he decided El Paso was a romantic-sounding name, and he'd like to write a song about El Paso. By the time he reached the other side of the city, he'd forgotten the idea. The next Christmas he remembered, "Well, last year I said I was gonna write a song about El Paso." But again, he drove through the city and forgot the idea before reaching the other side.[10]

The third time through, in 1957, he reminded himself he'd said he was going to write a song about El Paso. Right at that moment, a line popped into his mind: "Out in the west Texas town of El Paso, I fell in love with a Mexican girl." In later years, he enjoyed telling the story of writing the song. "It was a funny sensation," he said in an interview. "I'm driving across the desert from El Paso to Phoenix as I'm writing, y'see. The song came out like a motion picture, and I could never forget the words to it. I put them down after I got to Phoenix, but I couldn't forget it because it was like a motion picture. I didn't know how it was going to end. It just kept on coming out, and coming out, and the tune was coming out at the same time." "I was rushing real quick trying to get through it, saying the words as fast as I could because they were just coming out." He told Ralph Emery, "It was real exciting, and I kept waiting for the end to come to see what was going to happen. Finally it ended when it wanted to. I really didn't have too much to do with that song. It just came out."[11]

Marty recognized the name Feleena as belonging to a classmate in elementary school in Glendale. "There was nothing really true about the story," Marty said, "except I found out after I had written the song . . . that at the turn of the century there was a place in El Paso called Rosa's Cantina." He classified "El Paso" as a cowboy song "more like a folk song of the early American West. To me, there's quite a big difference in cowboy and country-and-western."[12]

Recording "El Paso" was out of the question while working with Conniff and Miller. Marty asked Don Law if he could record it during a Nashville session, and Law said 4:37 (four minutes thirty-seven seconds) was too long. So Marty sang it for his band. When on the road, he usually rode in the second of two cars, with Bobby Sykes and Jim Glaser and several others. "Bobby had a rich baritone voice," Glaser says. "Marty carried a little ukulele with him, and to pass the miles, he used to sing every song he could think of and Bobby Sykes and I would put harmony on them. Just to be doing something." The songs they sang included "El Paso." According to Glaser, "We'd get out in the middle of Texas somewhere, and he'd get his ukulele and teach us the new part of the song. He'd come on tour and he'd have a new piece of it finished. It was several tours before we knew what was going to happen in the song. I'd lay out the harmony for Bobby and me. So by the time we went into the studio, we had it down pat."

Don Law finally agreed to let Marty record an album of western songs. "I had no idea there would be a big market for it," Marty explained later. "It was different than what I had been doing." His band members started writing songs, hoping Marty would include theirs in the album. They also started practicing the songs selected for that first western album.[13]

Marty recorded the complete album in an eight-hour session on April 7, 1959. Sykes recalls hearing Marty tell Law during the evening, "Don, this album won't sell five hundred records, but it's something I've always wanted to do and I think Columbia Records owes it to me." Law responded, "That's fine, Marty, you never know. Let's do the best we can and see what happens." There were seven traditional western songs and five new ones, four written by Marty and one by Tompall and Jim Glaser. Marty's new publishing company, Marty's Music, owned those five songs. Although the Glaser Brothers are usually credited with providing harmony for "El Paso," it was actually Bobby Sykes and Jim Glaser, just as they'd practiced during those long miles while on tour. "I think it was the sixth complete take at the studio that was the final take," Glaser recalls, "and an amazing thing in retrospect."[14]

"Everybody was having such a good time that night," says Sykes. "Of course, when the lights went on, we all got serious. But we joked in between takes. In just about any session with Marty, he would clown around so much he would put you at ease. But then, if you got too loose, he would snap you back into shape in a second, I guarantee you." Sykes explains, "It was his career and one way or another he was paying for it. It didn't come out of his pocket right then, but eventually it would. The company paid for the recording session, but then they would deduct it from your royalties."[15]

Grady Martin played lead guitar and arranged the "El Paso" session. Sykes describes the Martin-Law-Robbins relationship as follows:

> Don always had somebody working for him on the sessions trying to get the right sound, the right arrangement. In many of Marty's sessions, that man was Grady Martin. I know I heard Don say many times before a session started: "Grady, get me a good sound on this." And he more or less left it up to Grady. Don would go into the control room and when he heard what he wanted to hear, he would say, "Okay, that sounds good. Let's do a take." Then they would play it back for Marty. If it was what Marty wanted to hear, fine. If Marty would say, "Let's change this or do that a little differently," I don't care who spoke up, that's the way they would do it.[16]

Along with recording sessions and business matters, Marty continued touring. "Jim Glaser and I did a lot of the driving," Babcock says. "We'd do a show, and usually go get something to eat after the show, then pack in, and drive all night. Most of our jobs were three [hundred] to four hundred miles apart. That was a hard life but we loved it—for awhile. We'd pull in at a motel about nine or ten o'clock, get a little sleep in the daytime, try to rest up, and do it again the next night." He adds, "We played a lot of those Texas dancehalls. Bobby Sykes usually fronted the show. He was a wonderful singer and played a lot of those old Bob Wills tunes. Marty hated those dances. He'd rather be where he could capture that audience. He wanted to sing to the audience and have them react to him. The dancers, y'know, they danced. Still, there were always a bunch of people up front when Marty came on to watch the show. It was a dance *and* a show."[17]

Glaser calls Marty "an incredible entertainer." He also remembers working big clubs in Texas and California. "We'd go out and sing our little hearts out," he says, "and Bobby Sykes would sing his little heart out. People would dance, and sit at the tables, and Marty would come up to the microphone, and the *whole crowd* would get up and rush to the edge of the stage and stand and watch him, in rapt attention. It didn't just happen once; this always happened. I looked at him and I thought, what is this charisma he has?"[18]

One reason Marty carried a band was to give him control in making his live shows sound like the records. When they played package shows, other singers wanted to use the Teardrops because few of them carried bands. "It made Marty sort of mad," Babcock says, "because he had to pay the band, the travel and motel and everything, so he started making them pay us a little money. He didn't get anything out of it, but he at least made them pay us a little bit for those package shows."[19]

Hal Willis remembers Marty as "one of the biggest-hearted guys in the world" but someone who enjoyed giving his band a hard time. Whenever a musician asked for an advance, Marty would cock his head and say, "Now look, you work for me. I pay you good money. Good money! And you're always coming back—you haven't been home three days—and you want to borrow money. What are you doing with your money? Are you burning it in the back yard? Are you throwing it to the wind? What are you doing with the cash?" After the harassment, he would reach in his pocket for money. "I've never seen him turn one down," Willis says. "But you knew he would give you some heck first."

Willis experienced this himself after Ginger stopped working for Marty, when the couple was preparing to go on tour. Willis went to Marty's office and said, "I need $1,400 for about two weeks, and I'll have it right back to you." Marty cocked his head and grinned. "Hal, you're making enough money." He went through the diatribe Willis expected. Then he said, "I haven't got it in my pocket, that's for darn sure. Let me holler at Jimmy." He called upstairs to Jim Farmer and asked, "Jim, we got any money in the publishing company? I'm going to send Hal up there. You write him a check for $1,400 for a loan." Farmer wrote a check and gave it to Willis, who repaid Farmer at the end of the tour. The next time Marty saw Willis, he immediately thanked him for returning the cash. "This is the kind of guy he was," Willis reminisces. "You can't help but love him. That one time I needed help, and he helped."[20]

April 1959 saw the release of Marty's fourth album while the western album was being finalized. *Marty's Greatest Hits,* unlike earlier LPs, actually contained his hits—the Melvin Endsley songs and recent teen ballads. Because Marty had no idea what to call the western album, he let Don Law choose a title. *The Music Reporter* announced in its September 7 issue: "Marty Robbins' newest Columbia album *Gunfighter Ballads and Trail Songs* caused a switchboard jam during the first local airing (WSM)."[21]

Almost fifty years later, Doug "Ranger Doug" Green of the western singing group Riders in the Sky would say, "For anybody that sings western music, the *Gunfighter Ballads and Trail Songs* album is seminal. It's part of Cowboy 101. It influenced all of us."[22]

The popularity of the flowing waltz music and riveting love story of "El Paso" grew so rapidly that Don Law released a single on October 26. The B side was the Glasers' "Running Gun," a song that sounded as if Marty wrote it. A shorter version of "El Paso" was also released, in an attempt to fit standard formats. It only added confusion and was not a success. Fans preferred the longer version. "I only recorded it one time," Marty said, "and so I know I don't sing any less on personal appearances than I do on the original recording. It's still four minutes and thirty-seven seconds long."[23]

Talent promoter Marty Landau in Hollywood could see what was happening. "'El Paso' took off on the West Coast," Joe Wright explains, "and we were like two or three weeks behind what was going on out on the West Coast. It took that long to get back to the East Coast. Once they got the single out, it went right straight to number one." The song brought Marty his first professional management contract. He hadn't had much luck with Eddie Crandall and Lee Emerson, whom he kept around out of friendship and charity. When Landau called, Marty turned over management responsibilities.[24]

El Paso itself paid attention. Marty was invited to various events during his lifetime and is remembered today in the Marty Robbins Recreation Center located at 11600 Vista Del Sol. When his flight to the West Coast stopped at the El Paso airport in 1976, Marty got off the plane to run in and get a taco. He heard a symphony orchestra playing an instrumental version of "El Paso" and forgot about his taco. "I thought it was so great they would play that," he stated. "It happens every hour on the hour." Another time he turned on the radio to listen to the Sun Bowl football game, and he heard a band playing "El Paso." So the next year he listened just to hear his song played again.[25]

In 1982 Marty called "El Paso" his favorite of all songs he'd recorded. "I do it every night, but I never get tired of singing it," he said. "There's not another song like it, I guess. Plus, it's cowboy music, and it's got a little bit of mariachi-type music in it, y'know, the Mexican border sound in it. That's kind of what I like, too. Maybe it's a combination of different things that makes it my favorite song." When asked how many times he thought he'd sung it, he answered, "Tell me how many personal appearances I've made since 1959, and then I will know."[26]

"El Paso" entered *Billboard*'s country chart in early November and reached number one on December 21, where it stayed for seven weeks. As a crossover hit, it captured the number one spot on *Billboard*'s pop chart on Christmas Day. Marty moved into the decade of the 1960s with his forever favorite song sitting at number one on both country and pop charts.

"Big Iron" followed "El Paso" as the second single from the *Gunfighter* album. Although it's been assumed Marty acquired songwriting ideas from his grandfather, he said, "I only wrote one song—'Big Iron'—that I could say was about a story he told me." Texas Bob Heckle, who died when his grandson was six years old, did leave a storytelling legacy. "I'm not too sure he was a Texas Ranger," Marty said, recalling Texas Bob's many stories. "But he told me one time how *bad* the people in Texas wanted him to stay there; they had a room for him, y'know, and at the time I didn't know Huntsville was the penitentiary. He told me he didn't want to stay because he thought he would be getting in their way, and so he had a horse, it wasn't a good horse, and so he traded this horse. To show good faith, he left this horse and took another horse, and he said so many people in Texas wanted him to stay, but he just couldn't stay, and he had to leave and come to Arizona."[27]

Marty was driving into Nashville one day when the radio played a bluegrass song by the McCormick Brothers. He thought they mentioned "big iron," and he told himself, oh, what a title for a song. Actually, they were saying "big eyes." When he reached his office, he sat down and wrote "Big Iron." He'd been carrying the idea for awhile, and the thought of big iron allowed the song to take shape. He wrote another song the same day, "Devil Woman," which would make its appearance several years later. "I remember singing them to Tompall Glaser," he recalled. "Neither one of them impressed him much."[28]

"Big Iron" reached number five on *Billboard*'s country chart and crossed over to number twenty-six on *Billboard*'s pop chart. An album cut, "The Master's Call," might have been released as a single if not for one almost imperceptible error. Marty, always a perfectionist, refused to publish a recording in which he sang "a miracle *preformed* that night."[29] When he rerecorded the song in 1963, he was careful to say "performed."

In early 1960, Marty prepared for a triumphal engagement in El Paso, Texas. He flew to Amarillo, the first show date on the tour, while his band and the Glasers drove the two station wagons from Nashville. The group included future Opry star Bill Anderson. "The whole tour was geared toward the excitement we knew a date with Marty Robbins in El Paso would bring," Anderson says. "None of us could wait to get there." When they arrived, the mayor welcomed Marty, and television and newspaper reporters interviewed him. Everyone looked forward to an overflowing auditorium for that night's concert. But fewer than eight hundred people attended the show. The promoter made the ghastly error of thinking the city's top rock 'n' roll station would generate a larger audience than the country station. After all, "El Paso" had been a big crossover hit in the pop field. Advertising and promotion targeted those listeners instead of Marty's true fans, thousands of whom didn't know he was in town. "It was one of the worst decisions I have ever seen made in my entire show business career," Anderson concludes. "I know it had to be among the most disappointing and frustrating nights of Marty's life."[30]

The *Gunfighter* album continued to make an impact. It was such a hit that Marty and his band spent the first half of 1960 working on a second western album. In six recording sessions Marty sang eleven songs to complete *More Gunfighter Ballads and Trail Songs,* released in September. Its one single, Jim Glaser's "Five Brothers" backed with Lee Emerson's "Ride Cowboy Ride," made an appearance on both country and pop charts. *More Greatest Hits,* which followed in April 1961, continued in the same vein and contained several songs from the two *Gunfighter* albums—as well as Marty's next number one single. Joe Babcock, Jim Glaser, and Lee Emerson contributed their songwriting skills. All songs written by Marty's group for these three albums belonged to two publishing companies, Marty's Music and newly formed Marizona Music. Jim Glaser laid out three-part harmonies for the first *Gunfighter* album and half of the second one. He used his normal Glaser Brothers arrangements on new songs and traditional western style for songs in the public domain. From then on, the Glaser Brothers sound became the Marty Robbins sound.[31]

During live performances, the Glasers provided two types of vocal backing for Marty. Jim Glaser and Joe Babcock did the trio singing on western songs. "We all worked on one microphone," Babcock explains. "When we sang 'El Paso,' it was Marty to my left, me in the middle, and Jim to the right. Marty always played that little guitar." For songs such as "White Sport Coat," Tompall joined his brother and Babcock on a separate microphone to provide doo-wap harmony.[32]

In late 1959, Jim Farmer quit traveling to work full time in Marty's publishing companies. Pete Drake handled Marty's steel guitar work until the following summer when he started his career as master sessionman, eventually gaining fame with his Talking Steel Guitar. "He liked chords," Babcock reminisces, "and he hit a real wild chord once, one of these soaring steel endings. Marty looked over and said, 'What the hell was that?' So Pete didn't do that anymore." Also in 1960 Marty fired Bobby Sykes. Although Marty admired his singing, saying "You don't run on to voices like that very often," he could not tolerate drinking. Drake and Sykes were replaced when Bill Johnson and Don Winters joined the band in September. Winters had been friends with Marty for several years, and he brought his steel guitar friend along when Marty asked Winters to work with him. "We had an agreement that I could sing my records on his show," Winters recalled in an interview. "He made me a featured artist on his show from day one."[33]

Their first show date was the Opry. The Glasers were not there that night, so Winters and Johnson sang Marty's background vocals in addition to Johnson playing steel guitar. "We had rehearsed prior to that," Johnson says, "but that was my first time to play the Opry, and it was almost like I was walking on air to the mike to sing behind him on the first song." Winters was playing rhythm, and Marty told him, "Don, back up. You're a little too loud." Winters backed up a few feet, kept playing, and Marty told him to back up some more. This continued until Winters stood at the edge by the curtain. Marty turned around and said, "Just right." At the end of the song, Winters returned to his original position, and Marty told him, "Don't play the guitar anymore. I don't like your rhythm playing. Just sing." Winters quickly got over his hurt feelings. "I kept singing and never did play a guitar again," he says.[34]

Winters eventually became Marty's permanent bodyguard and sidekick. Marty seldom went anywhere alone. He needed both companionship and a buffer to hold off people who wanted to fight and fans who wanted to get too close. Winters replaced Lee Emerson, whom Joe Babcock describes as "a colorful character. He was tall, wavy-haired, nice-looking man, athletic, strong, and a good fighter. Lee was good to us. He was our road manager for awhile. As a lot of people did back then, he took a lot of pills—amphetamines." One evening a drunk was heckling Marty during a show, saying, "Hey, Marty, come on down and fight." Marty said, "No, sir, I have a man who does that for me." The heckler shouted, "Well, show him to me. I'll fight him." Emerson worked his way through the audience, tapped the man's shoulder, smiled an evil smile, and said, "I'm that man." The heckler disappeared. "I think he went down on his hands and knees and crawled through the audience," Babcock says. "Lee could scare you like that."

Emerson's reputation didn't stop hot-headed Marty from challenging him. Babcock watched them arguing backstage one night. Although dressed for the show, they both peeled off their coats and squared off, ready to fight. Then Emerson turned and walked away. Marty looked at Babcock and said, "Joe, y'know, Lee just did me a big favor." Babcock says, "Marty was a pretty good man, but he would have been no match for Lee Emerson."[35]

They fought on the same side in one Georgia town. They were walking along a sidewalk when several hooligans whistled, making wise remarks about their cute little suits. Emerson wanted to beat them up. "I didn't want to do it," Marty explained later. "But I was with him, so I had to. It was three of them and two of us. We came out ahead."[36] Marty's insistence that he "didn't want to" may have been to protect his image when telling the story. He loved a good fight; it just wasn't appropriate for a man with a singing career and fan base.

Winters, although an ex-prizefighter like Emerson, had a different personality. "We would have some strong arguments," he says about Marty, "but we never got mad at each other. . . . We knew he was the boss and we tried to do it his way. But if we thought it was wrong, well, I'd tell him." Winters stayed close to Marty during and after shows to offer protection from "smart alecks" and Marty's own temper. "I can't see him fighting, so I'll sometimes do his fighting for him," Winters once told an interviewer. "I'd rather get whipped than see him get whipped." Marty described Winters as "kind of my best friend."[37]

By the time Winters and Johnson joined the band Marty was already singing "Don't Worry," which had been recorded in July and would be released as a single in December. The song idea came to him one night on his way home from the Opry while sitting at a stoplight on Thompson Lane. "This came to me real quick, and I hadn't been looking for anything," he said. "I wrote that in about four miles. I never did put the words on it down until I got ready to have it copyrighted. It was such an easy song to remember." Reaching his house, he played it on the piano for an hour, "not just to remember the song but because I liked the song," he explained to an interviewer. "I couldn't go to sleep very well, so I sang it over and over to myself." He said "Don't Worry" and "El Paso" were "the only two I might have written in my head and didn't forget. The others I put down on paper." To him, those two songs were unforgettable.[38]

Marty's piano skills, according to Joe Wright, who learned the same way, came from sitting in the studio and messing around with the piano until he could chord on it. "If he sang," Wright says, "he could play the rhythm to it. He wasn't a piano player; he wasn't Floyd Cramer."[39]

The July 12, 1960, session made history when the recording of "Don't Worry" unexpectedly gave birth to a new sound—fuzztone. "Nobody heard it while we were recording it, see," Marty recalled. "When they played it back, chooo, man, the studio went wild. They didn't know what had happened, y'know." Grady Martin on lead bass guitar had been playing the riff when something went wrong in his amplifier. Marty wanted to remove the distortion from the instrumental break. Law told him, "Well, Marty, we may have something here." He joked, "Let's call it Marty Robbins and his Bumblebees." Marty said, "No, no, I'll make a deal with you. We'll leave it in there, but don't put Marty Robbins and the Bumblebees on it."[40]

The distorted sound caused much discussion then, and the origin of fuzztone is still talked about by musicians fifty years later. "No one could figure out the sound because it sounded like a saxophone," Marty explained in an interview. "It sounded like a jet airplane taking off. It had many different sounds."[41]

Because Marty wanted his live performances to duplicate his records, it was up to his musicians to develop the fuzztone distortion in his stage shows. "I believe it was an electronic malfunction of Grady's amplifier that caused, electronically speaking, a square wave," Johnson says.

> But anyway, we had no way to recreate it on stage. So I thought about it, and on some shows, Jack and I were not too far apart on stage, and I would lean back

when it came time for that instrumental break and I'd put my fingernails lightly against the back of the speaker, and made it rattle—made it distort. We did it that way some, but it didn't thrill Jack too much. So that didn't last long. Eventually, a gadget came out on the market—a little gadget that would make that distortion sound. Jack didn't particularly want to use the gadget, so I did it on the steel. It was a tiny electronic gadget, and it was easy for me to plug it in and out of my steel. It had an on-and-off button, but after I'd do the break, I would unplug because it slightly affected the tone if it stayed plugged in, even though it was off. That's just a musician's preference.[42]

Jack Pruett's first attempt was simply to turn up the amp as high as possible to distort the sound. "Sometimes it would duplicate the fuzz," he says, "and sometimes it was clear. It would never do what you wanted it to." A steel guitar buddy on the West Coast made him a little homemade fuzz box "even before Gibson started making them," he recalls. "I used it for quite awhile." Engineers from the session figured out electronically what occurred and then drew up a schematic, Johnson explains. "I believe they eventually sold the rights to the schematic to Gibson." The first professional aid Johnson used was the Moseright Fuzz-Right, given to him at Moseright's guitar factory in California. Later he received a Jordan Electronics Bosstone, which he preferred. "It was much smaller," Johnson says, "and it fit right into the guitar. I didn't have to punch a button with my foot in order to kick it in."[43]

When Marty started performing the song on stage, he needed a piano to recreate Floyd Cramer's introduction. So he asked Babcock, "Cowboy, do you think you could learn to play that?" Because Babcock fiddled around with the piano, he said he'd give it a try. "That's how I ended up playing piano for him," Babcock states. "I learned that intro and a few other things he did, and I became the piano player. I played it exactly note for note like Floyd. Which was pretty easy to do because it was simple." Babcock acquired most of his piano skills during Texas dances. "I got to where I could play a few things," he says. "Louie Dunn would holler, 'Pound it out, Cowboy, pound it out!' I don't know exactly what it was, but I'd pound out something."[44]

"Don't Worry" became Marty's seventh number one single. It entered *Billboard*'s country chart in February 1961 and spent ten weeks at the top.[45] As a crossover hit, it reached number three on *Billboard*'s pop chart.

On April 12, 1961, the third annual Grammy awards ceremony took place simultaneously in New York City and Los Angeles. Marty's recording of "El

Paso" was announced as "Best Country & Western Performance" of 1960. Previous winners in that category were Johnny Horton's "The Battle of New Orleans" in 1959 and the Kingston Trio's "Tom Dooley" in 1958. "They looked down on country music so bad twenty years ago," Marty said years later, "that they didn't even have my name on the Grammy. I don't even think they had 'El Paso' on it. They just sent it to me." When it came in the mail, he engraved it himself with "1960" and four stars on each side of "El Paso."[46]

With great record sales, Marty could finally afford his third passion. "For me, auto racing comes right after my family and singing," he said.[47] Micro-midgets captured his attention in 1960.

[9]

Early 1960s

Micro-midget race cars evolved from three-quarter midgets, which evolved from pre-World War II midget race cars. An average micro-midget weighed 250 pounds and was 5 feet long and 34 inches high. "When you're that close to the ground," one driver remarked, "sixty miles an hour is a hell of a lot faster than one hundred twenty in a standard-size car." Motorcycle engines powered the cars.[1]

Marty indulged his love of auto racing by purchasing his first micro-midget, a number seven car he raced without repainting. He bought a second and called it "44 Junior" because he sponsored the number 44 car at the Fairgrounds Speedway. He named his next micro-midget "Big Iron Special" and gave it a triple seven number. His race cars throughout the 1960s carried number 777. Marty joked it represented the first money he won on a slot machine in Las Vegas.[2]

He raced "Big Iron Special" at Bartlesville, Oklahoma, on August 21, 1960, in a race sponsored by the National Micro-Midgets Association. "I was running second and trying to pass the leader," he said in a telephone interview after the fifteen-car race. "We came into a curve and my left rear wheel came off. I spun into the car beside me and it knocked my right front wheel off. The next thing I knew I was going backwards down the track and the car behind me crashed into me head-on. Then all three of us piled into the hay they stacked along the guard rail." The experience was "sort of fun," he said. "I'd never gone backwards like that before. We hit the hay pretty hard, but it was better than hitting the rail."[3]

This was no publicity stunt. Marty's recent "El Paso" fame had broadened his fan base and made his actions worthy of newspaper reportage. Readers could almost hear the excitement in his voice. He expected singing and racing to coexist, and when his passion for driving race cars increased in following years, it often collided with the singing career that enabled him to afford the cars.

To capitalize on the racing fad, Marty started building a micro-midget track in Smyrna, Tennessee, in early 1960, and he employed his band members so they could make extra money. "Marty was good to us," Joe Babcock says. "He tried to help us out financially because we didn't make much money on the road." Babcock remembers first hearing "Don't Worry" while working on the track. He was bolting down chairs in the seating section when Marty told him, "Joe, get in this truck with me. I want to sing you a song." The truck had a water tank on it, and a hose for hosing down the track, and they drove down to the river to fill the tank. Marty sang "Don't Worry" and then asked, "What do you think?" Babcock replied, "Chief, everything you sing sounds so good. I can't tell if it's a hit or not."[4]

Okie Jones came on the scene when Louie Dunn, his brother-in-law, got him a job at the track. Jones, five years younger than Marty, turned thirty while working there in 1960. "We worked for a dollar and a half an hour," Jones says. "Back then it was good money. All his band members worked on the race track. In fact, my boss was Pete Drake; he was playing steel for Marty at the time." All except Tompall Glaser, that is. "He wouldn't go out there and work," Jones explains. "He said some of his fans might see him working."[5]

The *Music Reporter* announced on September 12, 1960, "Marty Robbins, whose BIG hobby is racing micro-midget autos, has built a track for the speedsters south of Nashville."[6] He would sell it two years later, after it became a financial drain and his interests turned to faster cars. When talking in later years about the beginning of his driving career, he seldom mentioned micro-midgets.

Always willing to help young singers in search of record contracts, Marty put Johnny Seay and Norman Wade to work in his enterprise. He met Seay, who had come from the Louisiana Hayride to try for the Opry, on the steps outside WSM's studio and greeted him by name. "I could not believe he knew me," Seay marvels at the memory, "because he was God to me." When Marty learned Seay was a painter as well as a singer, he offered $500 to have Seay paint a mural for Rosa's Cantina, the restaurant at the micro-midget track. "That's the first painting I ever sold," Seay states, "and I sold it to Marty Robbins."[7]

The teenaged Wade first saw Marty playing a steel guitar in an Opry dressing room and didn't know who he was. Wade answered Marty's inquiries by saying he'd come to Nashville to write and sing and was staying at the YMCA. "He told me to go to 713 18th Avenue South and meet him there," Wade recalls. "I still didn't know who he was." He found out when he went to the office Monday morning, and Marty told Jim Glaser, "Give Norman a room next door and $57.50 a week."[8]

Okie Jones lived upstairs in an old house Marty owned next door to his office. When someone suggested putting furniture in the rooms to rent to musicians, Jones said, "Let's call it Hillbilly Heaven." He used the name given to Delia "Mom" Upchurch's boardinghouse for musicians on Boscobel Street, where he'd roomed in 1949. Jones installed a shower in the basement so anyone could come in off the street and clean up. It surprised him how much itinerant musicians used and appreciated that facility. Marty returned from a tour and related how a woman came up to him and thanked him for the wonderful thing he was doing in providing rooms for musicians. She said her son got his start in Nashville because Marty gave him a place to live. The woman's gratitude impressed Marty, who liked being given the credit, and he told Jones to stop charging rent.[9]

Johnny Seay considered Marty a genius and also someone hard to get along with. "I never had any trouble with him," he says, "but I noticed a lot of people had trouble getting along with him." One was Tompall Glaser. "Tom, when he came to Nashville," Seay says, "he worshipped Marty Robbins. I think all the Glaser brothers did. But Marty and Tom did not get along, and I never knew why. I guess they were too much alike."[10]

"We left Marty because we felt we were beginning to damage our own careers," Jim Glaser explains. "We starved to death, too. We were all married." They were becoming known as a backup group and none of their Robbins Records singles made the charts. "Marty wasn't happy when we decided to quit," Jim says, "and Tompall was at the forefront of that. He felt our sound was being usurped by Marty since the western album, and Marty was more interested in his own career." Marty would have been content to keep them as a vocal backing group. "I know he and Tompall had words over that," Jim says. "I don't think they ever resolved it. They didn't hate each other, but it wasn't like it was in the beginning."[11]

When Chuck Glaser came home from the Army in early 1961, Tom offered to keep Joe Babcock in the group. Babcock felt he would be "a fifth wheel" and chose to return to Marty, where he stayed another four years.[12] The Glaser brothers continued their recording careers, together and separately, and also became Music Row businessmen.

Babcock again took the baritone part of Marty's trio, allowing Bill Johnson to concentrate on steel guitar, and Don Winters stayed as tenor. When they sang "Don't Worry," Babcock would play the piano intro and jump back to the microphone. "I rigged a pick-up I could bolt to the back of the piano with a microphone so people could hear the piano," he says. "And I carried an amplifier with me."[13]

Although they usually traveled in station wagons and pulled a trailer, Marty sometimes chose the green-and-tan bus he had purchased in 1956. After converting the round-tail twenty-nine-passenger bus to hold eight bunks, nine seats, and two large clothes closets, he used it in good weather. They called it "Frog Eye" because of its frog-eyed appearance. Jim Glaser remembers traveling in the old bus, with "Marty Robbins" painted on the side to ensure it qualified as a business tax deduction. "The thing wouldn't always start," Glaser says, "so wherever we ate would have to be a restaurant up on a little hill. One time out in Arizona, we were all behind the bus pushing it down this little hill to get it started, and a car drove by, and they rolled down the window and said, 'Hey, which one of you is Marty?' And Marty yelled, 'Marty flies. He doesn't fool with this bus.'"[14]

During the summer of 1961, Jimmy Selph toured with the group and played rhythm guitar. Then Marty rehired Sykes, who needed a job and seemed to be controlling his drinking. The "Teardrops" name fell out of favor, and the band became known simply as the Marty Robbins Band. Marty hired a permanent musician for upright bass when Henry Dorrough came along the latter half of 1961. Prior to that time, the position had been filled by Lester Wilburn, Cedric Rainwater, Hillous Butrum, Shorty Lavender—whoever was available. Rainwater doubled as bus driver until he and Marty took Okie Jones out one day to test drive the bus. Marty hired Jones, who traveled along as relief driver for several trips before Rainwater left.[15]

Marty had purchased this 1947 GMC bus, "Big Red," to replace "Frog Eye." "It was an old-timey bus," Jones says. "No springs under it." He remembers driving down from Spokane when Joe Babcock was trying to read; the roughness gave Babcock a migraine headache.[16]

To give Jones a break, Marty sometimes drove the bus. Babcock spent many nights standing in the front of the bus because his migraines prevented him from sleeping. He remembers being out in the desert in the middle of the night with Marty at the wheel. They passed a truck whose driver indicated he wanted to race. That was a challenge Marty couldn't ignore. "Big Red" had the advantage on long uphill slopes, and the truck took the lead going downhill. They raced in the night for thirty minutes or so. "Marty was just laughing," Babcock recalls. "He was having the time of his life." When the trucker finally pulled off into the night Marty and Babcock "went back to the long hours of watching that old white line go by in the desert night."[17]

Marty felt he needed to be on the bus unless Jones had a relief driver—Earl White sometimes filled that role. The former Teardrop remembers receiving a late-night telephone call from Marty in Bremerton, Washington, asking him to fly out and drive the bus home. Marty bought White a plane ticket and then flew home himself as soon as White arrived. "He would fly home, and mess around, and get bored, and he would call us on the phone to meet him," Jones says. "He'd want to get back on the bus, like in Kansas City or somewhere, and we'd have to go to the airport to pick him up, and he'd ride the bus back with us." White was at the wheel when the brakes failed on the old GMC. "We kept trying to decide whether to tell Marty or not, because he was already mad about something," he says. "Then I ran through a four-way stop, and Marty was in his seat, and he said, 'Pull over, Big Earl.' I pulled over." They called a garage and had the brakes fixed.[18]

Louie Dunn named the bus "Big Red" because it was red. "Louie named everything," Babcock says. "He named me Cowboy, because I was from Nebraska and wore a western hat." Dunn made Marty laugh. "Louie and Marty were big buddies, always, and clowned around together," Jack Pruett explains. "I think my little bandy-legged, bony legs reminded them of a chicken. And I kind of have Oriental eyes and cheeks, so they hung the bandy-legged chicken and the Oriental wong on me, so that's where it come out with Bandy Wong. Most of the band members called me Bandy."[19]

Marty and his band members occupied themselves playing poker during the long bus trips. "I was the navigator," Babcock says. "Okie and I were up in the front, and the rest of the boys were in the back with their eternal poker game that never stopped in the six years I was there." Bill Johnson remembers a game that started in the parking lot of Marty's office and lasted all the way to Los Angeles. "Some would play awhile, then sleep awhile," he says. "We never played for high stakes; it was more or less for something to do." Marty didn't like losing, and his agitation could be actual or feigned. Pruett usually won the games, although he knew when he'd gone too far. "Marty would set over there and look at me like he'd kill me," Pruett says. During one game, Pruett called and Marty turned over three queens. Pruett shoved aside his queen high straight without showing it and let Marty win. "I'd won four or five hands," he explains, "and I knew if I'd won that pot, I would *still* be walking." Don Winters says, "Jack and Marty would get so mad at each other. . . . Marty was lucky; he would get the cards, even when other people were dealing. Jack was more of a bluffer, but he was a good bluffer." Winters adds, "When those two got to betting against each other, it was time to get out. I wasn't that good. It was a way to make it through the night. Then we would get to our hotel the next morning and check in and go to sleep."[20]

Babcock, navigating for Jones, once got them lost. They arrived at the theater just before show time. The worried theater owner came out and started cussing Babcock, who apologized and explained they'd been lost. "He just worked me over," Babcock says, "chewing me out." Marty came out of the bus in his stage uniform, beautifully dressed as if in a magazine advertisement, and heard the commotion. "Marty was a very emotional person," Babcock explains. "He was good to us, but you never wanted to be chewed out by Marty. When he did lose his temper, or *use* his temper, he was a master at it." Babcock watched as Marty "lit into this theater owner and chewed him up and down and around and sideways, screaming at him and cursing him for getting on to me." It went on for about five minutes, until the man apologized. "This guy just wilted and disappeared," Babcock says. "Then Marty was back to his old smiling self. He went in and played a wonderful show. He could turn it on and turn it off, just like that."

One year, on September 26, Marty commented it was his birthday. Jones stopped where they could buy a cake and candles, Joe Babcock wrote a poem, and the band held a birthday party on the bus. Marty said, "Boys, that's the only birthday party I ever had."

Marty was proud of his band and wanted everyone to look good. During one road trip, somebody went into a restaurant improperly groomed to the extent that Marty was embarrassed. He made an edict they would wear suits and ties in restaurants. "And so we did," Babcock says. "I don't remember how long that went on, but for awhile he laid down the law and made us really look nice to go into a restaurant."

Babcock believes Marty felt most relaxed when on the road in "Big Red" with his band. "We had been out on the road quite a while," he reminisces, "and although I loved playing and working with Marty, sometimes it gets a little tiresome watching that old white line mile after mile. Marty was in his seat, I was riding shotgun and Okie was driving. I was thinking about home, my darling wife and kids, and a little tired of seeing cornfields. Marty looked over and said, 'Joe, I thank the Lord every day that I can travel.'"

When not on the road, the band helped promote the publishing company and build a studio. "At the office, I was terrified of him," Babcock says. "I never knew if he was going to get onto me or was it going to be okay?" Babcock didn't realize until years later that Marty valued his opinion as a music expert. Ronny Robbins says he never knew what would set his dad off: "Sometimes he'd put up with all kinds of things, and sometimes it would just take one little thing. I think the road relaxed him. He never was really relaxed at home." Ronny recalls being eleven years old and playing with Janet, who was learning to walk. He would toss a football and pretend to tackle her. Once he accidentally pulled her feet out from under her. Marty stopped in the act of peeling a grapefruit and flung it across the room, catching Ronny on the back of the head.[21]

Working at his craft helped Marty relax. "He'd come to the office and sit at the piano in the little studio," Bill Johnson recalls, "and sing for a long time. Other times he would be on the bus and working on a song—I suppose maybe keeping his pipes in shape, and maybe familiarizing himself if he had a new song."[22]

Two singles and one album followed "Don't Worry" in 1961. Babcock wrote the title song of *Just a Little Sentimental,* an album released in October. None of the songs—mostly old favorites by other singers—were issued as singles. Two of Marty's original songs were released as singles without yet appearing on albums. "Jimmy Martinez," a western ballad using the name of Marty's high school boxing buddy from Glendale, made it to number twenty-four on

Billboard's country chart. "It's Your World" reached number three. Both songs topped out at fifty-one on the pop chart.

As 1961 drew to a close, Marty and his band headed northeast on a tour. One stop was Carnegie Hall in New York City. Although Opry artists had entertained there, this November 29 package show was by far the largest. Most of the performers flew to New York City in a chartered aircraft. Because Marty wasn't on the plane, a Patsy Cline biographer later wrongly claimed he "took the train because of his fear of flying." Pruett surmises that Marty didn't like the idea of flying with so many Opry performers, either because of the consequences of a crash or because he didn't want to be in such close quarters on the flight. Eight of the forty artists rated star billing. In addition to Marty, they were Faron Young, Patsy Cline, Bill Monroe, Minnie Pearl, Grandpa Jones, fiddler Tommy Jackson, and headliner Jim Reeves.[23]

Leo Jackson, one of Jim Reeves's Blue Boys, remembers Marty's Carnegie Hall performance as "Marty was hyper on stage. He couldn't keep still. He was a blast to watch. The crowd loved him, as usual. It was just Marty being Marty. He was always walking around the stage—running around the stage sometimes." Marty and Jim Reeves worked numerous shows together during this period, with Reeves always closing the show. According to Jackson, Reeves often checked the radio dial while traveling to see if his songs were being played. "The only time he would stop and listen to somebody else sing, it would be to listen to Marty," Jackson says. "Once in awhile he'd listen to Patsy Cline. But Marty—he *always* stopped. I don't care how many times we heard Marty sing, he'd always stop and listen to Marty."[24]

Bill Johnson recalls unloading their gear in front of Carnegie Hall and carrying it down "a long narrow alley from the street, along the side of the building, to the stage." The memory of playing Carnegie Hall would have to hold him for awhile. He received his draft notice and left for the Army at the end of 1961.[25] During Johnson's two-year absence, Pete Drake traveled with the band, but Marty seldom used steel guitars on his recording sessions.

[10]

Cowboy in a Continental Suit

In December 1961, when Marty had been at Columbia for ten years, Don Law negotiated a contract change from a two-year to a ten-year term. "I made so much money back in 1959, '60, '61, and '62, and I didn't even have a CPA," Marty told an interviewer in 1981. "By the time I got one, it was already too late. I'd spent a whole lot of my money and a whole lot of Uncle Sam's. I had an income tax problem for eight or nine years." To put the era in perspective, a 1964 Ford Mustang sold for $2,368.[1]

Financial insecurities always haunted Marty. "I've never had the feeling I had it made," he said a year before his death. "I've always had this fear it could all be taken away." The highest Internal Revenue Service (IRS) tax bracket in the early 1960s was 91 percent tax on net incomes above $400,000. That included Marty. The penniless boy had become a rich man, and he failed to allow for tax consequences. He made $500,000 in 1960 and spent it without thinking about setting aside tax money. Marty's Music and Marizona Music were casualties of his oversight.[2] He would have to sell the two successful publishing companies to cover his IRS debt. In doing so, he lost future publishing royalties from most of the songs he and his band members wrote between 1958 and 1964, including "El Paso" and "Don't Worry," the other songs on his *Gunfighter* albums, and his next three number one songs.

First of those was "Devil Woman," which Marty wrote the same day as "Big Iron." He didn't remember any inspiration for "Devil Woman," other than thinking "Big Iron" was such a great song he'd try to write another one the same day. He hit on a falsetto he liked and then developed the song around it. "I don't know the reason for that song, except that I wanted to do a falsetto," he recalled. "I was messing around at the piano. It's a funny song to come up with at the piano, because I don't play the piano well enough to write that type of song. It usually takes a guitar. But I wrote that one at the piano."[3]

To find a B side for "Devil Woman," he asked Don Winters for suggestions. Winters started singing his own compositions and Marty liked "April Fool's Day." Winters cheerfully states his song "sold as much as the other one."[4]

Marty sat in a chair while recording "Devil Woman," which required Winters and Joe Babcock to kneel. The one microphone hung low enough for all three to sing into it, with Winters to the right of Marty and Babcock to the left. Marty joked, "Boys, that's just how I want you—down on your knees."[5] Another song recorded during that April 10, 1962, session was Lee Emerson's "Ruby Ann" (written under his legal name of Lee Emerson Bellamy). The two singles became back-to-back number one *Billboard* hits. "Devil Woman" held the top spot for October and November, and then "Ruby Ann" grabbed it for one week.

Both songs were included on *Devil Woman,* his third album for 1962. Two previous albums were *Marty After Midnight* and *Portrait of Marty.* Consisting of a variety of songs Marty liked, mostly pop standards, they were recorded to produce sales rather than singles. From 1962 through 1964 Marty recorded seven albums, which together showcased his wide-ranging tastes and talents. He repeated his Hawaiian and western themes in 1963 with *Hawaii's Calling Me* and *Return of the Gunfighter.* 1964 brought *Island Woman,* an album of West Indian music, and a country album, *R.F.D.*

"On the bus you couldn't mention a song he couldn't do a part of," Okie Jones says. "If it had been played on the air, he heard it and he could sing it." Marty so loved music that he seemed to absorb everything he heard. "I was amazed myself that he did know so many different types of songs," Marizona stated after his death. "I was watching some of his shows this past week, and I couldn't believe he would have memorized so many different songs."[6]

The wealth of Marty's publishing companies expanded when Jeanne Pruett, wife of Jack Pruett and later a singing star herself, joined the enterprise. Marty, with typical chauvinism of the day, referred to her as "the greatest *girl* songwriter in the business." Louie Dunn nicknamed her Maude. Jeanne Pruett appreciated that Marty used the work of his own writers before seeking outside material. "I think getting cuts by somebody as famous and important as Marty," she says, "was the thing that kept me working hard at my craft. All the years I've been in this business I owe to that one man."[7]

A girl Marty worried about was his toddler daughter, Janet. One of Marizona's friends remembers going out to dinner after church with Marizona and her children. Janet recognized Marty's album cover on the jukebox, hollered, "Daddy, Daddy," and tried to climb up the jukebox. Marizona ran over and grabbed her, explaining to the friend that Marty didn't want people to know Janet was his daughter. He was afraid of a kidnapping.[8]

Marty's star power during the years 1961–64 is evidenced by the fact that Columbia released fourteen Marty Robbins singles: all twenty-eight sides (he wrote twenty-one of the songs) belonged to his publishing companies, both those he was to lose and the successor he created. He experimented with such publishing company names as Maricana and Maricopa, finally settling on Mariposa in 1964 as his major company. By then he had sold Marty's Music and Marizona Music. "I didn't have a manager or even a CPA that knew anything about the music industry, or I would have saved all those copyrights," he said. "I just got so mad over paying all that income tax that I sold them."[9]

He sold his micro-midget track in 1963. "That's one of the few things I think Daddy lost money on," Ronny says. Perhaps another reason for the sale was that micro-midgets had become too tame for Marty Robbins. A high-banked quarter-mile dirt track had opened in May 1962 at Ridgetop, north of Nashville. Marty sat in the turns in the front row to watch the modified races at Highland Rim Speedway, but officials would make him move. Oh, if I could have one of those, he'd tell himself. Finally he went to the garage where the cars were built and ordered a modified special. Preacher Hamilton built the 1934 Ford racer. The cover photo of Marty's *Devil Woman* album displayed the Devil Woman Modified, purple with yellow wheels and lettering. "I started racing at 37, 38," he said. "When most people are ready to stop, I started. I've always liked racing, but I never had the money to have a race car. Finally, I had a little car built to run on dirt tracks and I used to run on Friday nights." Although he'd previously owned six micro-midgets, he seemed to have forgotten about them. Marty would race Number 777 at Ridgetop for two years before moving into his third racing phase—at the Fairgrounds Speedway.[10]

The 1963 death of his good friend Hawkshaw Hawkins might also have decreased Marty's desire for his micro-midget track and its memories. Hawkins, a fellow Grand Ole Opry star, had run micro-midgets with Marty since 1959. He was so tall his specially built car was a third again as large as other micro-midgets. Even then, his feet stuck out in front. Hawkins and his wife, singer Jean Shepard, named their first son Don Robin, in honor of their friends Don Gibson and Marty Robbins. "I know they were pretty close," Ronny says, "as close as I ever saw Daddy get to anybody." Ralph Emery says, "Marty went to Hawk's funeral, the only one I ever saw him attend."[11]

Marty once reminisced about doing a show together. He'd noticed a steel guitar sitting on the stage, and he started playing it while Hawkins was singing. "I was doing all the fill-in," he said, "and I wasn't doing too bad, see, and he turned around and it was me, see, and it surprised him. So then, that dog, he went and got his fiddle, when I came on, and he was playing fiddle on 'White Sport Coat.'" Hawkins stood in Marty's blind spot, and he moved every time Marty turned his head to see who was playing the fiddle. "I could hear it," Marty said, "but I didn't know where it was coming from."[12]

On March 5, 1963, Hawkins, Patsy Cline, and Cowboy Copas were returning with pilot Randy Hughes from a benefit show in Kansas City when their Piper Comanche crashed near Camden, Tennessee. All four were killed. Several weeks later, after Jean Shepard gave birth to her second son, Marty told her he wanted to write a song for her. "Marty, you can't write a song for me," she said, "because you don't know how I feel." He asked, "Can I try?" She consented. When he presented her with "Two Little Boys," she realized it was a great song. "When I awake every morning and find that you're not here with me," the song begins, "tears start to fall without warning; then through a curtain of sorrow I see, two little boys." Marty gave songwriter credit to her sons, thus ensuring they would always draw the royalties. "It's a very touching song," Shepard says. "I didn't think he could do it, but he did, and I love him dearly."[13]

The end of 1963 brought Marty's tenth number one *Billboard* hit and the seventh he wrote. He recorded "Begging To You" in September on the first take. "I was ready with the song," he told Ralph Emery, "because I liked it really well. And Grady Martin liked it. It was such a simple song it was no problem." He called it "a simple session," with piano, drums, bass, and lead guitar. When Emery commented, "I didn't think anybody recorded with just four musicians," Marty responded, "That day we did." The Jordanaires later added background vocals.[14] The song spent three weeks at number one.

Marty also made another movie in 1963, a Hollywood adaptation that brought his songs "El Paso" and "San Angelo" into one story. *Ballad of a Gunfighter* was filmed in Kanab, Utah, in August. He played a Robin Hood-type outlaw named Marty Robbins in the town of San Angelo. One of the characters was Feleena from "El Paso." She spoke of her younger days and the young cowboy who died for her in El Paso. The movie climax followed the song's storyline, similar to a modern-day video, with Marty and Socorra dying in the street as the soundtrack of "San Angelo" played.[15]

The movie premiered in San Angelo, Texas, and Marty dressed in a European-style suit with a continental cut. During that period he usually wore Italian-made three-piece suits onstage. The local newspaper interviewed him, and the reporter asked, "Why don't you wear cowboy clothes?" Marty replied, "Well, I don't know; I like the continental look." The newspaper article said, "He looks like a cowboy in a continental suit." Marty thought it was a neat title for a song. "I have to be inspired to write," he explained, "and that inspired me to write a song." He described the finished product by saying, "He's dressed in a continental suit, and he comes to ride this big buckskin called the Brute. No one has ever ridden this horse, and anyone that can ride him gets a thousand bucks. And he opens the gate, and this buckskin comes running out, and he grabs him around the neck, and pulls himself up on the back of this buckskin, and rides him. No saddle, no bridle, no nothing." The horse was ashamed to have been ridden by a cowboy in a continental suit.[16] Released as a single in the summer of 1964, "The Cowboy in the Continental Suit" reached number three on *Billboard*'s country chart.

Marty purchased tickets for himself and his band at a West Memphis theater while they were on tour. Although Marty didn't like hecklers, "he didn't mind being one," according to Earl White. He scooted down in the seat and made comments such as, "Who's that with the big nose?" "Man, what ears! Look at the ears on that guy." "Just look at that nose!" Movie patrons didn't know it was Marty heckling himself. When he tired of his game, even though Okie Jones and the band members were enjoying *Ballad of a Gunfighter,* Marty took them back to the bus. It was strange behavior for someone so self-conscious about his nose.[17]

His style of drawing attention to himself probably developed as a way to compensate for his insecurities. Perhaps that's why some fans enjoyed his exaggerated displays of egotism. They understood it was a façade. Even so, few people realized Marty's extreme introversion. A 1964 newspaper headline announced "Robbins Seeks No Limelight." The article said, "It is virtually impossible to persuade the singer-guitarist to talk about himself or his commercial achievements." It quoted Marty as saying, "I don't think I've ever done anything so special that it should be recorded in print. I am merely making a living doing what I like doing. Is that news?"[18]

The more famous he became, the more he kept his private life private. In his interviews, he rarely mentioned his family. A 1964 magazine article included his comments about taking fourteen-year-old Ronny to races and allowing him to hang around the pits. Marty emphasized to his son the importance of shoulder harnesses and other safety precautions. He mentioned in the interview that Marizona played piano and was teaching five-year-old Janet. Ronny sang and played the guitar and was taking piano lessons. "I'm self-taught in music," Marty said, "but I want Ronny to learn music the right way. I can play chords on the piano, but I can only do hard songs in the key of C. I don't have the patience to learn music the right way."[19]

One of his quirks was washing his hair in the rain; he thought rain water made it feel soft. Around 4:30 on the afternoon of July 31, 1964, he was out on his lawn in a thunderstorm. "I was standing in that downpour with lather on my head and I heard an airplane up above," he told Ralph Emery several days later, adding he'd wondered, "What silly son of a bitch is flying in this weather?" Janet saw him outside and ran to join him. Washing his hair in the rain was one of her favorite things to see him do. They were laughing when they heard the crash. A strange look crossed Marty's face, and he pushed his daughter inside the house. He called the local authorities, and she remembers him getting upset because he wasn't taken seriously.[20]

Okie Jones picked him up shortly thereafter, with the Devil Woman Modified on the trailer, and they drove to Highland Rim Speedway for the Friday night race. Marty described washing his hair in the rain and hearing a plane go in the ground. It was the weirdest feeling, he told Jones, to know someone's life was snuffed out, just like that.

On their way home that evening, they learned Jim Reeves was missing. Emery announced on his WSM All-Night Show that a plane was down and the pilot was a famous entertainer. Then he confirmed Jim Reeves and his passenger, pianist Dean Manuel, were missing. Their plane seemed to have fallen out of the sky.[21] Jones dropped Marty at home and then spent all night with the searchers.

The next day, Marty told the pilot of the search helicopter where the plane had gone in, and the pilot said they'd searched that spot many times. Marty didn't want to be the one to find Reeves. Janet knew they were looking for the plane her daddy heard go down. The searchers were right down the street, across Franklin road, and she wanted to join them. She went to the edge of the road, and her mother called her back.[22]

The search lasted forty-four hours. "Marty, Eddy Arnold, myself and numerous others participated in the strenuous search," Emery recalls. "One-hundred-degree temperatures aren't uncommon in Nashville in August, and we were scaling the steep, snake-infested hills around Brentwood, Tennessee, looking for what we dreaded to find." The plane was found where Marty had said it would be. It had gone straight in, leaving no hole in the forest canopy to be spotted from the air.[23]

Jim Reeves, like Marty, was a stubborn, hot-tempered perfectionist with an amazing singing talent that crossed genres. Now he was gone. Marty continued to watch over his own family, manage his publishing companies, record, tour, race—striving to be his best in everything. In 1965 he would open the door for a young Canadian named Gordon Lightfoot by recording another number one song.

[11]

Still More Gunfighter Ballads and Trail Songs

"I don't go out and look for songs," Marty told an interviewer. "It's mostly just my own songs I write and record." He added, "If I hear a song and like it, I'll record it. I don't care who writes or publishes it. If it's good enough for me to sing, I don't care." One song he heard and liked in early 1965 was Gordon Lightfoot's "Ribbon of Darkness." The voice of the unknown Canadian on the demo tape intimidated ever-insecure Marty. "I had a hard time doing it, because he did such a good job," Marty said. "It took me awhile to get over *him*. Finally I got to where I could sing it."[1] He recorded the song March 2, 1965, using the same arrangement as the demo, and the single was released three weeks later. "Ribbon of Darkness" became Marty's eleventh number one *Billboard* country chart hit. (Lightfoot, now in the Canadian Music Hall of Fame, recorded it for his 1966 debut album.)

The flipside, a song about a little robin, Marty apparently wrote for six-year-old Janet. He gave her songwriter credit. "My dad was my idol," Janet says as an adult. "If he was on the road, and I got lonely, I'd play an album, put on a cowboy hat, become Marty Robbins, go out on the range, and then come back to earth and my real life. I always wanted to be able to sing as well as he could. I still do. I was Daddy's little princess."[2]

Marty recorded two albums in 1965. He had told Marizona and Ronny, "If you write a song, I'll put it in an album." His request inspired Marizona to write lyrics that came "from my heart; it was the way I felt." Fourteen-year-old Ronny wrote the music. It was the first song for both of them, and Marty made it the title track of his religious album, *What God Has Done.*[3]

The other album, *Turn the Lights Down Low,* contained a collection of songs from Marty's publishing companies. The title song belonged to Joe Babcock, who had finally tired of traveling. When he told Marty in February about his desire to quit, the response was, "Joe, I don't blame you. I wouldn't work the road for $25 a day." Marty agreed to let Babcock stay home and write songs and run the publishing company after he found a replacement piano player. Babcock called Bobby Braddock, recently arrived from Florida in search of a music career, and invited him to audition.[4] Following Babcock's advice, Braddock practiced the piano intros to "Ruby Ann" and "Don't Worry." He played them for Marty, who also had him sing harmony with the group. "I got the job right there on the spot," Braddock marvels. "I was thrilled to death. Because I was a *big* fan. It was like magic to me."

Braddock admits to sometimes sounding flat during background segments. One night he jumped up from the piano to sing his harmony part on "White Sport Coat," and Marty said, "Don't sing. Ever." By now Marty had perfected his western trio with baritone Bobby Sykes and tenor Don Winters. He used additional voices on the doo-wap teen ballads—until he told Braddock to quit singing.[5]

Sykes and Winters never knew what to expect from the third member of their trio. Ralph Emery once asked Marty if he ever forgot the words to "El Paso." Marty explained how that could happen, if he was listening for a guitar string going out of tune. "I've got to hear my guitar on the last part," he said. "If I try to get it in tune, I might forget a line. I'll hum a little bit but Bobby and

Don are singing, so I know nobody will notice it, y'see. And they don't know if I really forgot it or not. Then I'll look at one of them and say, 'Why don't you learn the song?' Like it was their fault, y'see."[6]

The band in 1965 included Henry Dorrough on upright bass, Bill Johnson on steel, Jack Pruett on guitar, and Louie Dunn on drums. Dunn continued to give everybody nicknames. Bobby Sykes was Roan Horse, Don Winters was Ox, Bill Johnson was Bluto (Popeye character), and Braddock was Blinky because of the way he blinked his eyes. Winters acquired his nickname when he walked down the corridor at the edge of the theater they were working, and a child asked if he was a wrestler. "Yeah, don't mess with me; I'm bad," Winters joked. Dunn told him, "You looked like a great big ox walking down through that hallway." "Louie was probably Marty's best friend, or certainly one of his best friends," Braddock says. "Whenever Marty flew, he would take Louie with him. Louie made Marty laugh."[7]

Marty brought a dream to life by filming a television series, *The Drifter,* in late 1965. It allowed him to play the Gene Autry role he'd so admired as a child, with a guitar appearing out of nowhere and his movie hero singing a song. "He had this burning thing that, I think, never went away," Braddock surmises. "He really wanted to be the cowboy star." Marty called a producer friend in Hollywood and asked for help. Bob Hinkle flew to Nashville, and they filmed thirteen of the planned twenty-six episodes. Filming took place in the WSIX-TV studios and on a farm Marty owned near Franklin. The format called for Marty to "sing his way in and out of various dramatic situations." Each thirty-minute show had one guest star, usually a western singer.[8] Marty financed the production, and his friends and associates wrote scripts. Braddock and his wife wrote several, as did Bobby Sykes.

Hinkle's sole script centered on Tex Ritter as owner of a little general store. Marty asked, "Whose guitar is that?" Ritter said, "Mine. Do you play it? Sing us a song while I fill this order for you." Sykes and Winters just happened to be there playing cards, and Marty asked them to help. At the end of the song, someone said, "Drifter, we wish you'd stay." On another week the show might take place in a saloon or around a campfire. The week the drifter stowed away on a boat to Hawaii, the guest star was steel guitarist Jerry Byrd. That gave Marty an opportunity to sing his Hawaiian songs.[9]

Eddie Crandall tried unsuccessfully to find a market for *The Drifter.* Marty, usually so forward thinking, had accepted Crandall's recommendation to film in black and white. It might have been an economical decision at the time, but it was a fatal error with color television on the horizon. The shows only aired in Oregon and Wichita, Kansas, in addition to Nashville. Reflecting on *The Drifter's* lack of success, Marty said, "I put them in the vault and took a big loss." He refused to sell them at a discounted rate. "I don't care too much about giving them to TV stations," he said.[10]

Columbia Records used that title for the first of Marty's two 1966 albums, both collections of western songs written mostly by Marty and his writers. *The Drifter* included "Mr. Shorty," a song he wrote for his brother Johnny. At five foot five, Johnny stood four inches shorter than the younger brother for whom he served as handyman. When Marty said, "Hey, shorty," Johnny responded, "It's Mister Shorty to you." Marty thought that was a great title for a cowboy song.[11]

Another cut on *The Drifter* album, "Feleena (From El Paso)," clocked in at eight minutes and ten seconds. "I'm really proud of that song," Marty said, "because it's eight minutes of real rhyming, real beautiful lines, I think. It tells about the girl, how she got to El Paso, how she met this guy and how he shot somebody; he ran out the back door, and then the next day she hears some rifle shots. She runs to the back door of the cantina and here comes her cowboy. He's shot from the saddle, and she can see he's dying. The rangers have gathered around. He's lying on the ground, and she grabs his gun and pulls the trigger and shoots herself. She dies with him. It's a very tender song." Marty worked for almost six weeks to finish it. "I wrote probably forty or fifty verses, trying to get two I wanted for the ending," he said. "I knew what I wanted to say, but I couldn't say it." While in Phoenix, he decided to fly to El Paso. "I checked into a hotel, looked out the window at the mountain, and I finished the song, two verses, in about two minutes."

When asked about naming his western albums, Marty said he couldn't think of titles for any of them. Don Law had titled the first *Gunfighter Ballads and Trail Songs*. From then on, fans referred to all of his cowboy songs as gunfighter ballads. The second album became *More Gunfighter Ballads and Trail Songs* and the third, *Return of the Gunfighter*. After *The Drifter*, Marty joked, "If we do another one, I wouldn't know what to call it. Maybe *Still More Gunfighter Ballads and Trail Songs*."[12] Actually, the next album was *Saddle Tramp*, with the title song written by Marty. It contained his previous hit, "The Cowboy in the Continental Suit."

As influential a songwriter and recording artist as Marty was, he ran into a wall when he recorded a political song. A conservative Republican, he had served as southern director of "Stars for Barry" in support of Barry Goldwater's 1964 presidential campaign. His responsibilities included directing campaign activities of country music performers throughout the South. Senator Goldwater, a Phoenix native, was one of Marty's heroes. In February 1966, Marty and Roy Acuff entertained at a Republican Party fundraiser with former Vice President Richard Nixon as guest speaker. A thousand guests from throughout Tennessee attended the $25-a-plate dinner. During Marty's performance, he praised Nixon, who moved from his seat to the stage and chatted with Marty for several minutes, briefly stopping the show. Then Marty gave a speech about the great Barry Goldwater. "The timing wasn't good," Bobby Braddock points out. "It was Nixon's affair."[13]

To express his strong political beliefs, Marty wrote a pair of songs and recorded them in April. Don Law assigned a release number for a single and sent the product to Columbia's headquarters in New York City. It was rejected as too controversial. Law supported the corporate decision, saying such material would detract from the popularity of a great artist.[14] "The country's full of two-faced politicians," Marty sang in "Ain't I Right." He talked about winning the war with communism by fighting it "here as well as Vietnam." He called the act of burning draft cards "a get-acquainted communistic kiss."

"I thought it was a hit," he later told an interviewer. "At the time there was a lot of trouble in this country. Everybody was protesting, so that was my way of protesting."[15] The backside of the single was "My Own Native Land," a complaint about foreign aid: "We give to those who quickly take it, posing as a friend, and just as quickly turn and bite that hand that's feeding them." The singer would gladly help this world, but it isn't selfishness to put his native land first, and he asks why "we should please the very ones who'd like to see our country on her knees."

The official recording log of Marty's Columbia sessions has a line drawn through "Ain't I Right" and a handwritten "Do Not Use" in parentheses next to it. Marty did not give up so easily. Bobby Sykes listened to the record and then sang both songs in Marty's studio, using the same arrangement and sounding like Marty. They released the new single under the name of Johnny Freedom on a private label. A Georgia magazine reported in October, "A great number of the country music stations in the Atlanta area are playing this record on the average of every thirty minutes per station." The disc reappeared almost two years later, along with erroneous reports that Marty had recently recorded it under the Johnny Freedom pseudonym for the presidential campaign of George Wallace, then Alabama governor.[16]

In mid-1966, Marty moved his family to his 250-acre farm on North Chapel Road near Franklin, mainly because of tour buses driving up and down Redwood Drive all day long. The large buses disrupted the quiet neighborhood, and Marty's swimming pool was visible from the road. "We'd be out in the pool, and a bus would drive by, and we'd hide if we didn't feel like displaying ourselves," Janet recalls. The tour bus frequency increased from weekly to daily to every half hour, and tourists started climbing over the fence to take photographs. "We could see the buses coming around the bend on Forest Acres Drive," Ronny says, "and we would hightail it to the back of the yard and wait for them to go by, and then go out and mow another three or four strips and here comes another one."[17]

The farm offered more privacy than Marizona and Janet wanted. They spent most of their time alone after Ronny turned eighteen and moved out. Eight-year-old Janet begged her father to take her to the recording studio. "I wanted to know what a recording studio was," she says. "I wanted to go to the office. I wanted to do all these things." Marty refused to allow any connection to the music business, although he often brought his little guitar to Janet's bedroom to sing to her. "That was probably one of my favorite memories," Janet says. "They weren't his songs," she remembers. "They were Spanish songs, traditional songs, cowboy songs."[18]

The studio Marty wouldn't let his daughter see had been built several years earlier by Okie Jones. It was used for recording demos for publishing companies. Because one of Marty's favorite sayings was, "Ah, you *dum*my," Jones replaced the normal on-the-air sign with one that read "Quiet, You Dummy." Jones engineered sessions, in addition to helping in Marty's three publishing companies, working on his farm, and driving the bus. Marty once asked if he would like to give up any of the jobs to quit having to do so much. "I kind of like doing them all," Jones answered, and Marty replied, "Oh, good."[19]

"We used to get mad at each other and maybe not speak for three or four days," Jones recalls. Marty would end the impasse by saying something to the effect of, "You think I can't do without you? I can hire three or four people to replace you any day." Jones would start laughing, and they'd be on good terms again.[20]

During a demo session with Jones at the control board, Jeanne Pruett sang a song she'd written, "Count Me Out." Marty had never heard her sing, and he gave her fulsome praise. "Oh, man, that's a housewife sound," he raved. "That'll sell records, Maude. We'll go find someplace to get you a good contract." And they did.[21] She became best known for her hit with "Satin Sheets." Marty recorded "Count Me Out" and released it as a single, with his "Private Wilson White" on the flipside. This Vietnam war song modernized the cowboy ballad: "Seven bullets found their mark, seven bullets near the heart, and the force of seven bullets knocked the soldier to the ground."

In 1967 Columbia issued three Marty Robbins albums, the first being standard fare by himself and his writers, *My Kind of Country*. The second was a Mexican-themed album, *Tonight Carmen*, whose title track started a string of thirteen top ten hits, including three number ones. "She was a girl I met one night in my dreams," Marty said. "I just got the idea for this song. I don't know who the girl was—I sure would like to know her—but I got the idea from a dream and wrote the song." Don Winters recalls having twin trumpets on the recording, and he says, "I believe on that particular song we sang on a separate mike from Marty. As a matter of fact, I think that was the first one we tried that on."[22] *Tonight Carmen* spent one week at the top and stayed on the *Billboard* country chart for four months.

The third album was *Christmas With Marty Robbins*. The cover showed a photo of Marty superimposed over a photo of Salt Lake City at night. Marty was on tour there when the photo shoot was scheduled. In midsummer he'd told Jeanne Pruett, "Maudie, I need a couple of good Christmas songs." She answered, "Will you promise me you'll record it? I'm not wasting my time in the middle of the summer writing a Christmas song if you're not gonna cut it." He assured her, "If it's good enough, it'll get on there." Pruett went home, put up a Christmas tree, turned on the air conditioner, decorated her house, and wrote two songs. Both "Christmas Is for Kids" and "One of You in Every Size" appeared on the album, which was released in October. So did Bill Johnson's "Christmas Kisses." He was inspired by the thought of soldiers in Vietnam looking forward to being home for Christmas kisses.[23]

Again in 1968, Columbia issued three Marty Robbins albums. One was the western-themed *Bend In the River*. The other two were mixtures of Marty's original songs and hits by other singers, *By the Time I Get To Phoenix* and *I Walk Alone*. Don Law had retired sixteen months earlier, and Marty now worked with Bob Johnson. They finished an album on July 1, 1968, and a few minutes of session time remained. Marty said he wanted to do an old Eddy Arnold song he frequently played at home. So Bill Purcell moved from piano to organ, and Marty sat at the piano. He quickly went through "I Walk Alone" to show the musicians what he wanted, and they did the first take. Johnson came running out of the control room, saying, "It's a hit; it's a hit!"

Marty's immediate reaction is incomprehensible to anyone who reflects on his talent and stature and accomplishments. He thought Johnson was ridiculing his piano playing. "I knew I couldn't play but that didn't bother me," he said later. "So I didn't pay any attention to him. I just wanted to take it home and listen to it. . . . I wanted to see what it sounded like with a whole group." Johnson finally convinced Marty he believed the song would be a number one hit. When he asked for a second take, Marty couldn't hit the right notes on the piano. "He had me so nervous then, y'know, I couldn't hit a barn with a bass fiddle," Marty explained. "So he took the first cut, and released it, and it went to number one."[24]

Ronny fondly remembers being at that session and watching his dad play the piano. He had graduated from high school and was in college by then, majoring in mechanical engineering. He also played electric organ and sang backup in a rock 'n' roll band called the Jades. While in high school he acted as a singing General Bullmoose in the musical version of *Lil' Abner*. Ronny's first road trip with his famous father had been in October 1966 when Marty headlined a package show, which also featured Faron Young, at a filled-to-capacity twenty-thousand-seat venue in Charlotte, North Carolina. It was the beginning of Ronny's performing education. "He let me learn for myself," Ronny says. "Rather than saying this is the way it needs to be done, he showed me how to do it by his experience and by being a good teacher."[25]

Ronny was practicing on his keyboard one night in the piano room of their farmhouse when his father entered the room. Marty complimented him, which surprised Ronny. Marty sensed Ronny's unhappiness with his current band and asked, "Would you consider learning three country songs and being part of my show for $50 a day?" That sounded good to an eighteen-year-old who was making $40 a weekend. Ronny already knew a good selection of such songs and he accepted the offer. His first tour was a five-day trip through the Southeast, beginning with a performance in Macon, Georgia, on September 8, 1968. "People liked him on the stage," Marty stated. "He didn't do any kind of a show, but he was just a young bashful kid. Young girls liked him, y'know." Then Marty joked, "He'd get a bigger hand than I would. So I knocked that off. I sent him home."[26]

Following the September tour, Ronny went along on a three-week Thanksgiving tour that covered the Northwest. Most dates were with Johnny Cash and his group, consisting of Mother Maybelle Carter and June and her sisters, plus the Statler Brothers and Carl Perkins. "We had worked in Seattle the night before Thanksgiving, and we were staying at a hotel close to the Space Needle," Ronny recalls, "and it had a Chinese restaurant. I was feeling kind of blue because it was the first time we'd ever not been at home for Thanksgiving. I didn't know where Daddy was." As he stared forlornly at the menu, the sound of someone speaking Chinese in the next booth began to get on his nerves. Suddenly, the foliage in the planter above the booth was yanked open, and a face poked through. It was Marty, chattering in a phony language. "It scared *the crap* out of me," Ronny says. "He could mimic anything, anybody."[27]

[12]

From Dirt Track to NASCAR

Marty's fascination with fast cars surfaced when he returned from the Navy in 1946 and spent spare time at Phoenix races. "I understood a little about working on cars and even put my own engine together," a 1969 newspaper article quoted him. "I built a little street job back then. I put together the complete body from part of a 1928 Chevrolet I got out of the desert. The back part was what they call a bucket, a Model T truck. I even put upholstery in and I was pretty proud of it."

When he began singing in nightclubs, he was no longer free to attend evening races. He continued to follow the careers of drivers such as his racing favorite and future Indianapolis 500 winner Bill Vukovich Sr. and local youths Jimmy Bryan and Bobby Ball. Ball died after fourteen months in a coma following a 1952 accident.[1] Vukovich was killed while leading the Indy 500 in 1955 and Bryan died in 1960 at Pennsylvania's Langhorne Speedway. Their early deaths did not deter Marty, who by then had begun racing micro-midgets.

In 1963 he started driving the "Devil Woman Modified" at Ridgetop's Highland Rim Speedway. Describing his first race, he told a magazine reporter, "I had a good time trial, but it scared me a little. When it came time for the heat race, I didn't want to get into the middle of the pack because I was afraid I might make a mistake and mess somebody up. It was one thing if I wrecked my equipment, but those other boys were racing for a living and I didn't want to cause them any trouble." He pretended something was wrong with his car that forced him to start in the back. "I'd never run with fast cars around me and I didn't know what was going to happen," he said. After three weeks, he started in his proper spot. "I didn't pass anyone, but no one passed me," he stated. "Finally, I got used to running with fast cars."[2]

When racing and winning at Ridgetop became too tame, he moved in 1965 to late-model sportsman cars at the Fairgrounds Speedway. His 1962 Plymouth, built by Preacher and Bud Hamilton, carried the purple-and-yellow color scheme and number 777 of the "Devil Woman Modified." His best 1965 showing occurred during the one-hundred-lap Labor Day race when he led most of the laps until his tires got hot and he tapped the wall; he came in third. In 1966 he won one of his nine races, beating the track champion, Coo Coo Marlin. "I decided I'd like to race with the top drivers," he said.[3] He ran his first NASCAR Grand National (later called Winston Cup, Nextel, and then Sprint Cup) race that year, driving a 1964 Ford in the Nashville 400 but dropping out due to an oil leak.

In October 1968 he drove a 1967 Dodge Charger in the National 500 at Charlotte Motor Speedway in North Carolina, his first race on a big track. He finished twelfth in a forty-five-car race. Marty didn't know until much later that he experienced his first heart attack during the race. Thinking indigestion was causing his pain, he gave the car to a relief driver for an hour and a half. He finished the race after the pain stopped. "I could not breathe deep," he recalled years later. "I had no idea what was wrong. I didn't even go to the doctor. I had no idea it was my heart. That one healed itself." Later X-rays showed scar tissue.[4]

Combining racing with other interests, Marty turned to making movies about a singer who raced cars. He starred in two movies produced by Robert Patrick and directed by Will Zens—*Road to Nashville* in 1966 and *Hell on Wheels* in 1967. Marty served as associate producer and Eddie Crandall as production assistant on *Road to Nashville*. The movie showcased performances by many of Nashville's country music stars. Unfortunately, the plotline followed a format common in country music movies, with a bumbling character pulling down the overall quality and detracting from the excellent music. The movie included film footage of Marty winning the feature race at the Fairgrounds Speedway the previous year. His performance of "El Paso" concluded the movie.[5]

Hell on Wheels was a racing drama filmed at the Fairgrounds Speedway and other locations around Nashville. Marty sang and raced as himself but belonged to a fictitious family. John Ashley played his younger brother, Del Robbins, with Gigi Perreau as Del's girlfriend. Marty's bachelor character sang "Fly Butterfly Fly" to his movie niece. Marty had written "Fly Butterfly Fly" after watching six-year-old Janet catch a butterfly by their swimming pool. It got away from her, and the thought occurred to Marty that Janet would someday fly away from him, like a butterfly.[6]

The film's world premiere on June 16, 1967, brought Hollywood pageantry to Nashville. "A red carpet greeted stars Marty Robbins, John Ashley and Gigi Perreau as they arrived at the Paramount Theater before a crowd of 3,000 fans," reported the *Nashville Banner*. They came in limousines, with Marty arriving last and without Marizona. Mayor Beverly Briley introduced the stars, who each spoke briefly before the movie began.[7]

In his early days at the Fairgrounds Speedway, Marty met the three Allison brothers, soon to be NASCAR legends. They lived in Alabama but came to Nashville because the track paid good purses. Bobby raced his own car, and Donnie and Eddie owned one together, with Donnie driving and Eddie serving as mechanic. "He was my favorite country music singer anyway," Bobby Allison says. "Then one day I got to meet him, and I raced against him." Allison offered advice to the novice driver and helped him compete in other races. "He actually raced pretty good," Bobby recalls. "He had finishes near the front and was a great competitor." The Allisons often left the fairgrounds late on Saturday night and dashed over to the Opry to catch Marty's show. They sometimes went backstage during his performance.[8]

Feeling comfortable with late-night crowds, Marty had overcome his earlier belief that people expected him to be serious on stage because he sang serious songs. "I figured everybody out there was half asleep anyway," he explained in a magazine interview. "So after I finished a song I stood away from the mike and said, 'Hey, Marty, that was great,' and I started whistling and cheering. The live audience laughed and the radio audience didn't know it was me doing it. Well, it got to be a thing with the late Opry audiences. The minute I walked on stage they'd start cheering and whistling, like I'd trained them. So I got looser and looser until finally I was doing the same kind of fooling around on my road shows and now everybody expects it."[9]

"Marty really created the 11:30 spot on the Grand Ole Opry," says Bud Wendell, who began managing the Opry in 1967. "He made it certainly one of the high points. When he came in at 11:30, he was stylishly dressed—but occasionally he did come in with a few scratches." Marty enjoyed finding new ways to surprise his audience. "We planted him in the audience more than once," Wendell recalls. "Unrecognized with a ball cap and glasses on, he would go sit down just like every fan, and have a remote mike with him. When the 11:30 show started and Hal Durham, the announcer, would say, 'And here's Marty,' he would stand up in the middle of the crowd and start singing. It was bedlam. Then he'd work his way up to the stage."

One night Marty quit a race he was leading at the Fairgrounds Speedway to get to the Opry, only to find the evening running behind schedule. Wanting to give his audience a complete show, he insisted on doing his full half-hour. The crowd loved it, and Marty turned that extension into an act. Hal Durham would threaten to close the curtains, and Marty would jump out and hold them as if upset at being shut down. WSM Radio was supposed to switch programming from the Opry stage to the Ernest Tubb Record Shop at midnight for Tubb's Midnite Jamboree. Marty acknowledged routinely running the show over by fifteen minutes, thus allowing him to sing extra songs. He said Tubb didn't care because he could cut into the disc jockey's time and the deejay didn't care because he could get some rest.[10] WSM continued to broadcast the Opry until Marty ended his performance. On the air Marty would say, "Hold on, Ernest, we're gonna get to you. Just one more song."

Sometimes Marty brought Ronny. They would each do a verse and a chorus, and radio listeners didn't know which was which. "Ronny could sound so much like Marty it was just unbelievable," Wendell says. "Those kinds of moments were something that pleased Marty."

"He almost had a cult following," Wendell marvels. "Audiences were enraptured by his performance." After the show, Marty would stand outside on the front steps of the Ryman and sign autographs for several hundred waiting fans. One regular was a city street sweeper with his broom. "He'd start sweeping around this crowd," Wendell remembers, "and the crowd would get smaller and he'd sweep a little closer, and finally he'd get right up to Marty. He and Marty would carry on a conversation. This guy was a great Marty Robbins fan." The man later described Marty by saying, "Rain or shine, when Mr. Robbins was on the Opry, he'd look to see if I was outside and stand and talk for a minute. He always asked after me, always took time to stop to say hello. He treated me like a real person. I was proud to keep the streets clean for him to walk on."[11]

After all autographs were signed, Marty might tell Wendell, "Let's go to the Pancake Pantry." At 2:30 AM, they and Hal Durham would eat pancakes and talk.[12] Although Marty's companions changed over the years, he seemed always to enjoy being out late at night with friends.

Every Thursday Wendell would call Marty's secretary, Lucy Coldsnow, to ask if her boss was available for the Grand Ole Opry that Saturday night. Coldsnow had begun working for Marty in 1967. He was looking for a secretary, a mutual friend recommended her, and he hired her without an interview. They hit it off, and she ran his office for the next ten years. Coldsnow remembers him as "easygoing and shy and very much of a clown." She says he liked traveling and entertaining and didn't want to have to worry about managing an office. Jim Farmer ran the publishing company and Coldsnow assisted. She listened to the constant flow of demo tapes that came in the mail and saved for Marty those she thought might interest him. She prepared royalty statements for the publishing company and copyrighted all songs. Marty usually wrote at night and he would come in the next morning with his lyrics scribbled on little pieces of paper. He would first sing the songs while Coldsnow wrote down the lyrics and then they recorded him singing to his own piano or guitar accompaniment. Coldsnow would send the tapes and typed lyrics to an individual who prepared sheet music, after which she submitted the songs for copyright. Marty Landau, the Hollywood agent, booked dates and sent contracts to Coldsnow. She made Marty's airline reservations and scheduled the bus. "Marty would bring the money back after the dates," she recalls. "He would give me, a lot of times, cash. I would count it all and put it in the bank."

When Marty learned Coldsnow could make shirts, he asked her to sew for him. He told her to buy the most expensive sewing machine she could find and he would pay for it. The busy young woman didn't want to spend her time sewing, but she agreed to do what Marty asked. She made shirts with wild colors, polka dots, and strange colors or strange fabrics mixed together, such as an orange shirt with brown polka dots. "He loved me making shirts for him," she says. "He enjoyed something someone would do for him. He liked that attention."

Coldsnow served as production coordinator for the television show Marty started producing in 1968. Thirty-nine episodes of *The Marty Robbins Show* were filmed at the WSIX studio. The musical format included a "Marty's Corral" scene where Marty (with Winters and Sykes) sang a western song each week.[13]

Ronny appeared on the show as Marty Robbins Jr. Because he was being drafted into the U.S. Army, as Marty explained several years later, "I thought, well, he might go to Vietnam and something might happen, so maybe the name Marty Robbins Jr. might help get his record played a little bit." Marty wrote two songs for his son and they recorded a duet, with Marty singing harmony on Ronny's first single release, "Big Mouthin' Around."[14] Marty introduced him on the show by saying, "This is the moment I have waited for. My boy baby will be on TV for the first time, my friends." He then made comments such as "C'mon, Junior, it's all right," and he asked, "You want me to carry you on? Pardon me, folks." He disappeared from camera view, and then Ronny appeared, carrying Marty in his arms.

A guest another week was thirteen-year-old Louie Roberts. After hearing him on the Ernest Tubb Midnite Jamboree, singing "Don't Worry" and "Tonight Carmen" with correct voice breaks and falsetto, Marty told Coldsnow to book the teenager. Roberts had been a fan since hearing "El Paso" at age five. The son of steel guitarist Kayton Roberts, who played for Hank Snow, Louie first met Marty at the Opry. "It was like meeting a president," Roberts says. "This man was my hero. I can remember that curtain going up—the Lava soap portion of the Grand Ole Opry. 'Tonight Carmen' was the first song I heard him sing. I remember the rawhide boots he wore." While filming *The Marty Robbins Show*, Roberts recalls, "I would cut my eyes to the left—he'd sit over there with his arms folded and watch me. That was so cool, knowing my idol was watching me."

Following the television appearance, Roberts often performed on the Opry during Marty's segment. "I'd do a Marty Robbins song," he says. "People would go nuts, and he would run out there, and clown around." When Marty wasn't racing, "He would come in the Opry about 10:30, go in the dressing room, and sit down at my daddy's 1951 Fender double-neck lap steel guitar. I would sit there with a guitar and I'd sing all those old songs, and that used to blow his mind because he couldn't believe I knew that many old songs. He would play the steel guitar while I would sing. That's how he'd relax."[15]

Wendell remembers Marty disguised with a hat and glasses and sitting at the side of the stage to watch Roy Acuff and his dobro player, Brother Oswald. "He was respectful of those senior people," Wendell states. "It showed genuineness in him, that he loved the music and the people and the Opry." Jeanne Pruett recalls how Marty would go onstage behind Acuff. "He'd have that little hat he'd pull down," she says, "thinking nobody knew who he was, and he'd sit out there and play music all during Mr. Acuff's portion."[16]

For the follow-up single to "I Walk Alone," Marty chose another Eddy Arnold recording, a former number one called "It's a Sin." Bob Johnson suggested Marty again record at the piano. "So I sat down and did the piano work by myself and he came in and overdubbed the music," Marty said.[17] His version reached number five on *Billboard*'s country chart and was the title track of his only 1969 album. As usual, most of the songs on *It's a Sin* belonged to his publishing company. One of Marty's most famous songs, which he never released as a single, appeared on this album when he recorded it a second time—the semi-autobiographical "You Gave Me a Mountain." Marty was "born in the heat of the desert," as the song proclaimed. He'd been "in a prison for something I never done" when arrested in Phoenix years earlier and taken to Yuma. "What inspired me to write this song was the way my father—y'know, my father didn't care too much about me, see—he didn't like me," Marty said. "Some of it's true and some of it isn't. I wrote it with some of the things in mind about my life."

Marty wrote "You Gave Me a Mountain" especially for Frankie Laine, whom he probably knew through Mitch Miller. Laine sang the theme songs for TV series *Rawhide* and movie *Blazing Saddles*. While trying to connect with Laine, Marty recorded an unreleased version during a 1966 session. Laine finally recorded the song in 1969 and it succeeded as a pop hit. Because he loved his father, and his father loved him, Laine changed "despised and disliked by my father" to "deprived of the love of a father."[18]

The song also became a top ten country hit for Johnny Bush that year. His record company, Stop Records, brought him from Texas to Nashville because label owner Pete Drake wanted him to cover Laine. It was customary for out-of-town singers to visit Ralph Emery's all-night show on WSM Radio, and Bush did so. When he walked into the control room, Marty was there. Bush told Emery he was in town to record and Emery asked if he knew yet what he would be recording. "One of his songs," Bush said, pointing to Marty. "Which one?" Marty asked. "It's a song called 'You Gave Me a Mountain,'" Bush replied. "Pete

Drake gave me a record, but I haven't listened to it yet." Marty said, "I'll sing it for you." So live on the radio, at three o'clock in the morning, Marty sat at the piano and sang, "You Gave Me a Mountain." Bush, in awe, declared, "Man, after I've heard you sing it, I don't know if I want to try." He didn't catch the difference in the one line, and he recorded Laine's version—as did Elvis Presley, who performed the song during his 1973 Honolulu concert, *Aloha from Hawaii*.

Bush appeared as a guest on *The Marty Robbins Show* and Marty's introduction concluded with his kidding tone, "And he gonna make it." Bush states, "To hear him say that, knowing he was my idol—it was the biggest thrill." Bush calls Marty "the greatest entertainer I ever witnessed." He remembers being on a Northeastern package tour on a winter Sunday afternoon between matinee and night performances. "Marty came in the room with his guitar," Bush says, "and it was just Ray Price, Marty Robbins and me, and a few of the guys in the band, and he sang for a solid two hours. He knew a thousand Mexican songs, in Spanish. Ray said, 'Where did you learn that?' He said, 'I would lay in bed at night with the window open, and we lived close to the railroad tracks, and these drunk Mexicans would be walking down the railroad track going home. I'd hear these songs and I learned them.' He sang those songs beautifully."[19]

Marty still occasionally found time for late-model races at the Fairgrounds Speedway, although a planned rule change would make his current 1964 Dodge obsolete. He said he could only afford one car. He announced in February 1969 that he would be driving a partially factory-backed 1969 Dodge Dart Swinger on NASCAR's Grand Touring (GT) Circuit the next season. These ponycars (Mustang, Barracuda, Dart, Camero, etc.) used the same tracks as larger cars. Marty had run several 1968 races in a Dodge Dart and he liked GT racing because, he said, "the races were long enough and the cars close enough to one another that the racing was fun. I liked it so much I went and had a Dart built."[20]

Marty never raced his new Dodge Dart. He understood oil pressure and manifold pressure but had no comprehension of the pressure building in his chest.

Martin David Robinson
and twin sister, Mamie,
age 8. (Courtesy of
Ronny Robbins.)

Martin, age 15, on high
school playground.
(Courtesy of Ronny
Robbins.)

Martin after his Navy discharge, walking the streets of Glendale, 1946.
(Courtesy of Ronny Robbins.)

Martin and Marizona on their wedding day, September 27, 1948. (Courtesy of Ronny Robbins.)

Marty teaching Ronny to box, in the front yard of their South Phoenix home, 1952. (Courtesy of Ronny Robbins.)

Sixteen-year-old Bill Anderson with Marty Robbins at WSM Studio, August 1954. (Courtesy of Bill Anderson.)

Janet being serenaded by her father, 1962. (Courtesy of Ronny Robbins.)

Preacher Hamilton, Marty, and Bud Hamilton with the Hamilton-built Devil Woman modified race car, 1963. (Courtesy of Steve Cavanah.)

Republican Party fundraiser at Nashville Municipal Auditorium, February 4, 1966. Left to right: Richard M. Nixon, Bill Johnson, Marty Robbins, Jack Pruett, Bobby Sykes. (Photo by Vic Cooley; courtesy of Bill Johnson.)

Marty with 777 at Fairgrounds Speedway, 1966. (Courtesy of Steve Cavanah.)

Movie set for *Road To Nashville*, 1966. Left to right: Sammy Pruett, rhythm guitar; Raymond "Snuffy" Smith, bass guitar; Bill Johnson, steel guitar; Don Winters; Bobby Sykes; Marty Robbins; Louie Dunn, drums; Bobby Braddock, piano; Jack Pruett, lead guitar. (Courtesy of Bill Johnson.)

At the Nashville airport when Ronny left for Germany, October 20, 1969. Left to right: Ronny, Marizona, Janet, Marty. (Photo by Hubert Long; courtesy of Lucy Coldsnow.)

Marty's racing publicity photo. (Courtesy of Kathy Baucom Baker.)

Lucy Coldsnow
at Marty's Fan Fair
booth, 1973. (Photo
by Kathy Baucom
Baker.)

Marizona and Marty at their twenty-fifth anniversary, 1973.
(Courtesy of Ronny Robbins.)

BMI awards show, 1973. Left to right: Lucy Coldsnow, Roger Sovine (BMI), Ronny
Robbins. (Courtesy of Lucy Coldsnow.)

Marty on stage in Ottawa, Ontario, 1977. (Photo by Robert Gardiner.)

Members of Marty's Army at Fan Fair, 1980. Left to right: Glenda Stevens, Carol Hutson, Kathy Baucom. (Courtesy of Kathy Baucom Baker.)

Marty accepting award at *Music City News* Awards show, 1981. Left to right: Dottie West, Marty, Barbara Mandrell. (Courtesy of Kathy Baucom Baker.)

Barbara Mandrell and Marty Robbins at *Music City News* Awards show, June 7, 1982. (Photo by Robert Gardiner.)

Marty Party at Opryland Hotel during Fan Fair, June 10, 1982. WSM disc jockey Chuck Morgan interviews Marty Robbins. (Photo by Robert Gardiner.)

Marty Party with "Superlegend" banner behind the band, June 10, 1982. Left to right: Don Winters, Bill Martinez, Marty, Bobby Sykes. (Photo by Gary DelBalso.)

All-American Country games at Vanderbilt University Stadium during 1982
Fan Fair. Left to right: Louise Mandrell, team captain Barbara Mandrell, Marty
Robbins, Irlene Mandrell, Dave Roland of "Dave and Sugar," and Rex Allen Jr.
(Photo by Robert Gardiner.)

Marty on the Grand
Ole Opry stage, 1982.
(Photo by Robert
Gardiner.)

Ronny and Marizona accepting Marty's posthumous award at *Music City News* Awards show, June 6, 1983. (Courtesy of Kathy Baucom Baker.)

[13]

A Hot Dog Ready to Pop

Driven to compete with himself in his passions for singing and racing, Marty searched for hit songs and faster cars, combining an amazing number of activities in the 1960s. While continuing to keep his family life private, he built his publishing companies and recording portfolio, made movies and television shows, and handled a heavy touring schedule. Because he enjoyed traveling, he usually rode the bus instead of flying.

Bobby Braddock remembers Marty's competitive nature and how he didn't like losing poker games. "My relationship with him was very pleasant," Braddock says, joking that "it was because I didn't play poker." He calls Marty "a very funny man. He was hilarious. He loved pulling jokes and had a quirky sense of humor. It was a blast working with him." Marty didn't always appreciate the quirks of others, though. "I used to do this imitation of a background singer who had this real high-pitched voice," Braddock says, "and Okie told me that was getting on the chief's nerves, and not to do it. I used to make up names and have people paged in hotel lobbies, and Okie told me Marty didn't like that either. But Marty never confronted me."

Braddock enjoyed listening to Marty sing on the bus. "He would serenade us sometimes for two or three hours. He loved to sit around and sing. He was a great singer, and he knew it. Oddly enough, most of his favorite singers were female."

Marty recorded two Braddock songs, "While You're Dancing" and "Matilda," and released them as singles. When Don Winters had called to say, "Chief said to come down here to the studio," Braddock arrived to find Marty cutting his songs. "Boy, talk about ecstasy," says the man whose songwriting aspirations brought him to Nashville. "I thought, maybe I really *am* a songwriter." With his new confidence, Braddock asked for the songs he'd placed in Marty's publishing company. Marty returned rights on all but those for which he'd already paid to have demo tapes made. Braddock stopped traveling in May 1966 but continued to play piano for Marty on the Opry for the next year. He also provided all piano backing in the movie *Road to Nashville.*

Now a longtime member of the Nashville Songwriters Hall of Fame, Braddock says, "Marty gave me my start. I never talked much to him after I left the band. I wish I'd told him how much it meant to me to be in his band, and him recording my songs."[1]

In late 1966 when traveling became physically difficult for Louie Dunn, he left Marty's band to go into the booking business. Buddy Rogers replaced him as drummer. During his trial two-night tour with the Marty Robbins Band, Rogers decided to show off his jazz background by turning "El Paso" into a jazz waltz. "I was worrying whether he was gonna like me or not," Rogers explains. "I was playing with these brushes on the snare drum, going t-chu, t-chu, t-chu, and I thought, this is easy." Marty, speaking into the microphone, turned and asked, "What are you doing back there, Whitey? It sounds like a dog trotting through dry leaves." Everybody laughed, and Rogers relaxed and simplified the beat. Marty hired him full time. In the movie *Hell on Wheels,* the drummer's blond head can frequently be seen behind Marty. Like everyone else, Rogers had a nickname—although he never knew why Marty began calling him "Lance."

Their show uniforms, styled like business suits, were custom made by the finest clothiers in Nashville. "One was a midnight blue with a little pinstripe, and one was a grey with a pinstripe," Rogers says. He also remembers wearing "jeans and a western shirt and rough-out boots."

Marty loved playing jokes. The bus stopped one afternoon at a seafood restaurant along the coast near Mobile, Alabama, and the group found seats at different tables. When the band members finished eating and went to pay for their meals, they didn't notice Marty back in the crowd, near his table. Suddenly he yelled, "Hey, you boys didn't leave any tip." Of course, they had left tips. "Everybody in the whole place looked at us like we were the biggest cheapskates in the world," Rogers recalls.

One of Marty's traveling rules was that everybody wore pajamas on the bus. He didn't want to see anyone in underwear. "We had pretty high standards, and I always appreciated that," Rogers says. When not on the road, drivers Okie Jones and Skip Slayton worked to customize the bus with its six bunks and a small room for Marty. Jones installed a hot wire under Marty's seat in the front. When Marty came from the rear, whoever was sitting in his seat had to move fast, or Jones would flip a switch and "electrocute" the person. "Oh, I wouldn't do it to Marty," Jones says when discussing the memory. "I didn't have *that* much nerve."[2]

"When Okie drove the bus, it was like being on a cloud," Rogers remembers. "It was so smooth, no matter where you were. But if Marty couldn't sleep, he drove. You could tell he was driving because you'd roll back and forth in your bunk. You'd go left, right, left, right." He calls traveling with Marty "an opportunity to see the whole United States—twice. It was beautiful. One state would be rolling plains and the next would be mountainous."

Marty enjoyed discussing music with Rogers, whose formal music background included high school and college bands and the U.S. Air Force band. "He was *so* much fun," Rogers says. When in a Mexican restaurant, Marty would make up Spanish-sounding words and order something like *chiles goldarnya* and *gluecamole* salad. "He could order a whole meal like that," Rogers marvels. "He would say it so fast in a real Mexican accent. They didn't quite know what he was ordering, but it sounded right."

Rogers left Marty's band in 1968 to open a music store on Lebanon Road. Across the street stood Preacher Hamilton's Garage, where Marty's race car was maintained. Knowing Marty liked to drink strawberry soda, Rogers kept his cooler stocked with that exact brand and flavor. Whenever Marty stopped by the garage to check on his car, he would go across the street to grab a soda. Travelers registered at the motel next door to Rogers's store would come in to look at guitars and be amazed to find Marty Robbins standing there. Rogers says, "Of course, Marty always showed off for them, and that made their day."[3]

A reporter who rode the bus during a tour described in *Harper's Magazine* Marty's patient interaction with a fan. The reporter quoted Marty as saying, "They buy your albums, they love you, they're loyal. They'll do damn near anything for you except leave you alone." Marty objected to the quote, later telling reporter Stacy Harris, "I know who said I said that, but I never said that. I was careful not to say anything he could print that would be bad, 'cause I knew he was trying to rip up country music and the fans. He had me using profanity—and I will use profanity when I get mad. I use a lot of it, too, when I get good and mad, but I don't use it as everyday language." Marty insisted he did not swear "around children or women, and if I don't know a person, I make sure I don't use it around them."[4]

May 1968 brought a major change in Marty's business life. After a concert in Phoenix, he flew with his longtime booking agent, Marty Landau, to Los Angeles. Bob Hinkle delivered them from the airport to their destinations. That night Landau died of a heart attack. Hinkle notified Marty and took him to Landau's house. Although in shock over the death of a friend, Marty understood his business responsibilities and asked Hinkle for assistance in managing contracts and bank accounts. "I reluctantly agreed to do it for one year on a trial basis," says Hinkle, who felt he lacked expertise. "That one year turned into more than a decade. Every January he paid me in advance for the upcoming year, all with nothing more than a handshake." According to Lucy Coldsnow, Marty was fond of Marty Landau but never talked about his death. Bobby Sykes took over the booking portion of Marty's business. "You didn't have to drum up business for Marty," Hinkle states. "He turned down more jobs than he took."[5]

Eddy Fox replaced Buddy Rogers as drummer, and he also became backup bus driver. Marty flew to El Paso for a concert and the band met him there. Marty had given specific instructions not to stay at a certain hotel in El Paso. The bus overheated during most of the trip, and Okie Jones was exhausted by the time they arrived. The only hotel he could find with a safe place to park was the one Marty prohibited. Jones sent Fox to pick up Marty, while Jones slept so he could drive to Phoenix. Marty flew, and when they met in Phoenix, he wouldn't speak to Jones. After that show they loaded the bus and headed to Los Angeles. As Jones drove out of town, he apologized to Marty for staying at that particular hotel. Marty reacted by throwing his soft drink at the windshield, where it splattered. "I wasn't going to say anything about it, but now that you brought it up," he said through clenched teeth, adding, "You forget who the boss is." Jones retorted, "Hell, I cain't forget it! You keep reminding me every hour." The band members quickly retreated to the sleeping area, and Jones described the bus trouble and how he'd needed to find a place to rest. He then pulled the bus off the road and asked, "You want me to get off here, or do you want me to wait until the trip is over?" Marty told him, "I don't give a damn what you do." Jones decided to finish the trip. They traveled in silence for twenty miles until Marty walked up behind his driver, leaned over his shoulder, and said, "Okie, if I didn't love you like a brother, I wouldn't know what to say to you, because I never apologize to anybody." With a peacemaking "I didn't know you had that much trouble," Marty returned to his friendly self.[6]

One never knew what to expect from Marty. Larry Jordan, a teenaged newspaper editor who wanted to interview Marty at the All-Iowa Fair in Cedar Rapids, got his chance when he saw Marty walking down the midway with several band members. Marty agreed to an interview right there, after stipulating not to ask him any questions about his family, and Jordan turned on his tape recorder. The interview went fine until Jordan asked, "What do you like to do when you're not on tour?" Marty glared at him, almost shouted, "I *told* you not to ask questions about my private life," and stomped off. Jordan, embarrassed, considered going home but decided to use his press credentials and stand near the stage during the matinee. "Marty was introduced to thunderous applause," Jordan recalls. "To my surprise, the minute he came on stage, he spotted me. He leaned over the edge of the stage and shook my hand as if we were old friends! For the next hour, he repeatedly mugged for my camera, asked me if I liked this song or that, stopped in mid-refrain to hold a pose—telling me out of the corner of his mouth to snap his picture because he had such a good profile—and generally hammed it up, making me part of the show." Jordan was so impressed by Marty's showmanship that he returned for the evening performance. When Marty noticed him in the audience, he introduced Jordan and commented on their enjoyable interview. "I was totally won over," Jordan marvels, "and his little temper outburst earlier in the afternoon was forgotten."[7] Such was Marty's way of apologizing and expressing regret.

Most of the time, his charm and consideration predominated. Mildred Harper of Louisville, Kentucky, remembers Marty's attention to a Catholic nun, a great fan, who was dying of cancer. Before Marty's appearance at the Kentucky State Fair, Harper wrote a letter to Lucy Coldsnow to request Marty call the nun while in town. He went to the nursing home with Don Winters and a state trooper and a photographer, and she had her picture taken with him. When Marty was leaving, she asked if she could walk him to the door. He put her house shoes on her feet and she escorted him out. A few weeks later, the Harpers drove to Nashville to see Marty at the Opry on Saturday night and he asked how their friend was doing. Not so well, Harper told him. He asked for an address, Harper wrote it down, and Marty stuffed the paper in his shirt pocket. On Tuesday the nun called Harper and said, "Guess what I got? Flowers from Marty." She died a few months later.[8]

Marty spent most of 1969 touring and working on *The Marty Robbins Show*, with no time for racing. Taping began in late 1968 and ran into July 1969. After finishing those shows, Marty took time to assemble a full-sized trampoline for Janet. Ronny arrived home for the weekend from missile school in Huntsville, Alabama, and saw his dad pulling on a grappling hook to tighten the springs. Marty was sweating, and his arms were shaking, and his face looked ashen. Daddy's starting to age, Ronny thought. Then he realized what appeared to be grey hair was actually blond, from the Lemon Go-Lightly Marty had begun using earlier that year. Still, it was a son's first realization that his father was getting older.[9]

Marty then left with his band for a three-week engagement at the Bonanza Hotel in Las Vegas. From there Okie Jones drove them to Ohio for a tour of one-nighters.[10]

Steel guitar player Bill Johnson remembers being in the front of the bus while traveling down the Ohio Turnpike from Toledo to Warren on Friday, August 1, 1969. Eddy Fox sat at the table and worked on an adjustment for his snare drum. Johnson saw Marty coming up the aisle, holding his chest, and immediately knew something was wrong. Marty said, "Okie, you better get me to a hospital." Jones floored the accelerator and headed east toward Elyria, driving like a maniac and trying to attract attention for a police escort. As he pulled up to the hospital, a patrolman came running over. He ordered Jones to stay and talk to him, and Jones said, "You wait a minute. When I get this man inside, I'll talk to you, and not until. I've been trying to pick up one of you guys for the last half hour." During the forty-mile ride, Marty sat at the card table, with Johnson and Don Winters rubbing his hands and forearms and talking to him. His skin looked orange and he acted distressed.[11]

"I couldn't hear anything they were saying," Marty later explained. "I couldn't feel them touching me. I felt like I was a hot dog, just ready to pop open, y'know. I had such a terrible pain in my chest. But I am a believer, and I believe in prayer. So I prayed. I felt that I was in hell, and the flames were getting higher and higher and higher. I said what am I going to do? I don't want to die. Maybe that's why I couldn't hear anybody. Because I was praying, boy, I was talking. I said please let me live, so I can testify. I know when I said *that*, the flames started going down. The pain started to go away, but not all of it."[12]

When they reached the hospital, Marty walked off the bus and into the emergency room. Johnson recalls the hospital trying to find an EKG machine. Jones remembers Marty asking, "Is somebody going to do anything?" And the doctor said, "I'm observing you." The noise of an electric drill in a corner bothered Marty so much he ordered, "Stop that damn thing! I'll do it." When he started to get up, the maintenance worker shut it off. The doctor asked if he wanted something for the pain, and Marty answered, "Yes! That's what I'm here for." Johnson told Jones, "Oh my God, they'll give him a shot, and he'll think he's all right, and we're going to do that show." Jones replied, "No, we're not either." Johnson said, "Oh, yes, that's the way it works. He'll feel better, and he'll go do it." Jones insisted, "We're going back to Nashville." Johnson surreptitiously told the head nurse, "You ought to take him to Cleveland in an ambulance." She said, "We can't make him do what he doesn't want to do."[13]

The doctor told Marty he'd had a heart attack and would have to stay in the hospital for three days. Marty answered, "I can't; we have a show date this afternoon." The doctor refused to release him but finally acquiesced when Marty promised to go to nearby Cleveland and catch a plane to Nashville. Marty signed a release form, and the doctor gave him a shot for the pain and some pain pills.[14] Once back on the bus, he said, "Let's go do the show." Jones protested, "You can't *do* that." Marty looked at Jones and said, "Let's go do the show."

"And I knew we was gonna go do the show," Jones recalls. "I had made up my mind I wasn't going to, but I couldn't fight with him." It was too late for the matinee, but Marty hoped to make the evening show, still over a hundred miles away. Once when Jones checked on his boss, he saw Marty lying on the bed with his hands across his chest. Jones let out a horrified "Oh, my God!" Marty opened his eyes and said, "I'm not dead yet, Okie. I think I can make it till tonight."[15]

During the performance in Warren, Ohio, Marty sang without his usual animation. About twenty minutes short of the normal show length, he told Sykes to order a security escort to get him back to the bus. Then he cut the show short with the words, "Head for the pass, Bandy." That was Jack Pruett's normal cue to play the "El Paso" intro. At the end of "El Paso," Marty handed Don Winters his guitar, gave Sykes a blank look, and said, "Boy, I like to have not made that."[16]

Jones headed the bus back toward Cleveland. Marty told him, "Okie, you gotta get me to a hospital. But not quite as fast as you did this afternoon." They reached Cleveland Metropolitan General Hospital near midnight, and Marty walked into the emergency room. Jones and the band members waited more than an hour until Marty was rolled back out in a wheelchair. He said he'd had a heart attack and might be in the process of another. He told them to return to Nashville and to cancel the show scheduled for the following night in South Carolina. When asked if he wanted any of them to stay with him, he said no.[17]

Marty hadn't believed the doctor in Elyria. "In fact," he later told an interviewer, "I didn't believe it until I went in the hospital in Cleveland. I couldn't figure out how I could have a heart attack, because I wasn't overweight. I weighed one fifty seven. I was in pretty good shape, so I thought. But the bottom part of the heart had stopped beating and I did a show that night, and I was jumping around on the stage having a big time, because the pain killers had taken the pain away. I'm lucky to be alive. I thank God for that."[18]

When Jones returned to Nashville he advised Marizona to go to the hospital in Ohio. Jones lived and worked on Marty's farm. Marizona assured him, "I just talked to Marty on the phone, and he said he was fine; he's just getting a checkup." Jones told her, "That is *not* the truth. You get yourself up there." Marizona said she had no money for a plane ticket. Jones gave her money from the gate receipts of the recent show dates.[19]

Marizona waited for Ronny to drive home from Huntsville, and they flew together to Cleveland. Newspapers lacked clear information about what had happened to the famous singer, with reports of "severe exhaustion" or "apparent heart attack" or "acute indigestion." Finally, the hospital's chief resident announced a clot in an artery.[20]

"They had to run a wire from my arm all the way around to the bottom of my heart to give it an electric shock to get it started beating again," Marty later told an interviewer. "I was given a fifty-fifty chance of getting out of the Cleveland hospital. Even after they took me off medication, it still hadn't dawned on me how serious it was. My only thought was racing."[21]

Marty stayed in Cleveland fifteen days. After being shown scar tissue in his X-rays, he realized the pain during his Charlotte race the previous year had actually been a heart attack. He returned to Nashville at noon on August 16 and entered Park View Hospital. "WSM flew me back in a private plane, which I thought was very nice of them," Marty said. Bill Johnson was in the crowd that met the plane at the Nashville airport. "When he got off the plane," Johnson says, "it was obvious he was not well." Marty spent eighteen days at Park View Hospital, before going home for further recuperation and to celebrate his forty-fourth birthday.[22]

Okie Jones worked on the farm and did not visit Marty in the hospital. "Nobody will come and see you when you're feeling good, but as soon as you look your worst and you're in the hospital, everybody comes to visit you," Jones grumbles, "and it just irritates me to no end. So I didn't bother him." The band sought temporary jobs. Jack Pruett and Henry Dorrough joined David Houston's band. Eddy Fox went with singer Johnny Darrell, and Bill Johnson became a member of the Moss Ross publishing staff. Bobby Sykes and Don Winters made no plans as they waited for Marty to heal. "We were still on call," Johnson says, "whenever Marty had any shows."[23]

When Marty came home from the hospital, he saw Jones bush hogging a field and he and Marizona drove to where Jones was working. Marty walked to the fence, shook hands with Jones, thanked him and handed him a $50 bill. "I didn't know what it was for," Jones says. "He didn't ever give nobody money at all, unless it was an emergency, or something he was doing to help people."[24]

Marty couldn't remain inactive. He went into the studio at the end of October to record a few songs. Then he and his band flew to Las Vegas in November for a two-and-a-half week engagement at the Fremont Hotel. He wrote a letter to Ronny, who had been transferred to Germany in October, and proudly commented he'd set a Freemont attendance record. "He was excited about it," Ronny recalls. "I figured he was pretty well healed up at that point."[25]

In December Marty went unannounced to Madison Square Garden to see the Johnny Cash show. "I had on this big gangster-type overcoat," he remembered, "and I was sitting on the front row. The stage went round and round, y'see. Well, the first time around, Carl Perkins smiled real big, see, and I didn't smile. So next time around, he looked, and smiled some more, and I didn't smile at him. He nudged one of the guys in the band, and they looked, and they smiled, and I didn't smile, I just looked at him, y'see. . . . And Johnny Cash then got to looking, and I wouldn't do a thing." Cash finally recognized the Columbia executive sitting next to him and introduced Marty to the crowd. "That was funny, though," he reminisced. "Carl Perkins—I'll never forget the look on his face when I wouldn't smile at him."[26]

[14]

"I Want To Race Again"

On January 2, 1970, Marty went into the Columbia studio and recorded "My Woman, My Woman, My Wife" as the title track of his next album. Although he often said he wrote the song for Marizona while in the hospital, he probably fine-tuned it there. Ralph Emery asked him, "Where were you when you wrote this song?" He answered, "In a bus." Okie Jones says Marty wrote it before the Las Vegas trip in July. Marty said his hospital stay showed him "what a woman has to go through in life, and I dedicate that to all of the ladies in the world because they do go through a lot. They say man works from sun to sun but a woman's work is never done. A woman has it hard in this world."[1]

"I was really quite honored," Marizona said years later, during the seventy-fifth birthday tribute for her deceased husband. "I appreciated it, and naturally I cried. He said he'd wanted to write a song for me for a long time. He jokingly said the reason he wrote it was because I didn't make him eat hospital food; I would take him fried chicken." She quickly explained she did take food to him but "it probably wasn't fried chicken, because he wasn't supposed to be eating fried chicken."[2]

Marty also recorded "A Very Special Way," a song he wrote to thank his fans. Because he couldn't possibly answer personally the volumes of mail he'd received in the hospital, he sang, "And thanks again for helping when I needed you. Oh, it seems so little, what else can I say, I love you in a very special way." On a session two weeks later, he finished the first half of the album. He also completed a photo shoot for the album cover. Looking back later, he said, "I look at those pictures and I think, hey, I don't look too healthy."[3]

He wanted to compete in NASCAR again, but first he needed medical clearance. Dr. William Ewers, Marty's internist, wanted to wait until May to give him a coronary arteriogram, but Marty convinced him to do it earlier. Marty checked into St. Thomas Hospital in Nashville on January 20 for diagnostic tests. The heart-muscle arteriogram was a newly devised process that injected a special substance into the heart's three main arteries to color them for X-rays. Marty's X-rays showed significant cholesterol congestion.[4] The results shocked him. "It showed that of the three leading arteries, two of them were 100 percent blocked and the other was 80 percent blocked," he remembered. "It was so bad it scared the doctor when he saw it." Marty's blood-thinner medication was keeping him alive.

Wanting to have some time to think about surgery, Marty asked how long he had to live. "If it was me or my wife or my children, I'd say do it today," Dr. Ewers replied. He couldn't promise how much longer Marty would live even with surgery—or if he would get off the operating table.

That scared forty-four-year-old Marty. "I've always been pretty religious, as far as believing," he said later. "I don't do all the things I should do—I never have. But that night I prayed and prayed. Finally, I realized living was not the most important thing; it wasn't life that mattered. So I prayed that regardless of what happened, my soul would be saved, and in the morning when I woke up I would have the answer. Well, the next morning, everything was peaceful.

I had the answer. I told the doctor I wanted to have the operation as soon as I could. And I never worried after that."[5]

He and Marizona contacted the American Red Cross for assistance in getting Ronny home.[6] The Red Cross notified the U.S. Army, and Ronny was granted emergency leave to fly home from his duty station in Germany.

Marty gave an interview on January 23 while lying in his hospital bed. To avoid any appearance of asking for sympathy, he allowed no photographs. "I've got a 1969 Dodge Dart ready and I want to race it," he said. "I didn't want to start racing again until I took these tests and found out everything was all right, so I came and took them and found out nothing was all right." Because of his excellent physical condition, he couldn't answer the question as to what caused his heart attack. "I don't know," he said. "Some of the doctors said it might be heredity." The evening before his surgery, he consented to a television interview in his hospital room. He told his fans and friends, "I am ready for come what may, and I have been praying a lot here of late. I want everybody else to be offering prayers that this will come out all right." He said he wasn't nervous.[7]

Two surgeons conducted the five-hour operation on January 27, 1970, beginning at 8:30 AM. They used a new surgical technique, one that involved bypassing blocked coronary arteries with veins taken from the legs. According to the hospital newsletter, Marty was "the seventeenth patient to undergo this type of surgery at St. Thomas and is one of only about three-hundred such patients in the nation." He was the first at St. Thomas to have three arteries bypassed. "He'll feel like a truck hit him when he wakes up this afternoon," a cardiovascular specialist said. "Chest discomfort will be the worst part of it, because in this operation they have to split the breastbone to get to the heart." When Marty was wheeled from the recovery room to the cardiac care unit late that night, Marizona and Ronny and Lucy Coldsnow were standing in a nearby waiting area. Marty smiled and said, "Hello, baby."[8]

St. Thomas's cardiac facility received nationwide attention as a result of Marty's surgery. According to the hospital newsletter, its communication office supplied "seventy-three news feeds to radio stations from coast to coast, nearly twenty press reports and six reports to national news wire services. In addition, there were three live radio interviews and a TV interview. WSM-TV filmed interviews with Robbins prior to his surgery. A news conference was held at St. Thomas immediately after the entertainer's surgery."[9]

Marty later described his triple bypass surgery by saying two and a half feet of veins had been taken from his legs, tied in above the heart and wrapped around the heart. "So it was called a vein bypass," he said. "A lot of people get it mixed up with open heart surgery, but it wasn't open heart surgery." He'd been told he was the fifteenth person in the world to have three arteries bypassed.[10]

"The doctor said I died while I was on the operating table, y'see," Marty explained later. "Now maybe I was dead, maybe I wasn't, but I saw a river—I've never told this to anybody except my wife—and I saw underneath this tree on the other side, I saw Jesus Christ. I saw him, in a purple robe with a white something, maybe it was another robe underneath it, with about two or three inches of the white robe hanging out. I wanted to walk across this river to him, and he shook his head."[11]

"I've had a lot of pain in my life, and it's hard to say which one is worse," he told an interviewer years later. "But when they sew you back up, you've got about nine hundred stitches on the inside and about sixty stitches on the outside. They have to put the breast bone back together. Have to go through five layers of tissue. It would hurt so bad! I was in terrible pain! I was still in intensive care, and I said, 'Oh, God, I don't think I can take it any more. Just take me right now.' But as soon as I said that, I realized what I'd said, and I said, 'God, I didn't mean that. I'll take all the pain, if you let me live.' And you know it wasn't forty-five minutes till the pain was gone."[12]

By Thursday he could sit briefly in a chair, and he helped shave himself. Drainage tubes inserted in his chest during surgery were removed. On Saturday, January 31, he moved from the cardiac unit to a private room, and a hospital spokesman projected he would be home by Valentine's Day. Monday morning he walked up and down the corridor outside his room and then returned to bed. "I got a terrible headache," he told a visiting newspaper reporter. "Too much exercise, I suppose. But I hate to be inactive." He said he planned to be in Las Vegas in April for a one-month engagement at the Fremont Hotel. Lifting his pajama top, Marty showed the reporter the scar that ran from an inch above his navel to his collarbone, straight up the middle of his chest. He explained how the veins transplanted to his heart had been removed from the inner part of both legs, between groin and knee. The hospital estimated he had already received more than five thousand pieces of mail, plus hundreds of telephone calls. "I'll never be able to answer all that mail," Marty said. "However, I am going to read every bit of it."[13]

Coldsnow remembers watching him try to walk; he was so sore. He some-times called her to say, "Lucy, go get me some steak and biscuits at Ireland's," or "Go get me a Whopper at Burger King." She would take him the food and remind him, "Marty, you aren't supposed to eat much of this. You've got to be careful." She found out later that he also called other people to bring food.[14]

Marty went home February 10, two weeks after his surgery. The previous evening he described his plans for returning to work, telling a newspaper re-porter, "I've been singing the past several days. Not to anybody in particular—mainly to myself and not too loud. I didn't want to disturb any of the other patients." He said, "I'm now able to take a full, deep breath, something I haven't been able to do for almost a month."[15]

Immediately after Marty returned home, Okie Jones was shocked to see him out on the farm with a gun, trying to kill wild dogs chasing his cows. When Jones chastised him, Marty said, "I'm holding it out like this," as if holding the gun away from his chest would avoid tearing his wound open. He showed Jones his scar, which looked like an old one. Jones acknowledged, "My God, you heal fast." Still, he did have pain. Bill Johnson went to lunch with him one day, and Marty explained how his breastbone had been cut and how it had to knit back together. It was giving him a lot of trouble, and he said he would never go through that experience again. Marty told Johnson the surgery would last about thirteen years.[16] And it did.

"Robbins's recovery was remarkably fast," stated St. Thomas's newsletter. "He was released from St. Thomas ahead of the usual schedule and was able to attend the Nashville Auto Show and then participate in the local Grammy Awards where he received a standing ovation." It bragged, "St. Thomas is proud of its role in restoring the famous entertainer to health. His case, which was so publicized because of his international recognition, should point up the advances made in medical knowledge, surgical and hospital techniques."[17]

Marty called the heart attack "probably the scaredest I've ever been—up till then." He went on to describe an experience that scared him more. A month after his surgery, he was looking at a bull he'd bought the day before and the bull charged him. Marty ran to a fence ten feet away and dived under it. Sliding along the frozen ground tore the skin off the side of his face. "The doctor had just told me, don't get excited about anything," Marty stated.[18]

On March 20 Marty returned to the Columbia studio and recorded five final songs for his new album. The following day, "My Woman, My Woman,

My Wife" hit number one on *Billboard*'s country chart. It had been released as a single in February. On *Billboard*'s pop chart, it peaked at forty-two. The album *My Woman, My Woman, My Wife* would be released in May. Although that song is known as Marty's love song to Marizona, the true love story of this couple is better shown in two other songs. He wrote "I've Got a Woman's Love," which says, "She gives me contentment when my day is done, gave me a daughter, gave me a son." The song concludes with "I'm happy and free cuz I've got a woman's love." Marizona is credited with writing "Three Little Words" about a woman wanting reassurance she is loved. "Your eyes sparkled with laughter when you saw I was after these three little words, I love you," she says. "You didn't disappoint me though you teased me a bit." She is happy because "you spoke these three words I was waiting to hear."

The night Marty and his fans (and his band) had been waiting for came March 28, 1970, when he made a triumphal return to the Opry stage. His last appearance had been in mid-January, three days before he entered the hospital. Marty arrived at the Ryman forty-five minutes before show time and was mobbed by fans and fellow performers. A fan from Georgia went backstage to see if she could find Marty for an autograph, and suddenly she saw him walking toward her. "Smiling, looking great, he had on a baby blue jumpsuit," she remembers. "He was happy. He introduced himself, and I told him how glad we all were about his recovery and we had prayed for him. He put his arm around me and said 'I love you.' I almost died!"[19]

In the dressing room, Marty announced he wanted to sing Porter Wagoner a new song. The normal noisy activity of the crowded dressing room turned to silence as he sang a Wagoner-style sad song. With the Opry running behind schedule, Marty's 11:30 show began at 11:45. When the curtain opened, the roar of the crowd drowned out the first song. After several songs, he sat down at the piano and said, "I had so many things I was going to say tonight. I want to thank all my friends for their concern and I want to thank God for letting me be here. Now I can't think of anything to say, so I guess I'll have to sing for you." As the time moved past midnight, Marty would check his watch before beginning each new song. Before he finished it, the crowd would start screaming, "More!" The curtain finally closed at 12:27, in spite of screams for more songs.[20]

Two nights later Marty was Ralph Emery's guest on a one-hour television special that began at midnight on WSM-TV and was simulcast as part of Emery's *Opry Spotlight* radio show. Marty sat at the piano, with Emery on a stool nearby, and the two carried on a conversation between songs. Fans from across the nation sat in the studio audience, some having come to Nashville for the Saturday night Opry and staying over for the welcome-back TV special. Don Winters and Bobby Sykes were in the audience, and Marty invited them to sing harmony on several songs. The show ran over by eighteen minutes because so many calls and telegrams were coming in from across the nation. When television coverage finally cut off, Marty stayed with Emery for his all-night radio show.[21]

On April 13 Marty was in Los Angeles where he attended the fifth annual Academy of Country and Western Music awards banquet held at the Hollywood Palladium. There he received the organization's first "Man of the Decade" trophy for the decade of the 1960s. (With the award renamed "Artist of the Decade," later winners would be Loretta Lynn, Alabama, Garth Brooks, and George Strait.) His speech included his usual sentiment, "I thank God for allowing me to be here tonight."[22] He then went on to Las Vegas for his month-long gig at the Fremont Hotel.

Although he could accept being forced to give up grueling bus rides and one-nighters, he couldn't accept the loss of racing. "I want to race again," he said in early July. "If I had not asked for the operation because I wanted to race, I know I would be dead now. The doctors said they doubted I would have lasted past May if I had not had the operation."[23] As much as he wanted to race, in those few months after surgery he had to settle for being grand marshal at NASCAR's Paul Revere 250 and Firecracker 400 in Daytona, Florida.

[15]

Back in the Groove

Marty worked mostly with Bobby Sykes and Don Winters for the next several years. He sold his bus, and Okie Jones found other employment. *My Woman, My Woman, My Wife* was Marty's only album in 1970, with Columbia releasing two compilation albums. He appeared regularly on the Opry.

"He made a striking figure up there on that stage in a white suit with navy pinstripes, a deep blue shirt and white patent footwear," says Louise Mayer, vice president of his fan club, in describing his Opry appearance on July 11. "Thunderous applause brought about the encore we wanted so much. . . . Hal Durham closed the show against the will of the clamoring thousands in the Ole' Opry House!" Fan club members moved outside to wait for Marty to appear on the front steps. "It was long after the Opry show was over when finally all autographs were signed," Mayer writes, "all pictures were taken, all fans had a chance for a little visit with him, that he'd found himself willing to leave." Just as Marty was getting into his car, driven by Don Winters, a taxicab brought a load of autograph seekers, and Marty graciously signed autographs for them before he left.[1]

In August he headed back to Las Vegas for another four-week engagement at the Fremont Hotel. Winters and Sykes sang harmony. Jackie Knar, a fan who attended the show on August 16, said Marty "looked great, dressed in a striped sport jacket and gold pants." Knar sat "with a lump in my throat looking at this man up there on stage appearing the picture of health and obviously enjoying every minute of what he was doing, then thinking of the many prayers I had said for someone I'd never met."[2]

Two singles followed Marty's number one "My Woman, My Woman, My Wife," and both reached the top ten as 1970 closed. He'd recorded "Jolie Girl" in April and rerecorded it in July, along with "Padre." Both songs (neither of which he wrote) appeared on his *Greatest Hits, Volume III* album the following April.

In a letter to his fan club, Marty addressed complaints about his choice of songs. "I thank all you fans for continuing to accept my records, even though some have not been as country as others," he wrote. "Some people have been dissatisfied with the song 'Jolie Girl.' 'It isn't country,' they say." He reminded his fans, "I love all kinds of music, but country music is my favorite." He said he wanted more people throughout the world to listen to and purchase country music. "I believe by recording different types of songs I stand a better chance of reaching more people than the artist that records one particular way," he explained. "It's the same old Marty Robbins that is doing the singing regardless of the type of song."[3]

Some fans also criticized his changed appearance. Several members called him a hippie and resigned from the fan club when Marty's hairstyle changed with the times. Fan club president Peggy Ann Munson took them to task for complaining about his "slightly longer hairstyle." She said, "His hair is still short, compared to some of the C&W stars. It's just style, girls, and probably will not last any longer than your mini-skirt."[4] Actually, Marty's wide sideburns were a more drastic change than the length of his hair, by then noticeably blond.

He definitely embraced the '70s look when he appeared on Ralph Emery's October 13 simulcast during the annual deejay convention. Emery paired him with Merle Haggard for the midnight show because "I knew how much Marty loved Merle Haggard's singing, and with Merle the feeling was mutual." Marty wore a blue-and-white checked sport jacket over a red shirt, and Emery told him, "You may not outsing Merle tonight, but you've sure outdressed him." While sitting at the grand piano, Marty started on a political lecture about pollution and environment and how politicians and unions were to blame for the mess. "Merle Haggard looked like he wished he could fade into the stage backdrop as he stood there watching Marty carry on," Emery recalls. When the show resumed after its scheduled break, Marty apologized and said he hadn't meant to offend anyone. A highlight of the evening came when Haggard wore Marty's jacket and sang a near-perfect imitation of "Devil Woman," even stretching for the high notes. Marty acted amazed and impressed, as if he'd never seen Haggard's performance before.[5]

When the television portion ended, Marty began signing autographs and posing for photos with fans who surrounded him. He then returned to the piano and—live on Emery's radio show—rehearsed his songs for the next evening's Country Music Association awards show. "He told stories of what life was like for him in his climb to the top rung [on] the ladder of success," wrote Mayer in the fan club journal. "Times may have been hard, but [with] Marty telling it the way only he can tell it made it all sound hilariously funny. Ralph is a jewel in the way he draws Marty out." Marty again signed autographs and posed for photos when the radio show ended, not leaving until after 4:30, when most of the crowd was gone.

Mayer and a friend visited Marty's office that afternoon, where they met Lucy Coldsnow, whom Mayer called "as gracious as she is beautiful." Marty blew in through the front door, carrying a powder blue suit for the awards show. "If we had any doubts about his health, they were dispelled in a hurry," Mayer wrote, "after seeing how he came in and practically flew up the winding stairway to get ready." The CMA awards show was televised live from the Ryman. Marty sang "My Woman, My Woman, My Wife." The song was a nominee for both Song of the Year (songwriter) and Single of the Year (performance) but didn't win either category. Marty was nominated for Male Vocalist of the Year, an award that went to Merle Haggard. Those CMA award nominations would be the only three of Marty's career.[6]

Marty seldom attended awards shows. "I don't ever remember him going to anything unless he was performing or presenting," Coldsnow says. "And I don't ever remember Marizona going with him." Marty frequently won awards as a BMI (Broadcast Music, Inc.) writer but would not go to the BMI awards show. Coldsnow always accepted his songwriter awards, sometimes with Ronny beside her.[7]

One awards ceremony Marty did attend was the Thirteenth Annual Grammy Awards show on March 16, 1971, emceed by singer Andy Williams and staged at the Palladium in Los Angeles. This marked the first nationally televised live broadcast of the National Academy of Recording Arts and Sciences awards. The big winner, with six awards, was Simon and Garfunkel's "Bridge over Troubled Waters." Bob Hinkle remembers Marty wanting to leave early and catch the midnight flight back to Nashville, as the nominated songs had been prerecorded.[8] But he stayed long enough to receive his second Grammy, this time a songwriter award for 1970's Best Country Song, "My Woman, My Woman, My Wife." He bounded up the steps, accepted the gold-plated miniature of an old-style phonograph from presenter Lynn Anderson, and concluded his brief comments with, "I thank God for this, and I thank God for my woman, my woman, my wife."

July found Marty at the Fremont Hotel in Las Vegas for his first of two 1971 engagements there. As always, Winters and Sykes were part of his show. On July 18, about thirty minutes before show time, Marty received word that Fred Kare was in the audience. He hurried down the aisle to his old friend's table, shaking hands with fans along the way. He embraced the elderly Kare, kissed his forehead, and chatted for a few minutes before being called away to talk to other out-of-town visitors.

When his show began, Marty introduced Kare and explained how he worked at Kare's nightclub when he began his performing career in Phoenix more than two decades earlier. "Fred has been like a father to me," Marty said, describing how Kare took him to Nashville for his first Opry appearance and to Los Angeles for his first recording session. He sang "Strawberry Roan" for his mentor, doing the song without orchestral backing because it hadn't been rehearsed.[9]

Marty was honored on his forty-sixth birthday with a celebration following the Friday Night Opry on September 24, 1971. WSM moved the broadcast of Ralph Emery's all-night *Opry Spotlight* to the stage of the Ryman because of the expected crowd. Members of Marty's fan club came from all over the United States and even Canada. In addition to a regular birthday cake, Emery gave a special one to his friend. Against a background of colorful autumn flowers, his nickname for Marty, "Golden Throat," was written in gold letters and "Happy

Birthday" in brown. A fan provided a third cake, this one shaped like a grand piano, complete with piano bench, and decorated in Marty's racing colors. As the crowd sang "Happy Birthday," Marty hid his face and pretended to be embarrassed by the attention. During the night, he sang his own hits and other currently popular ones. Winters and Sykes also sang, and Emery spun records.

The party continued Saturday night during the Opry's 11:30 time slot when Hal Durham presented Marty with a fan club gift of a polished wooden plaque in the shape of the United States and inscribed with a list of Marty's hits. Marty said he had the best fan club in the world. One fan described him as "so handsome in white trousers and shoes, red and white jacket with shirt and tie to match." Marty invited his fans to meet him in front of the Opry House, and he stayed for an hour and a half, a fan recalls, "granting every request for pictures, signing all autographs asked for and visiting a little with each fan. We knew the time had come; Marty would have to go as Don was waiting with the car at the curb."[10]

Marty wrote to his fan club, "It's time to say I Love My People publicly again in our *Drifter.* I do love all of you in a very special way." He thanked them for his birthday party, saying, "I was one tired but happy man as I looked out over all those smiling faces of My People and in my heart I kept thanking God for the strength and health to enable me to be there and sign just one more autograph. And from somewhere I kept getting more strength." Remembering the plaque presented to him on the Opry stage, he said, "I almost lost my voice. This thought kept running through my mind. Those seats out there are full of the wonderful folks that made this possible and I can't say a word. Well, folks, the words were there, the love was there, but for some reason I couldn't get them to come out." He thanked WSM and Ralph Emery and "all my fans who saved and planned their vacations so they could come to Nashville to help me celebrate. The most Beautiful People In The World Are In My Fan Club, My People, And I love you all."[11]

Marty recorded only one album, *Today,* in 1971, from several small sessions spread out during the year. Two songs were released as singles, "The Chair" and "Early Morning Sunshine." Both made it into *Billboard's* Top Ten. Marty wrote "The Chair" several years earlier, on the same day as "You Gave Me a Mountain." He said he usually wrote two at a time.[12] It must have been a depressing day for him to write about being despised and disliked by his father and then about a condemned criminal who dies in an electric chair.

His relationship with Columbia Records was also depressing. After twenty years on the label, Marty felt unappreciated. "I got mad and left," he explained years later. "I got my feelings hurt. I didn't feel like my records were being placed right in the record store."[13] He recorded his last Columbia session on October 28, 1971, two songs released on the same single, with "The Best Part of Living" becoming his last in a five-year string of thirteen top ten hits. Columbia continued to release compilation albums for the next several years.

On New Year's Eve, Marty called Bob Hinkle in Hollywood and said, "I've got an idea for a movie. Come on down tomorrow. I want to do a country music movie." So Hinkle flew to Nashville to discuss the idea. They agreed to ask Sammy Jackson, Marty's good friend and a disc jockey on KLAC in Los Angeles, to follow Marty around with a pretense of doing a story on him. That would provide an excuse for racing scenes and traveling to Los Angeles and Dallas. "Marty Robbins has written a script for a movie which he'll bankroll, produce and star in," the Nashville Banner reported on January 6, 1972. Filming would begin at the Grand Ole Opry House on February 15. Bob Hinkle directed Country Music, Marty was the producer, and Lucy Coldsnow served as assistant to the producer. "I got all the talent together," she says, "and paid bills, and whatever I guess the assistant to the producer would do."[14]

The movie began with Marty on tour, playing on a Las Vegas stage, going to a race in Pomona, and then stopping in Fort Worth to see disc jockey Bill Mack before returning to Nashville for the Opry. "It was raining and that old Ryman auditorium was full," Hinkle recalls. "We shot Marty's show, and then I went back and did all inserts and cutaways and different things we needed to do. The audience stayed until we finished at two o'clock in the morning."

The movie was released in September by Universal Pictures as part of Marty's new recording contract. Hinkle, with his Hollywood connections, takes credit for connecting Marty with Universal and its parent company, MCA, which also owned Decca Records. Marty wanted to make a series of Gene Autry-type singing westerns, and Hinkle told him, "Let me call Universal, and I'll call MCA, and see if I can get us a deal out there so we can do some movies. And then you cut albums for them." Marty said okay, Hinkle called the MCA/Decca president, and Mike Maitland agreed immediately. He sent someone to Las Vegas to negotiate contracts with Marty and his manager.[15]

Decca Records hosted a fifty-guest luncheon in Nashville on June 27, 1972, to announce Marty had signed a five-year recording contract and already recorded his first single. Maitland joked that the luncheon at the King of the Road Motor Inn had been scheduled a week earlier but they couldn't find Marty to sign the contract. "He is involved in so many different things," Maitland said, "movie-making, auto racing, recording." Marty explained he thought Decca would give him "a little more attention" than Columbia had. Although possibly not realizing he was summarizing what drove him in life, he said, "And I really love attention."[16] He craved approval.

His first Decca release, recorded on June 15 (before he signed the contract), was a song he wrote, "This Much a Man." It reached number eleven on *Billboard*'s country chart. At the same time, Columbia issued a cut from Marty's *My Woman, My Woman, My Wife*, thus forcing him to compete with himself for airplay and chart action. "I've Got a Woman's Love" peaked at thirty-two.[17]

In late July Marty and his crew went to Phoenix to film his singing western, *The Drifter*, at nearby Apacheland. They changed the movie's name to *Guns of a Stranger* at the request of Clint Eastwood's company, so as not to conflict with Eastwood's latest movie, *High Plains Drifter*.[18] This must have disappointed Marty, who used the drifter theme in his first television series and in numerous songs and had long wanted to make the movie. He seemed to carry the drifter persona, perhaps originating with his childhood on the desert.

Universal Pictures provided funding and screen credits listed Robert Hinkle as director and producer, although Marty was the producer. Coldsnow served as Marty's assistant and as script supervisor. "I had no idea what a script supervisor did," she says. "The film editor depends on script notes, so I had a meeting with the film editor, and he told me what to do. So I did that, along with paying bills and taking care of whatever needed to be done. I remember having to rewrite the script at night, type my notes, so it was a twenty-four-hour job. But I loved it."[19]

Marty and Hinkle, both experienced horsemen, wanted a horse already accustomed to the Arizona climate. They hired Flax, who had appeared on television in *The High Chaparral*.[20] Ronny Robbins and Melody Hinkle, son and daughter of producer and director, played a young married ranch couple. Ronny, in his movie debut, had been discharged from the military long enough to have an appropriate '70s-length hairstyle.

In the *Shane*-type movie, Marty played a guilt-ridden former marshal named Matthew Roberts, usually called Drifter. As he described the movie, "I was a marshal in a little town, and they made me up to look a lot younger than I am, y'know, and did a very good job. I have to kill a seventeen- or eighteen-year-old kid, because this kid wants to make a name for himself, see. So I have to shoot him. Well, then, I turn in the badge, and I start riding. All I do is drift—it was just like one of those Gene Autry movies, see. And I ride in, and I aid this little kid; he's out practicing the fast draw because he's going to shoot somebody that shot his father. I give them a hand, and I help them save the ranch. And then I ride off into the sunset."[21] The drifter called on Bobby Sykes and Don Winters to help herd cattle and sing with him. In one scene, he said, "The boys and I will sing at the drop of a hat," and he tossed his hat on the ground. Marty pulled a song from his 1966 *The Drifter* album, "Oh, Virginia," to sing to the rancher, Virginia. He also sang "Lonely Old Bunkhouse," a song he wrote for his uncles, all of whom had spent their lives as genuine Arizona cowboys.[22] Several songs from the movie, including "The Dreamer," would not appear on record until his 1979 album, *All-Around Cowboy.*

Several scenes showed Marty in a sleeveless undershirt, exhibiting his healthy-looking physique. His action scenes included a boxing match, and he did not look like someone who underwent triple bypass heart surgery less than three years earlier. A magazine reporter commented, "After seeing him on location at Apacheland, working in 110- to 112-degree heat in heavy, brown Western clothing, and with the big, heavy gun strapped around his slim waist, you can see the movie business . . . is hard, demanding work."[23]

Marty lost his temper once. "He whipped the dog manure out of a long lean cowboy twice his size," Bobby Sykes remembers. "He called Marty a son of a bitch. Marty hit him three or four times and it took them five minutes to bring the guy to. And the guy never did hit Marty once!" Sykes adds, "Marty was a nice guy, and easy going, but he did have a temper and he was *not* afraid of *anything.*" Hinkle thought the man was a movie extra because he wore old western attire. He'd been drinking, and he started harassing Marty, who "knocked the hell out of him," Hinkle says. "Marty threw his arm out when he hit him, and was sore for a week. And it was the time we were doing the fight scenes."[24]

Marty returned to Nashville and called his band together for a show at Mockingbird Hill Park on August 13, 1972, in Anderson, Indiana. They played the Opry on Saturday night and then drove to Indiana for two Sunday shows. Their rental bus blew its engine south of Bowling Green, Kentucky. Don Winters hitched a ride into the city to get a taxicab, and several of the men returned to

Nashville to rent cars to complete the trip. They reloaded everything and made it to Anderson in time.[25]

Bobby Sykes opened both shows, followed by Winters and then Marty, who announced it was his first personal appearance with his band since his surgery. He said he had promised the owner of the park he would do his first show there, as a replacement for the one cancelled when he had his heart attack. "He said they wanted to come in the worst way and that was how they did come," a fan recalls. Ronny sang several songs after being introduced as "my little boy" by his dad. When he came onstage, he raised the microphone so high Marty had to stand on tiptoe to reach it.[26]

In his annual letter to his fan club, Marty asked his fans to see the new movie. "It will be My People's decision in the end," he wrote, "if many more movies are to be made as they cost a pile of money to make them. But My People has put me where I am today, and I stand confident you are all with me all the way." He encouraged everyone to attend Fan Fair the following June, saying "Both myself and my 'LITTLE BOY' Ronny will do our very best to try to meet you all at Fan Fair 1973."[27]

[16]

NASCAR 42

When Marty applied for his NASCAR license in 1970, he chose number forty-two from a list of available car numbers. Lee Petty had used that number from NASCAR's beginning in 1946 until he retired from racing in 1962. Richard Petty writes in his autobiography, "Daddy picked it by looking around the garage until his eyes stopped on the license plate of his passenger car. Four and two were the first two numbers, so that was it. Somehow there should have been a more exciting reason for picking the number that someday would become one of the most famous in NASCAR history."[1] He doesn't mention Marty's role in making the number famous.

In a letter dated September 23, 1970, Marty wrote to his fan club, "I intend to start racing in the month of October. Since God has seen fit to heal my body, I see no reason for not enjoying life. I firmly believe if God did not want me to race again he would not have made me physically fit to do so." He went on to say, "I do not appreciate letters condemning me for enjoying this sport. . . . If some of you have dreams or visions about my racing, try not to tell me about them. Instead, if you think I should not race, although you know I'm going to, pray for me." He assured his fans, "Bobby Allison is seeing that my car is in perfect shape. Bobby is a Grand National driver and in my estimate is one of the greatest drivers in the business today."[2]

Marty chose the major NASCAR Grand National circuit over the smaller Grand Touring circuit he'd planned to run before his heart attack. He sold his brand-new 1969 Dodge Dart Swinger to a driver in another racing circuit. "I ended up buying a Dodge Daytona from James Hylton and I ran at Charlotte in the October race in 1970," Marty said. "He bought his first Grand National race car from me," Hylton agrees. "The first time I met Marty, I'd been out on an errand and came back to my race shop at Inman, South Carolina, and heard this music—acoustic guitar playing and Marty singing, sitting on one of my workbenches, singing. I'm one of his biggest fans, or maybe *the* biggest fan of Marty Robbins. I think he's probably the greatest songwriter, performer, of all times."[3]

With "42" and "Marty Robbins" emblazoned on the freshly painted purple and yellow and green Dodge Charger Daytona, Marty drove in his second National 500 at Charlotte Motor Speedway two years after his previous run. Engine failure knocked him out after 105 laps. He later told an interviewer, "I guess I was a little discouraged after that. Besides, my wife was upset with my racing so I sold the car and went back to running an occasional modified race."[4]

Although Marty returned to racing his 777 sportsman at the Fairgrounds Speedway, the 1971 season drew him again to NASCAR. "We made a trade deal in which he ended up with my '71 Dodge Charger," Bobby Allison says, "and I ended up with his '67 Dodge, which I went ahead and sold somebody for a sportsman car." Allison also provided a trailer to transport the car and a van for hauling race equipment. To complete the trade, Marty tossed in a Lincoln Continental and a Black Angus bull.[5]

Marty competed in five races in the renamed Winston Cup Grand National Series in 1971. While in Charlotte for the World 600 in May, he visited record shops to sign autographs. Before the race he appeared in front of the grandstand and sang several songs. He finished the race in fifteenth place and without problems. Next came the Dixie 500 at Atlanta Motor Speedway in August. There, after several spin-outs, he finished thirteenth.

During prerace activities at the Southern 500 in Darlington, South Carolina, on Labor Day, Marty served as a judge to select Miss Southern 500 and he rode in the parade. Toward the end of the race itself, he got so tired his heavy helmet pulled his head sideways, and he felt unsafe to stay on the track. He pulled into the pits and turned his car over to a relief driver for a few laps. "A life-saving crew immediately descended on Marty and offered him oxygen as he slumped over a tire," reported a fan. "Marty took a few whiffs and jumped to his feet, shadow boxing and saying, 'Let me at 'em.'" The more experienced Richard Petty has described the feeling by saying, "My neck gets tired from holding my head up straight with that heavy helmet on, when the G-forces are trying to pull it to the right. The pain goes all the way down your shoulders and back." Marty finished seventh, his highest place to date, and he won the Fireball Roberts memorial trophy for rookie of the race.[6] A steering problem knocked him out of the National 500 at Charlotte the following month.

When Marty mentioned he had no one in Nashville to get his car into top condition, the Allisons told him to bring it to their shop in Hueytown, Alabama. Eddie Allison worked as Marty's full-time mechanic during the week and stayed with the car through its inspection and qualification phases. Then he switched to Holman-Moody's pit crew to take care of Bobby's car during races. The Allisons hired someone to drive Marty's vehicles to the racetrack. If Marty had a show date nearby, he usually performed first and then ran the car on Sunday.

Eddie's first race as a member of Marty's crew occurred in December 1971 at Texas World Speedway in College Station. After Marty dropped out due to engine failure, he invited his crew to a Japanese steakhouse. "He put on a show with the Japanese cook," Allison recalls. "He and that cook fit together instantly, and it made the evening so pleasant and so enjoyable."

Ronny liked to build motors, and he would sometimes build an engine for his dad. Marty was hauling one of those from Nashville when he ran out of gas on the interstate highway a few miles from Hueytown. He parked along the road and walked to a house to use the telephone. Eddie Allison brought the gas, and he remembers, "Those women, when they found out who he was, they went wild. They wouldn't have ever known if we hadn't told them, because he didn't.

He wasn't that kind of person." After they installed the engine in the race car, Marty called Eddie's wife and said, "Go get some steaks and we'll have steak for supper." At the Allison house, Penny asked how Marty wanted his steak cooked, and he told her, "Get everybody else's cooked and I'll do mine." He put it on the grill, turned it over, and put it on his plate. Penny placed a circle of salad dressing bottles around the plate so she didn't have to look at him eating raw steak.

Marty worked with Eddie Allison on a sportsman car they took to a track in Birmingham for a shakedown and they went out to eat pizza after the race. Marty got up on the stage and played piano and sang for the customers. "It was two o'clock in the morning, and the manager was wanting to go home, and the people was wanting to listen to Marty sing," Allison remembers. He adds, "Even with him being a celebrity, he was so lovable with everybody. Around the racetrack, he was trying to be one of the racers and not be a celebrity." Don Winters was always close by, though, serving as Marty's bodyguard and watching to ensure no one messed with him.[7]

NASCAR moved into a new era in 1972 with fewer races and a points system designed to reward winners and motivate teams to run more races. To decrease speed, rules mandated either smaller cars or smaller engines. Marty went to Cotton Owens, who had a Plymouth, and said he wanted a Dodge. "So I took this Plymouth and made a Dodge out of it by changing the body," Owens says.[8] Eddie Allison prepared the new 1972 Dodge for the upcoming Miller Highlife 500 in Ontario, California, on March 5. This was during the filming of the *Country Music* movie, and director Bob Hinkle filmed the weekend. The group stayed at a Riverside motel. After practice, everyone gathered in a room and Marty sang all night. "As long as somebody was listening," Allison says, "he'd sing." Marty wrote "This Much a Man" (which became his first Decca single) that night in the motel.

Allison was amazed by Marty's ability to handle two physically exhausting professions. "If he'd had a show date on the weekend, it took a lot of his time and energy, so by race time he'd be tired out," Allison explains. "We got to be at a few show dates, and the energy he expended in entertaining people was unbelievable." Allison and his two crewmates attended Marty's concert in Long Beach the night before the Ontario race. They wore their pit uniforms, and Marty brought them onstage. "People went wild," Allison says. "He told the singing promoter he had to go on early because we had to go home and get in bed to be at the race track early in the morning. Dottie West was on the program, and when she found out, she cried, 'Marty, there's no way I can go on after you!' But she survived."[9] Marty finished the race in eighth place and received the Sportsman trophy.

Richard Petty describes racing: "The stress alone that's placed on you in the race car, where the temperature may be 140 degrees, is unbelievable, and when you're drafting at, say, 200 mph, it keeps you so tense that you can feel it in every muscle. . . . To do it for four or five hours is one of the most physically and mentally demanding things a man can do." He adds, "When you do it with a whole track full of cars, lap after lap after lap, it wears you down. . . . You can't even move your hands from where you have them on the steering wheel. If you do, you have to put them right back where they were, because that's the only place that won't burn you. . . . There have been times after a long, hot race when I had to have help to get me out of the car."[10]

Marty thrived on such experiences. He and his crew began preparing for the upcoming Winston 500 at Talladega's Superspeedway, which would be Marty's first race at what he later called "my favorite track, and it's the fastest track in the world."[11] The race on May 7, 1972, would also be his most famous—or infamous—one.

Because the new track was faster than tire technology could handle, NASCAR issued a rule to require restrictor rings in carburetors. Choking down air and fuel flow to the engine slowed the cars by approximately thirteen miles per hour and prevented tires from blowing. Marty wanted to know what it felt like to run with the leaders, so he asked Eddie Allison for help. Allison designed an arrangement to drop the rings into the intake manifold and hold them. According to crewmember Charlie Wright, they used epoxy glue that the gas would eventually loosen enough to release the inserts.[12] "I was illegal, but I wasn't cheating," Marty insisted later. "There is a difference, y'see. If you are illegal, then you confess. But if you cheat, you go ahead and you don't tell nobody, see. So I was just illegal."

When the restrictor rings melted off and the full horsepower kicked in, Marty "played around all day and made about forty or fifty pit stops, having a big time, y'know. I didn't want to pass anybody; I was just having a good time." With about forty miles to go, track officials called a temporary halt because of rain. Just before the restart, Marty told Allison, "I'm gonna catch the leaders. I want to see how fast I can go." His top wrench answered, "Go ahead; do it." Marty caught the leaders in two laps. Buddy Baker, Bobby Isaacs, and David

Pearson were running bumper to bumper, and Marty stayed behind them for a few laps while he thought about what to do next. "There were about seventy thousand people, and all of a sudden at the end of the race, here I am, pulled up right in back of the leaders, y'know. So I knew the fans knew I was there. I said to myself, I want to pass them, but where should I pass them? I didn't know whether to pass them on the front straightaway or the back straightaway. I wanted everybody in the stands to see it. But I got to thinking, well, now when I go into that turn, I'm going to be doing close to two hundred miles an hour, and I have never been that fast before. And so, I said if I don't make that turn, the first stop will be Daytona Beach. And that's a long jump, see. I said I don't think I'll do it."

Marty was washing his face and getting ready to go home when someone came to tell him, "You've been voted rookie of the race, and they want you in front of the grandstand to accept the award." Marty answered, "Well I can't take it; I was running illegal today." The man stood there, undecided as to whether Marty was joking, and said, "Hurry up, they're waiting for you." When Marty repeated, "I can't do it," the man realized he was serious and reported him to the officials. Marty explained to them how he qualified legal but was illegal when running.

They disqualified him from the race and dropped his finishing position from eighteenth to fiftieth. "I knew that when I told them," he said, "they would set me back to last position regardless of where I finished. So I was sure I wasn't going to win any money. I was doing it for fun. I didn't care about winning—I was just having a good time." He began to understand his actions had hurt some feelings.[13]

The consequences for Eddie Allison were drastic. "It caused some real havoc," Allison says. "Even though he took the blame for the deal, it rolled back on us because we did it. He wanted to do it, and we knew how to do it, and if he hadn't said anything nobody would have ever found out." Bobby and Eddie Allison were two of many who were appalled when Marty turned himself in. "We tried to explain to Marty that there were several other people doing that same thing," Bobby says. "There was no need for him to take any blame with NASCAR. It was one of those things we did." A magazine article reported, "By turning himself in, Robbins had violated a code of old-time racing ethics, NASCAR style. . . . The assumption has long been that whatever you can get to the starting line with is yours, legal or not. This little game between NASCAR inspectors and top wrenches has been played for years, but no one, *no one*, ever turned himself in."[14]

Although the Allisons and others believed Marty reported his actions because of a guilty conscience, such was not the case. Once confronted with accepting an award he hadn't earned, there was no alternative but to explain the reason for his speed. He would certainly have never risked his mechanic's career intentionally. Even then, he insisted he figured out for himself how to "let these little ol' restrictor plates slip out of the carburetor down into the manifold."[15]

But NASCAR officials knew better. They fined Eddie (with a disproportionate amount for such an offense) and permanently revoked his license. Marty paid the fine but couldn't restore the license. "Eddie's never been back in NASCAR," Bobby says. "There were a couple of inspectors at NASCAR that did not like the Allison family. Those inspectors were the ones that were involved heavily in the discipline of Marty Robbins." Eddie found employment with a masonry construction company as an equipment mechanic, and he continued to admire Marty and consider him a friend. According to Eddie, the incident led to better enforcement of NASCAR rules. "The inspectors had to get better because we could beat them to death," he says. "The drivers were outsmarting them."[16]

Bobby Allison appreciates Marty's overall contribution to NASCAR racing. "He helped people become aware of how big this racing thing was," Allison says. "He had a big fan base in the music business, and he brought more fans into NASCAR."[17]

Associated Press reports of Marty cheating and being caught by NASCAR officials so angered Marty that he considered giving up racing. He told a reporter, "It embarrassed me and it really embarrassed my wife. She thought I cheated, too." Concerned he had also embarrassed his many fans, he visited Ralph Emery's *Opry Spotlight* to explain what happened. Letters and telephone calls from around the country urged him to continue racing.[18]

And so he did. He called Charlie Wright, who had helped Eddie Allison at Talladega, and Wright agreed to be his mechanic at Texas World Speedway in June. They drove to College Station several days before the race to allow time for qualifying. They stayed at the Holiday Inn, and every night Marty and Don Winters sat by the pool and sang for anyone who came by. Their group was eating dinner at a restaurant when a teenager came in and saw Marty and asked, "Has anybody ever told you that you look like Marty Robbins?" Marty said no. "Well, are you Marty Robbins?" When Marty identified himself, the youth said, "My dad has every record you ever made." Marty said, "Well, I'd like to meet your dad." The amazed teenager asked if Marty really wanted to meet his dad, and Marty told him they had no other plans for the evening. "So we followed the kid out to his dad's house," Wright recalls, "and Marty went in, that kid introduced him to his dad, and went out and gathered up some neighbors, and Marty sat there in the den, and they brought him a guitar, and he played and sang, and that man sat over there in a rocking chair, and it looked like he had a halo over his head."[19]

Marty blew an engine during the Lone Star 500 and returned to Nashville to sign his Decca recording contract. After filming *Guns of a Stranger,* he raced in three more NASCAR events during 1972. One was the Southern 500 at Darlington on Labor Day. When the heat exhausted Marty on lap 230, he turned his car over to a relief driver, who took it to a ninth place finish. "Robbins watched Mayne push his #42 around the track," wrote a reporter. "He was chewing a cup of ice, but he took in every rotation of the yellow hub caps and black tires, and felt every throb of the motor. It was written in his face." After the race, Marty signed autographs and posed for photos with fans. "He was still signing autographs when he was almost pushed into a waiting car, to catch a plane," the reporter wrote.[20]

In late 1972, for the first time in his life, Marty grew a mustache. When Ralph Emery teased him about looking like the Frito bandito, he said, "I've been called that a number of times. But I don't care. I really do like it. I'm gonna keep it." He also let his hair go back to its natural color, instead of being lightened by the Lemon-Go-Lightly he had used for several years. When he performed at the Nugget in Sparks, Nevada, his change in appearance sparked a newspaper article that said he had been known for a "boyish face, the result of shiny blond hair and a candid, open expression. But suddenly the hair has turned brown and a moustache imparts a rakish look." Peggy Ann Munson, who by now had been Marty's fan club president for twenty years, added this handwritten note to the Sparks article reprinted in the fan club magazine: "Girls, stop throwing fits over the mustache. . . . I think it's cute on him—bad grammar—but I 'likes' it!" A fan who hadn't seen the new look wrote, "I just can't see him hiding any part of that beautiful face behind a bunch of superfluous hair, but if it makes him happy, then that is what counts."[21]

One night somebody yelled from the audience, "Why you growing the mustache?" Marty joked, "I'm going to do a western called *Pride and the Badge.*" He decided it was a "pretty good title" and wrote the song.[22] He later recorded "Pride and the Badge" for his *All-Around Cowboy* album in 1979.

Sporting his new look, Marty celebrated twenty years as a member of the Grand Ole Opry in January 1973. Most of his out-of-town appearances that year were engagements in Las Vegas, Lake Tahoe, Sparks, and Reno, Nevada, where he worked with a house band. He used a fifteen-piece orchestra for a show with Merle Haggard at the Hollywood Bowl, and he answered "He's not country" arguments by saying his songs were arranged right off his records. "So there's nothing pop-sounding about songs I do on stage," he said. "I do a country sound." He appeared on a few package shows but felt he could not afford a bus or a band, and only Don Winters and Bobby Sykes traveled with him. "I'm a long ways from being the wealthy person people think I am," he told a reporter.[23]

After a March package show headlined by Sonny James in Greensboro, North Carolina, one fan described forty-seven-year-old Marty as having "the looks and vigor of a twenty-year-old man. His hair, although it looked great blond, was back to its beautiful natural color. His mustache looked great." A fan who saw him at the Sahara Tahoe in Nevada earlier that month said he was "dressed in a white-with-black-stripes mod outfit, with yellow shirt and white shoes. Don and Bobby [had] jackets matching Marty's outfit and they wore red pants, pink shirts and white shoes." Comedian Steve Martin opened the show.[24]

This Much a Man, Marty's first MCA/Decca album, had been released the previous November. "Walking Piece of Heaven," the follow-up single to "This Much a Man," entered *Billboard's* country chart in March 1973. With no further competition from Columbia releases, it climbed to number six. The B side was "Franklin, Tennessee," a song Marty wrote about the town where he lived. In return, Williamson County Jaycees honored him with a "Marty Robbins Day."[25]

The Decca name disappeared when the label changed to MCA Records. Marty's second album, released in July, was simply *Marty Robbins.* It contained the Jeanne Pruett song that became Marty's next top ten hit, "Love Me." Marty explained to Ralph Emery that the single would be one verse shorter than its album cut because "the people at MCA" thought it was too long for airplay. He said, "I remember I had a hit one time that was four minutes and thirty-seven seconds long. It was called 'El Paso.' So I say, if it's on the record, they'll play it. And if it's not, they won't play it."

The flipside of "Love Me" also appeared on the *Marty Robbins* album. Marty got the idea for "Crawling On My Knees" when flying home at the end of a Las Vegas engagement. "We rushed real fast and caught a 2:40 plane," he said. "We got through at 2:00, had everything packed, all we had to do was jump in the taxi with what we had on. We got on the plane and were flying along, feeling real good, and started hitting some bumpy weather, and the stewardess fell down. She was crawling on her knees—I thought that was pretty funny—so I wrote the song, 'You got me crawling on my knees.'"

Marty obtained an MCA recording contract for Ronny, with legendary Owen Bradley as his producer. He recorded as Ronny Robbins, rather than Marty Robbins Jr., the name Marty wanted him to use with Columbia before his military service. When Marty was asked if he produced Ronny's records, he said, "I wish I could produce a hit for him, see, but I always thought it would be a lot easier for him to get along if I wasn't near the session." When Ronny was looking for material for his album, he asked his mother what songs she liked. Marizona told him an old Fred Rose song, "No One Will Ever Know," was one of her favorites. "I listened to it and I liked it," Ronny says, and he recorded it.[26]

Marty wrote a letter to his fans in July and thanked them for coming to the 1973 Fan Fair celebration where he appeared briefly and where fans raved over Ronny. He mentioned that the Nashville heat "doesn't bother a desert rat like me." He invited them to see *Guns of a Stranger,* although, he said, "I am sure it won't win any kind of awards since it has no sex scenes or vulgar language." He then said he had "some hay I want to rake and bale tomorrow so this winter my cows will say, 'Here comes Marty with some more great hay, girls.'"[27]

Twenty-four-year-old Ronny appeared with Marty in September on a new radio program, *The Ralph Emery Show.* Emery, while still on WSM, no longer worked the all-night *Opry Spotlight.* He asked Ronny what it was like to be the son of Marty Robbins, and Ronny answered, "Well, it's hard to say, because it's the only life I've ever known." Emery asked if sounding remarkably like his father would be a handicap in building his own career. Ronny agreed the name provided instant recognition but said it led people to expect more of him. Marty joked, "Let me remind you, I'm not selling too well right now, Ralph. I hope he doesn't have my problem."

When asked about Las Vegas appearances, Ronny said, "I've sung there one time, when I was traveling with Daddy before I got drafted." Marty whispered, "You don't say Daddy; you say Marty." They talked about fourteen-year-old Janet, who was five-foot-seven and as tall as her mother. Ronny said he and Janet were both bashful, and he explained how he handled working in front of a crowd: "If it's an auditorium show, I take the glasses off. I can't see anything, and it doesn't bother me. But when it's up close, if it's like a few people, I can't sing in front of people. I have to build up to it."

Emery asked if Marty wanted Ronny to get married. "I think if he falls in love with somebody, and she falls in love with him," Marty answered, "I think it would be nice to be married. But it's a fast world, and you have to be sure of a lot of things before you get married. A lot of lives can be ruined, just because some people *think* they're in love, and they get married. So the best thing to do is *find out* if you're meant—." Emery interrupted to ask if Ronny had heard this lecture before, and Ronny answered, "Not today." Marty made his point by saying, "When you're married and you're in show business, it's a rough life for the wife."[28]

Marty recorded his last top ten hit for MCA in October. He wrote "Twentieth Century Drifter" for those drivers who "don't have much of a chance of winning," he said. "They're kind of operating on a shoestring, y'know. They make just enough from one track to get to the next track. They're all great drivers, but they don't have the right equipment to be first." He saw similarities in his two chosen professions: "There's a lot of singers, y'know, if they had the right break, they could be big. But they will never get that right break, and the same goes for drivers."[29]

[17]

Twentieth Century Drifter

"Every time I go to a race," Marty once said, "I feel I have as good a chance of winning as anybody, y'know, because so many things can happen. That's like when I put out a song; I think I have as good a chance as anybody of having a hit."[1]

Marty wrecked his 1972 Dodge during February 1973's Daytona 500. "On the sixty-third lap he was the low man as three cars came side by side through the treacherous number four turn," a *Sports Illustrated* article explained. "Marty's right front fender was tapped just enough to send his car and three others into a long, long slide. Robbins stayed cool, holding his car up perfectly against the outside wall while the rest of the pack skittered by him as best they could." Don Winters watched from the pits. "I was scared," he stated. "Marty was sliding backward, and that wall was hitting right next to where the gas tank was."[2]

"I was so embarrassed when I got out of that car," Marty said. "I was lucky I got out because I was doing 170 when it turned around. I'm glad it didn't turn over. Here's one thing I did that no one else can say they did. I went about a thousand feet backward at 170 miles an hour. I think that's a record." Marty felt partially at fault. "I was gonna pass the guy on the inside," he explained, "and coming off the fourth turn there's a bad hump, and it throws you to the left a foot or two. I was going a little too fast to be down in that lower lane, see." When the other car hit the hump and bounced into Marty's path, "He barely touched the front end of my car, and got me completely out of control," Marty said, "and up against the wall going backwards. Well, I sang in a higher key for three or four weeks after that."[3]

After Daytona, Marty purchased a 1973 Dodge from Cotton Owens, who maintained the car and kept it at his facility in Spartanburg, South Carolina. Owens, already a member of the National Motorsports Press Association Hall of Fame, had retired from driving and from fielding a regular team. Marty first raced his new Charger at the Texas World Speedway in June. Two nights before the Alamo 500, he stood on the Holiday Inn patio and sang for an inebriated crowd of two hundred. Sometime after midnight he introduced "Twentieth Century Drifter" when asked if he'd ever written a song about stock car racing. He said he had one that wasn't finished. It was a song for independent race car drivers who had no sponsors and were "doing all they can do to get from one race to the next." He sang about a driver who "knows he's never going to win, but he's never lost the dream that he's going to win first place."[4]

Marty arrived in College Station too late to practice driving his brand new car. Still, he qualified for the tenth starting spot at the Alamo 500. "My car had to be at least three miles faster than any car out there," he said. "That's the only time I was ever close to winning." "I started in tenth place, and in four laps I was in fourth place, and caught Cale Yarborough and was getting ready to pass him. Richard Petty and Buddy Baker were first and second, Cale was third, I was fourth. Then the distributor caved in and that was it. But it was the best thirty laps I ever had." Richard Petty won. (Marty's three races at Texas World Speedway marked the high point of that track's relationship with NASCAR, which now uses Texas Motor Speedway near Forth Worth.)[5]

The following month Marty returned to Daytona, this time for the Firecracker 400 on Independence Day. He finished eighth in his new car. At the Talladega 500 in August, he started tenth and led one lap, for the first time ever.

But a timing chain broke after eighty laps, and he was out.[6] "Marty could have been a great race driver," Cotton Owens says, "if he'd got into it when he was young. Because of his music, he didn't devote the time it took to be a first-class race driver."

Although Marty worried about fitting in as a driver, "it was *his* concern," Owens says. "They didn't resent him at all. They accepted him and liked to hear him sing." The staff at the Ramada Inn in Talladega pulled a piano into the motel when Marty was scheduled to stay there. The racing crews gathered at the motel after track practice each day to hear Marty play and sing. "He'd sing 'til midnight or longer," Owens reminisces. "He'd entertain all the people at the restaurant and the motel. He was an enjoyable person to be around."[7]

In addition to Marty's impromptu singing, he often gave scheduled performances in conjunction with races. Lucy Coldsnow coordinated those from the office in Nashville. "Racing was his passion," she says. "He was always excited about it. I would order his fire outfits, his jumpsuits, and get him all ready to go." Marty would call her and say, "Lucy, get the car ready," and she would make telephone calls to get it sent to wherever it needed to go. She would ask how much money was needed and then write checks. She unhesitatingly called NASCAR founder Bill France Sr. if Marty needed something. "A guy gave me tires for my car one time," she remembers. "In return, I probably got him some albums or some Opry tickets. NASCAR was a small organization."[8]

Glen Wood of Wood Brothers Racing remembers asking for complimentary Opry tickets. When he went to Marty's office to get the tickets, he was surprised to have front row seats. Marty came onstage that night, sang a song, and then said he wanted to introduce a friend. He told Wood to stand. "I thought that was pretty cool," Wood reminisces. Marty often said he appreciated the drivers talking with him, and he felt honored they would do so. He didn't want to intrude or steal their headlines. Wood told him, "Marty, you got it the wrong way around. It's an honor for *us* to be able to talk with you."[9]

Marty completed his first three races in 1974, two at Talladega Superspeedway, his favorite track. He started in fifteenth position in May and finished fifteenth. In August he ran the Talladega 500. When his name was called during the introduction ceremony, "the entire grandstand section was on its feet applauding and cheering," said a magazine article. Marty waved and pretended to be embarrassed by the attention. He kissed the Winston girls and playfully tried to kiss the track announcer. Walking back to the pits, he posed and waved and smiled for the fans yelling and taking photos. During the race he followed one car for eight laps and then pulled his number 42 between that car and the wall. "The grandstand audience was on its feet," the magazine reported, "and a gasp rose through the hot summer air as Robbins missed the wall by less than six inches on his right and with clearance so scant on his left that one couldn't see daylight between the two autos as they came into the number one turn." Marty pulled in front of the other driver and finished ninth. Richard Petty commented, "He's a lot better race driver than I could ever be a singer." Marty joked he purposely didn't win races because he didn't want NASCAR drivers competing with him as singers.[10]

Marty's career-best NASCAR finish occurred June 16, 1974, when he took fifth in the Motor State 360 in Brooklyn, Michigan. Cotton Owens had rebuilt the 1973 Charger into a 1974 model because of new rules. Marty let Gary Bettenhausen pass him on a caution light "because I thought he belonged up there," he said. "I didn't know where I was running. When the race was over and they told me I finished fifth, I about passed out." "Marty didn't want to take money from those guys by beating them," Owens says.[11]

"He gave me the hardest race I've ever run," said Richard Childress, who later brought Dale Earnhardt and his number 3 Chevrolet to fame. "We had raced wheel to wheel for the last thirty laps of that race, then on the last turn I bumped the wall, he took advantage of my error and cut down to the inside to beat me." Childress concluded, "Marty Robbins is one man I don't mind trusting my life to at one hundred eighty mph."[12]

That happened four months later at the National 500 in Charlotte. It is probably Marty's most remembered race, other than the 1972 restrictor ring incident. Marty flew in the day before and qualified almost without practice laps. "The $161,877 race was marred by a spectacular ten-car crash that put seven vehicles out of the running and injured country and western singer Marty Robbins," said a newspaper article. "Robbins plowed his Dodge into the wall on the first turn to avoid the wreck." A rookie driver had lost control and cut across the track to the infield. The resulting dust storm destroyed driver visibility.[13]

With his vision obscured, Marty decided, "All I could do was hit the wall and hopefully bounce off and maybe take some speed out. When I turned that thing, it went right so quick I hit the wall at about 150 miles an hour. Oh, man, it hurt so bad, I didn't care if I was dying."[14]

Childress remembers getting hit by a car and being turned around on the front stretch. He and several other cars were spinning and sliding, and his car halted sideways. Then he saw Marty coming down the track. "Marty turns right and goes into the wall instead of hitting me," Childress marvels. "Probably if he hadn't done that, if he had not been a good experienced race driver, I may not be here today." When Marty bounced off the concrete wall, he hit Childress's door. "Robbins is into the wall," came the announcement, and the crowd watched in a hush. Then Marty climbed from his purple and lime-green Dodge and walked to the infield. The crowd cheered while ambulance attendants placed him on a stretcher. Reports from the field hospital said he suffered only facial cuts and multiple bruises.[15]

"I never fear death, but I am afraid of getting hurt when I race," Marty told a magazine reporter. "I chose to hit the wall because I could see it and thought I was prepared for it. What I wasn't prepared for was the stretch. . . . When I hit that wall it stretched my body at least a foot, because those shoulder straps don't give and the steering wheel was at least a foot away, and they found my face and bones *buried* in it." He said, "I had four broken ribs and a broken tailbone. I hit that wall with such force that by all rights the seat belt should have torn loose and I should have been killed."[16]

A NASCAR official stated, "What he did out there today saved at least one life and probably kept some other drivers from being maimed. He could have killed himself moving into the wall that way. But in the split second that counted, he chose to possibly give his life over hurting somebody else." Marty was taken to Charlotte Memorial Hospital, where thirty-two stitches closed the gash between his eye and eyebrow. During a radio interview at the hospital, he said he knew there were people in those wrecked cars and "I couldn't hit one of them because they'd probably not walk away from it." He returned to Nashville that night and left the following day to do a scheduled show for President Gerald Ford.[17]

"He had a love for race cars and going fast," Childress says. "He was a good solid racer, and didn't get himself in trouble, and raced hard all the time. If you were a NASCAR fan, you were a Marty Robbins fan. It definitely helped NASCAR by having Marty in the field. And he always had those loud colors on his car so you couldn't miss him. Lime yellow and purple or something—a real bright yellowish green. Most definitely, his color scheme stood out."[18]

"He was a driver," Darrell Waltrip says, "more than what we refer to as a crash artist. Guys that don't race a lot have a tendency to come in and they're not used to the car and the track, and they get themselves in a lot of trouble. Marty was conservative enough and intelligent enough to know the difference between going too fast and ever how fast Marty wanted to go."[19]

As for Marizona, "I don't tell her when I'm going to race," Marty said, perhaps jokingly. "I call her afterwards to let her know I'm okay." He said he tried to convince her he was getting free publicity from racing, but he acknowledged, "Smashing up $30,000 cars isn't exactly free, is it?" Cotton Owens repaired the car, and Marty looked forward to the 1975 racing season and the Daytona 500. He told a reporter, "I only know one thing for sure and that's the only walls I ever want to bounce off again will be the four walls in someone's home with the stereo on or in the recording studio."[20]

After the Charlotte wreck, Marty would lower himself carefully onto the piano bench and tell his audience he used to be a race car driver until a wall jumped out in front of him at Charlotte and broke his tailbone. "Did you ever try to find a comfortable position on a hard piano bench? They don't make 'em," he said.[21]

His next Winston Cup race, February 1975's Daytona 500, brought more trouble. In turn three of lap three, another driver lost control and came down off the wall in front of Marty, who could not drop lower because of a car already in that spot. "I wanted to make Daytona because it was a big track and I liked the speed," he said later. "I didn't want any more collisions. So I decided ahead what I'd do if it happened again. I would turn left and hit the brakes and get down in the infield, regardless. Because I had had all of the steering wheel I wanted." When he saw a smoking car ahead of him, he decided to pass it before the engine blew and spewed oil all over the track. He'd accelerated to 190 miles an hour when the other driver hit the wall and ricocheted off. "I'd always heard, go where you saw the car last, because it won't be there, so I tried that, and it worked," Marty explained. "But what I didn't know, there was another eight cars involved. Coming out of the smoke, I'd already gotten back down on it, and here's this car setting right in front of me—stopped. I turned left and let up on the gas, but it didn't do a lot of good. It tore both cars up, but I didn't get hurt."[22]

Marty's third consecutive crash occurred at Talladega on May 4, 1975. "I was running real good," he said. "I'd have probably finished fourth, because I started seventeenth and at the time I was running eighth." His speed was close to 190 miles an hour, and he even led the race for two laps. Then spectators saw three cars smash together, followed by a bright orange ball of flame. On the sixty-second lap, Ramo Stott's car blew an engine and burst into flames. Marty tapped the car as he slid to avoid it, and James Hylton slammed into Marty's driver-side door. Two drivers jumped out. "Robbins is still in the car!" yelled the announcer. Then Marty slowly crawled out and started walking down the track.[23]

"All that flame and smoke and I hit the brakes and turned left and the tires went pop-pop-pop-pop," Marty recalled. "All four of them blew, just like that." His car turned sideways and slowed to about 150 miles an hour. Hylton hit him so hard Marty's head slammed against the car frame. He didn't remember getting out of the car. "I knew who I was and what business I was in," he said. "All I could think of was, you've really done it this time. I've messed up my mind and I wouldn't remember the words to my songs. That's what haunted me. I told the doctor I didn't want to see anybody, and he told me to sit there and rest. And I sat there and said all the words of 'El Paso' to myself, and that's when I knew I was going to be all right."[24]

Hylton says, "If he got involved in a wreck, he'd apologize to whoever was in the wreck."[25]

Marty's band members were listening over the radio. They had worked a prerace event with Marty and left early in the race because they wanted to get home. The bus was forty miles out of Talladega when the accident occurred.[26] Concern for their jobs must have mixed with concern for their boss.

The car seemed too badly smashed to repair. "I can't buy one and it's too late to build one," Marty told an interviewer a week later. "I wanted to run the Fourth of July down in Daytona, but I won't get to run because I won't have a car. I told people I was going to quit, but I'm not really going to quit. I don't think people would want me to quit, maybe because it's something I enjoy doing. . . . I'm racing against the best stock car drivers in the world. And when I can finish in the top ten, y'know, that's not bad, because I only do it four or five times a year, and they do it every weekend. They run five hundred miles a week plus all the practicing, see. They practice more than I run."[27]

Marty sponsored himself under the name of Robbins Racing. "I know what my chances are of winning," he said, "because I know how underpowered my car is, y'know. I can't afford to spend the money on an engine that Richard Petty, Buddy Baker, or David Pearson can spend. So I go with almost an obsolete engine when I race."[28] He estimated his three wrecks cost him $100,000.

Without a car to distract him, he realized he'd been letting his hobby interfere with his singing career. When doing an oral history interview for the Country Music Foundation in November 1975, he said he enjoyed the music business, "not because of the money, but because I enjoy singing and being on the stage." Then he confessed, "I've let racing interfere much more than I should have for the past ten years. I'm almost out of contact with what's happening. I should be listening to the radio, seeing what's being played, watching television, instead of waiting for the next race. I thought of that more than I thought of the business, much more."

"There's no telling how much time I spend thinking of racing," he admitted. "All year, every night, I'm thinking about it, whether I'm going to do it or not." He must have been referring to himself in the lyrics of "Twentieth Century Drifter" when he wrote, "My woman sleeps in my arms and I lie here thinkin.' Half awake half asleep I run and re-run the race." Marty settled his racing versus music conflict by vowing, "I'm not going to let it interfere with the business I'm in. I'm going to make a big change, get back in the business, and have me some hits. I've went too long without one."[29]

$$[18]$$

Return to the Road

The Ryman Auditorium had been home to the Grand Ole Opry since 1943, ten years before Marty arrived. Built in 1892 by Nashville riverboat Captain Thomas Ryman and called the Union Gospel Tabernacle, it contained enough wooden pews to seat 3,755 people. From its beginning, the tabernacle hosted secular events, and it became known as the Ryman Auditorium after Captain Ryman died in 1904. The National Life and Accident Insurance Company, owner of WSM Radio and the Opry, purchased the Ryman for $207,500 in 1963 and changed its name to Grand Ole Opry House.[1]

In 1974 the Opry moved from the Ryman to the new Opry House in the center of Opryland USA, a multimillion-dollar entertainment complex being built nine miles east of downtown. Feelings were mixed about leaving the "Mother Church of Country Music." The old building lacked air conditioning and dressing rooms and was located in a seedy part of town. But it was where Hank Williams had drawn his encores and most Opry members had begun their careers. Minnie Pearl cried during her final show. She talked about memories but also looked forward to using the dressing rooms in the new Opry House—where there were mirrors with lights around them and "they've even got places to sit down!"

Marty Robbins closed the Saturday night performance at the Opry's old home on March 9, 1974. Although one last Friday Night Opry would be held the following week, Saturday was considered the Opry's finale there. As usual, the audience couldn't get enough of Marty. He continued with his jokes and songs and antics for more than an hour past midnight until the curtain closed on him as he shouted, "No! They want more! They want more!"

Moving the Opry from an area of panhandlers and massage parlors to a family vacation park helped modernize country music's image. *Country Music* magazine described the new building as "big and high-class, the most sophisticated entertainment/broadcast/television studio in the world—but the architects have done their best to make it comfortable for the mind as well as the body. The shape of the place is very like that of the Ryman: the seats are bench-style, like the Ryman; the dominant colors are dark and earthy." Spacious dressing rooms and a private parking lot, not to mention controlled temperatures, appealed more to performers than Ryman nostalgia.

Just as Marty closed the last Saturday show at the Ryman, he closed the invitation-only opening Saturday in the new Opry House on March 16, with special guest President Richard Nixon. In an appearance described in *Country Music* as his "first attempt to get down home with the folks since Watergate hit the headlines," Nixon appeared a confident entertainer, telling jokes and performing yo-yo tricks with Roy Acuff.[2]

Marty began touring with his band again in early 1974. The previous October, he'd asked Haskel McCormick to play banjo on the "Twentieth Century Drifter" session. McCormick had been in the bluegrass group that years earlier sang "big eyes" when Marty thought they said "big iron." After completing the one-song session, Marty invited McCormick to join his band. They made a verbal agreement for the year of 1974. McCormick also worked with Marty over the next few weeks to finish recording the *Good 'n Country* album, which had a distinct bluegrass flavor. Bill Johnson played on the "Twentieth Century Drifter" session, using fuzztone to make his steel guitar sound like a car engine.[3]

Marty recorded over seventy songs for MCA Records in a three-year period, with three albums released: *This Much a Man* in 1972, *Marty Robbins* in 1973, and *Good 'n Country* in 1974. "My favorite albums are the *Gunfighter* albums," Marty once commented. "That *Good 'n Country* is my favorite besides them. I've never gotten tired of playing and listening to it. Not for hearing myself sing. Just because I think the music was good on it, and I think the songs were in good taste, and I think they were good for country fans." The album's failure to sell frustrated him. "I did the best I could," he said. "But something happened. Either the records weren't available or people didn't like it."[4]

Returning members of the Marty Robbins Band, in addition to Don Winters and Bobby Sykes, were Jack Pruett on lead guitar, Eddy Fox on drums, and Bill Johnson on steel. New members, along with McCormick, were Larry Hunt on electric bass and Ken "Cadillac Johnson" McDuffy on fiddle. Marty hadn't used a fiddle since the 1950s and had never included a banjo. He added those because "he wanted to change the sound of his music," McCormick recalls. "He did fifty-one shows that year. He flew us almost wherever we went. It was like a paid vacation to me."[5]

When they flew to Redding, California, in April 1974, the airline lost their luggage. Marty apologized for appearing onstage in basic denim attire. A fan later wrote, "Marty was wearing a dark blue Levi jacket with rhinestone emblems, blue Levi-type shirt, light blue Levi pants with tan belt and brass buckle and brown boots. No matter what he wears, he's so handsome, everybody loves him anyway." When Marty sat down at the piano, he said he knew a few simple country and western chords. Then he said, "Oh, I may surprise you," and he played a melody that sounded like a concert pianist.[6]

Bill Johnson left Marty's employ the summer of 1974. Although he enjoyed playing shows, traveling had worn him down, and the upcoming birth of his son made him decide to stay home. Eddy Fox knew Don Powell from working gigs around town, and he asked if Powell would be interested in working with Marty. "Well, yeah, of course," Powell replied. During his audition in Marty's office, he explained he already had a full-time job with Acuff-Rose Publishing Company. Marty assured him most dates would be on weekends.[7]

One weekend they changed planes in St. Louis on their way to Peoria, Illinois. Baggage handlers set the instrument cases on the ground outside the plane—all except McCormick's banjo, which he carried. As Marty and his band stood in the little waiting room and watched the loading process, a deluge came down. The musicians knocked on the window to get someone's attention, but no one responded. Their instruments sat in the downpour until baggage handlers eventually loaded them. Marty was furious. He threatened to sue the airline if the rain ruined his little Martin guitar. "That was the first time and the only time I ever seen him real mad," says Powell.

When they retrieved their luggage in Peoria, Marty took his guitar out of its case, turned it up, and poured water out. "It didn't hurt the guitar at all; it beat all I ever seen," marvels McCormick. "Marty got aggravated, but after it was all over, it didn't hurt the instrument, so he didn't pursue it." When Powell opened his steel case, a towel in the bottom was soaking wet. "We were all unhappy," Powell says, "because we had to dry our guitars and clean them out before we could even play. They still worked, but Marty was afraid his guitar would come apart. That water sure didn't help it any."[8]

Marty's group usually flew first class, and the booking agency scheduled auditoriums that furnished sound and amplifiers and drums. "All we did was walk on the stage and set our guitars up and play," Powell recalls. The number of scheduled show dates increased. They flew to Canada for an eight-day tour, and they played out-and-back dates in Los Angeles. Marty's Charlotte NAS-CAR crash in October occurred two days before a scheduled performance for President Ford at a function in Warrenton, Virginia. "We thought, oh well, this is going to be canceled because he can't go," remembers McCormick, "but he went anyway." Dan Rather emceed the show for numerous White House officials and members of Congress. President Ford was unable to attend because of his wife's breast cancer surgery. Marty and his band wore tuxedos. "He had his tailbone broke, ribs broke, pretty bad cut over his forehead," McCormick says. "He was all bandaged up, sore, I'm sure, but he still did the show."[9]

While with MCA Records, Marty frequently traveled to Los Angeles, because he and Bob Hinkle worked with the West Coast office rather than the Nashville office. Sometime after the Charlotte wreck, he asked Hinkle to find him a plastic surgeon. The gash over his eye had healed unevenly and he wanted a less visible scar. There were also calcium deposits above his eyebrows, which the surgeon scraped. According to Coldsnow, Marty "was always concerned about his little beady eyes and his little flat nose." His eyelids drooped and blurred his vision somewhat, and the surgeon lifted the eyelids. "He was always real self-conscious about his nose," says Ronny. "He broke his nose in the Navy when he was boxing." Hinkle remembers Marty saying that when he reared back, it looked like a double-car garage with the doors open. Coldsnow doesn't remember him doing anything with the nose, although Ronny says his dad "had it chiseled on a few times in the later years." The plastic surgeon also tightened the skin on his neck. Marty stayed in Bob Hinkle's home for several weeks while he recovered.[10]

At his 1974 office Christmas party, Marty called in his band members and talked to them individually. When it was Powell's turn, Marty acknowledged the travel schedule was increasing, and he said he would find a new steel player because he didn't want to jeopardize Powell's job with Acuff-Rose. "I'm going to change the whole band around, as a matter of fact," he said. Haskel McCormick's one-year agreement had been fulfilled, so Marty's experiment with a bluegrass band ended when McCormick and McDuffy left.[11]

Katsuhiko "Katz" Kobayashi replaced Powell. Marty had done a Canadian tour in 1973, traveling with Winters and Sykes, and R. C. Bannon's "R. C. With Ice" from Seattle backed him. Guitar player John "Jay Dee" Hoag compared Bannon to an army sergeant for the amount of practice he required of his side-men. "The band was so good," Hoag explains, "Marty would stand off on the side and smile." Steel player Kobayashi formerly had a band in Osaka, Japan; he learned to speak English after he came to the United States and started working with Bannon. At the end of 1974, Marty hired both Kobayashi and Hoag.[12]

In March 1975 Marty took his band to Wembley, England, for the International Festival of Country Music, organized by promoter Mervyn Conn. The reception surprised and pleased Marty, and he gave his standard disclaimer to applause: "Oh, please. Please don't. Don't stop." He told the crowd he "was a little in doubt" as to whether people in England had heard of him, because only "Devil Woman" and "El Paso" had been hits there. "For the past fifteen years, I've been asked to come over here," he said. "I never did want to come over here. I didn't think anybody knew me."

When introducing "My Woman, My Woman, My Wife," he said he usually played a piano while singing that song. "I don't know how it's gonna turn out with me playing the guitar," Marty joked, "because I don't play the guitar very well—although I'm not bad on it. You'll notice the way I play, it's usually in this one position. If you've ever watched Chet Atkins or people like that, they play all up and down the neck like this, y'know. You know why? Because they're still searching. I have found it. It's right here."[13] It was a masterful way to turn his inability to compete with Chet Atkins into a triumph and a laugh.

Interviewed two months later, he said, "I'd have been over there before if I'd had any idea people knew me. Because I've had some pretty good records, and I guess every man in the business has a little pride, y'know, and I wanted to be with people that had heard of me."[14] Great Britain's Country Music Association named him Entertainer of the Year in November. Sadly, he never won such an award in the United States.

Marty's last MCA sessions took place in April 1975. "There's a new style of music coming in called southern rock," he said, describing his upcoming single, "Shotgun Rider" and "These Are My Souvenirs," as southern rock on one side and a ballad on the other. Both songs would be on his new album, which was "all ready, but I don't know what the title will be."[15] The title was *Ten Sides of Marty,* and it was never released. "Shotgun Rider," like the three singles before it, charted briefly.

Marty thought MCA focused on "four top artists that didn't need their help: Conway Twitty, Loretta Lynn, Olivia Newton-John, and Elton John." He said MCA "forgot they might have had forty other artists on that label that weren't doing a thing—and I was one of them. I'm not one to be left out and keep my mouth shut. So I proceeded to tell the wrong person what I thought." Disagreement over a western album also soured his relationship with MCA. Marty started recording songs but was told not to finish the album. "Well, I knew then I wasn't going to stay with them long," he said. "I wanted to leave them, and they wanted me to leave."[16]

Marty pulled out of his contract two years early, in mid-1975, and took sixty master recordings with him. Bob Hinkle says, "I had them give Marty all of his masters as part of the deal. So MCA never could release anything after that."[17]

With no recording contract and no car to race, Marty concentrated on touring. He was in Connecticut when the Nashville Songwriters Association named him to its Hall of Fame. Ronny attended the Friday night celebration on July 11 to accept the award.

Coldsnow typed Marty's itineraries but never sent them to Marizona. "If I was running an office now," she says, "I would send the wife the itinerary, but me being so young, I didn't think about that then." She rarely saw or talked to Marizona, who "stayed home, raised her children, and was active in her church. I'm sure Marty took home the itinerary so she knew where he was," Coldsnow says.[18]

For short tours, within 150 miles or so of Nashville, Marty used a large motor home. Sykes and Hoag handled the driving. Hoag enjoyed both driving and
hearing Marty say "Hoag, grab the guitar." Then he would accompany Marty's
singing while traveling. When not singing, Marty apparently spent time thinking
up practical jokes. On one trip, when they reached Nashville, Indiana, Hoag
remembers Sykes telling everyone to stay on the bus while Marty went into
the hotel. After waiting awhile, Sykes looked at his watch and said, "Okay, we
can go in now." The band members followed him to the front desk, where the
hotel clerk completed paperwork and handed them keys. Then the clerk said,
"Oh, by the way, when Marty Robbins comes in, see that gentleman sitting over
there on the couch? He wants to see him." Sykes answered, "That is Marty." The
priceless look on the clerk's face was the payoff Marty wanted. He stood up,
slapped his leg, laughed, and told the clerk, "Hey, good job," as he handed over
tickets to his upcoming performance.[19]

Marty always found time for fans. He walked into a hotel restaurant and
gift shop in Missouri one day, and a twelve-year-old boy rushed up to him and
asked for an autograph. "He politely reached for my placemat and signed his
name on it," Scott Lindley remembers. "I thanked him and went back to my
table. When we went to the lobby to check out, Mr. Robbins was checking in.
My dad started talking to him. His bodyguards started to approach [and] he
waved them off and told them it would be all right. We stood in that lobby and
visited for about two hours." Lindley calls the experience "one of the highlights
of my life" and Marty "one of the most courteous men I have ever met."[20]

Marty's concern extended to his animals. He was dressed up and on his
way to Nashville in September when he couldn't cross a bridge because a cow
stood in the middle of it. She wouldn't move, even when he honked the horn.
He thought perhaps her calf was under the bridge, so he checked and saw a
cow in the water. It had fallen off the bridge and broken its back. Marty stepped
into the creek and held her head above water to keep her from drowning. "I
stayed down there for about an hour," he said, "before somebody came along.
She would swing her head and get it going into a circular motion to keep from
going under. I kept dodging, and one time didn't dodge, and she hit me right
in the chest. In the shoulder, see. It didn't bother me too much that day, but the
next day it was really bad." Diagnosed as a shoulder separation, "it took eight
months, almost, before I could really raise my arm," he said.[21]

Still, he continued touring. His opening act during a show in Denver was a
young Nebraska woman who lived in Nashville. As a child, Diane Jordan had

watched the Glaser Brothers on local television. "I was influenced by Marty," she says. "I heard his falsetto break, and I remember going down to the barn and experimenting with it. I found out I could sing 'My Isle of Golden Dreams.'" After listening to Jordan in Denver, Marty told her to come to his office when they returned to Nashville. She did, and he offered to produce a session to help her get a recording contract. He paid for the session where she recorded one of his songs. She worked several shows with Marty after that, although, she says, he "didn't allow anyone to use his band, so the promoter had to have a band for me." Marty explained to Jordan that his band was part of his show, and if they backed someone else, the audience would have already seen them when he came on stage. Marty negotiated a recording contract for Jordan with Columbia Records, and he later told her he charged Columbia half the actual session price "so you'd have a better chance of getting signed."[22]

Marty called his 1972 exit from Columbia Records "the biggest mistake I ever made in my life in this business." He realized he should have discussed his differences with Columbia executives, "but I had my feelings hurt." Having been "in this business as long as I have—and I've had some pretty big hit records," he said, "I had my pride." He'd also given his word. "I'd already talked to MCA," he explained to an interviewer. "It was too late then. I had to go. I regretted it the day I signed." When he broke his MCA contract in 1975, he was free to go back to Columbia. "I got a good contract when I came back, but not *as* good," he said. "Because I asked to come back, and that's different from when they ask you."[23] He returned to Columbia's label at the end of the year, with a new western song ready to record.

He also had a new home. Marty and Marizona and Janet moved from the Franklin farm in December 1975 to a spacious luxury home along Holly Tree Gap Road in Brentwood. They paid $140,000 for the five-thousand-square-foot brick house on a steep hillside in the Country Road Estates subdivision. "We'd been on the farm forever," Janet explains. "I was almost seventeen. I didn't want to be out on that farm." When she saw "this really great house," she showed it to Marizona and hoped her mother would convince her father to buy it. "He must have been okay with it at that time to move," Janet says. "I think Mom was also ready to move closer into town."[24]

[19]

Back on Columbia Records and in the Spotlight

About the time Marty returned to Columbia, the company released another compilation album. *No Signs of Loneliness Here,* which came out in November 1975, contained a selection of singles from the 1960s. The title track belonged to Lee Emerson, Marty's former road manager and sideman. His occasional reappearances over the years frustrated Marty because of Emerson's violent and unpredictable drug-related behavior. The end would come in December 1978 when Barry Sadler of "Ballad of the Green Berets" fame shot and killed Emerson, who was sitting in a car outside the apartment building of a woman they'd both dated. Sadler eventually pled guilty to voluntary manslaughter.[1]

Marty went into Columbia's recording studio on January 27, 1976, to begin his long-awaited western album. He recorded "El Paso City," which he'd been holding for two years because MCA wouldn't let him record it.[2] Circumstances of writing the song were similar to those of "El Paso," except that Marty flew over the city instead of driving through it. He'd had a song idea for several years but "never could get anything going," he said. Every time he flew over El Paso, he would wake up three or four seconds before the pilot announced the location. "And it always happens that way," Marty recalled. "Well, this time I woke up just as the pilot said, 'Off to the left is the city of El Paso.' I got the idea right there, and I started writing. By the time I got to Los Angeles, I had the song written, the tune and everything." Bob Hinkle brought Marty to his hotel, where Marty sang it and Hinkle exclaimed, "It's a hit!"

Marty planned to write about an airline pilot married to a flight attendant who flew for a different airline. "He flew over El Paso on his way to Los Angeles," Marty explained. "He was pretty certain when she reached El Paso she would be taking off her wedding rings. He was trying to compare his love for this woman to the cowboy's love for Feleena in the song 'El Paso.' I thought that was a pretty good idea, see." Instead, the song evolved into reincarnation, with the airline pilot wondering whether he had been the cowboy in "El Paso." Marty's attitude on reincarnation varied over the years. In 1977 he said, "I'm not saying I believe in reincarnation; I'm not saying I *don't*. El Paso comes to me so many times, y'know, and sometimes I might wonder, is there anything to reincarnation?" In 1981 he said, "I don't believe in reincarnation, y'know. I don't want to make people hot at me because that's the way I believe, because I don't get hot at them if they believe in reincarnation. I just can't see their reason for it, see."

In addition to "El Paso," his eight-minute "Feleena (From El Paso)" album cut, and "El Paso City," Marty wrote but never recorded a fourth song in the series. After the release of "El Paso City," he received numerous letters telling him he was "a brother, a husband, a lover, whatever, a friend, back in another world," he said. "The Mystery of El Paso City" talked about "the cowboy that rode in and out of El Paso, and why people say it was me." He joked about writing more songs, such as "Right After I Left El Paso" or "It Happened Between El Paso and Las Cruces."

Marty returned to Wembley, England, for the International Festival of Country Music in April 1976. The visit included a ten-day tour of the United Kingdom.

"I got quite a surprise last year," Marty said, "because it was my first visit to the country here, and I didn't think people knew me or many of my records, y'know, and it was a good surprise, because any time anybody asked for a song, it was mine. It wasn't Johnny Cash, or somebody else, y'know, and it made me very happy." He was named Best International Male Vocalist during the festival, with the female vocalist award going to Dolly Parton, also on the tour.[3]

Jay Dee Hoag had left in November 1975 to care for his ailing father; piano player Del Delamont was the newest member when they went to England. He played piano, trumpet, and trombone. Marty nicknamed him "Duck" but never explained the reason. "Marty was famous for firing you if you did something he didn't like during the show," Delamont recalls. "I got fired and rehired nine times in the three years I was with him."[4]

When Ralph Emery asked Marty in 1976 about his children, Marty said Ronny was singing. As for Janet, "About all she can do is spin the tires off the back of her car. But she does a good job of that." He added, "She works for me now. She is one of my little secretaries." He joked, "Y'know, it's hard to believe a man thirty-three years old—how old did I say I was?" "Thirty-six," Emery replied. "Well, it's hard to believe a man thirty-six years old can have children as old as Ronny and Janet," fifty-year-old Marty said. Although Emery could ask Marty about his family, band members dared not. "He didn't talk about his personal life; he didn't talk about Marizona," Delamont says. "I never met Marizona. Oh, no, we didn't ask about personal issues. He never discussed anything about his family or home or Ronny or his daughter."[5]

Janet dropped out of high school during her junior year, shortly after her seventeenth birthday. Marty asked Lucy Coldsnow to take her as an assistant and help her learn business skills. They worked together for a year, and Coldsnow considered Janet "a really sweet, sweet girl."[6] It must have been a major concession for Marty to finally grant Janet such exposure. "He so didn't want me in the business," she says. "He was overprotective, and thought it was not a place for me." Janet was given a small office on the top floor. She listened to the constant flood of incoming tapes to decide which songs might interest her father. Coldsnow taught her about licensing paperwork and obtaining copyrights.

"Do anything you want to do in your life, but don't go in the music business," Marty told his daughter. Those were his only words on the subject. He said the music business didn't treat women well and was not a place for women. Janet, even though she'd taken piano lessons for years, wasn't interested in music. Still, she didn't appreciate his advice. "I wasn't exactly following directives from my parents at that time," she says, "because I pretty much rebelled."[7]

"El Paso City" became the first single released under Marty's new Columbia contract, and it hit number one in June. "Nobody had a lot of faith in the song, but I did because I knew it was different," Marty told reporter Stacy Harris. "There was no competition, really, because I didn't have to compete with Charley Pride or Merle Haggard or Buck Owens because it was not a love song. It was absolutely different, so I knew it had to be a big record."

Even so, it didn't sell as well as he'd hoped. "I think if I had put a little bit of funky guitar on this 'El Paso City,' it would have got more attention from pop stations," he said. "The beat wasn't real exciting, but people listened to it."[8]

El Paso's Convention and Visitor's Bureau took advantage of the publicity by hiring Marty to narrate a short film to promote the city. The film's executive producer said "El Paso" told of a "small, dusty, gunfighting town highlighted by Rosa's Cantina. His latest hit, which hit the top of country western charts this week, is 'El Paso City,' which updates the image from town to city and provides a more modern view." Marty said the twelve-minute commercial would be shown "all over the world in five different languages."[9]

He headlined a "Bicentennial Tribute to Marty Robbins" package show at the Sun Bowl Stadium in July and was introduced as "putting El Paso on the musical map of the world." Mayor Don Henderson presented him with the Conquistador Award and gave him several gifts, including a pair of Bicentennial boots. "I was made a Conquistador, which is the highest honor the city of El Paso can give to anybody," Marty said. "That's what the mayor told me. So, it was all right with me." He and his band wore custom-made Nudie suits from California.[10]

Marty worked with producer Billy Sherrill to complete the *El Paso City* album. They had time for one more song during a May 1976 session, and Sherrill asked Marty what he wanted to do. Although the others were western songs, Marty played a bit of "Among My Souvenirs," which had been a hit for Bing Crosby in the 1940s and Connie Francis in 1959. Sherrill agreed, "Yeah, man, I like it. Let's record it." Marty said, "Okay, let's get the words." "Don't you know them?" Sherrill asked. Marty said he didn't know enough of them, and Sherrill told him, "Sing what you know." Marty sang the verses he knew, later recalling how "everything was laid back and real nice, y'know, and the musicians were digging the song." The first take turned out so well that Sherrill added it to the

El Paso City album, which was released in August. He also issued "Among My Souvenirs" as the follow-up single to "El Paso City," and it became Marty's second number one record of 1976. Marty called it "one of the most beautiful songs I've ever heard in my life."[11]

In early 1977 Marty lost his personal assistant when Lucy Coldsnow left for Los Angeles to pursue her dream of being a film editor. Her earlier work as Marty's movie production assistant had identified what she wanted for a career. Still, she loved working with Marty, and few people understood why she would give up such a position. She'd taken a leave of absence to help a friend shoot a movie in Nashville. "When I got the opportunity to go to Los Angeles to finish the film, I knew I needed to move to Los Angeles," she says. "I wanted to move forward, and I wanted to work in film." Evelyn Lamb—who worked for Marty's accountant and business partner, Charlie Mosley—substituted during Coldsnow's leave of absence and stayed permanently with Marty. Janet moved from her parents' house into Coldsnow's vacant apartment.

Coldsnow calls her ten years with Marty "a great work experience and I feel like I gained a friend. I absolutely adored him. He was so sweet and so funny." She remembers driving Marty around Nashville in her little Volkswagen. "He would have me take him to run errands," she says. "Sometimes we'd just drive around and look at things, and I wonder what was going through his mind. Was he laughing at me?" She doesn't understand why someone who liked to drive fast and who owned expensive cars would want to ride with her. But it was exactly the sort of personal attention the insecure Martin David Robinson craved. When she left Nashville, he told her, "Lucy, if you decide you want to come back, you will always have a place in my office. I will always make room for you." Over the next few years, they occasionally called each other, until Coldsnow became immersed in her new career.[12]

Marty recorded two albums in 1977, *Adios Amigo* and *Don't Let Me Touch You*. As follow-ups to his two chart toppers, all four singles from those albums made *Billboard*'s top ten. "Return To Me," which had been a hit for Dean Martin twenty years earlier, reached number six in early 1978 and became the last top ten hit until 1982.[13]

During the summer of 1977, ShowBiz Inc. filmed twenty-four episodes of a syndicated television show called *The Marty Robbins Spotlight*, with the first show airing on September 4. "It's kind of a talk-and-sing show," Marty explained, "and it spotlights a different guest each week, with little cameos of different artists appearing on the show to say something about the guest. There's one spot where we do a medley. The guest will pick three or four songs, and I'll do bits and pieces of three or four songs."[14]

Musical director Timmy Tappan came with experience from similar shows. He describes his role as "helping choose the music and arranging the music and conducting the orchestra and working with Marty to make sure he was comfortable with the songs and keys and the guest songs." Del Delamont played keyboard and assisted Tappan with the arrangements. Marty played a blue-and-white-checkered grand piano specially designed by the show's scenic designer, Don Shirley, after arriving unfinished from the Kimball factory. Shirley soaked three-inch squares of white, dark blue, and light blue denim in a glue-water solution and covered the piano for a gingham effect. Strips of white tape simulated stitching, and the entire surface was sealed with eight coats of acrylic finish. The top, cut from a sheet of half-inch Plexiglas, was also patterned in the three-inch gingham design. After completion of the two-hundred-hour project, the piano served as a distinctive centerpiece when Marty opened each show.[15]

The first episode "took from noon until 4:00 the next morning to do one half-hour show," Marty remembered. "Then it got better. We could do one in six hours." After filming the first season at the Opryland Theater, Marty told Emery, "I enjoy doing that show. I don't particularly care about television, and if it's live, I don't like it at all. I'm a nervous person, and—I know it doesn't seem possible, Ralph—but I can make mistakes."[16] Filming in advance wasn't any better, although perhaps Marty only remembered the singing segments. He obviously didn't see himself as others saw him on the set.

"TV is a hard business, particularly for musicians and entertainers, because so much time in the studio is sitting around waiting," Tappan says. "Marty was not the most fun guy to be around at those times, because he got very frustrated, and he didn't have the patience to wait." He sometimes sat in a corner with a guitar, playing and singing to himself. Numerous technical problems held up production, and the orchestra required much coordination. Tappan remembers Marty doing "not much to help it move smoothly and at times exacerbated the problems. You could tell he was happiest when he was sitting at the piano or with the guitar and singing a song by himself."[17]

"I think filming the show was very stressful for him," Delamont says, "because he wasn't in control. He was used to the freedom of running his own show. A television production is scripted, and you've got to do what they say when they say."[18]

"It takes twelve hours for them to do two one-half hour shows, y'see," Marty told an interviewer. "And that's a bit too long for me in the studio, because, y'know, I just can't stay put that long."[19]

Marty enjoyed interaction with his guests, but scheduled commercial breaks made timing difficult. Retakes frustrated him. "It's hard to ad-lib," he told an interviewer. "When you're afraid you're going into overtime, you can't get into anything real interesting." He called the process "really hard for me" and said, "I'm not putting anybody down, but I know it wasn't my fault. They would do retake, retake, retake. If you said anything funny and got any kind of response from the audience, they'd make you do it over again, and I'm not going to repeat a joke. Not to the same crowd. Because you're never gonna get no laugh."[20]

"Marty demanded perfection from himself, but he couldn't do that with other people," Tappan says. "After we'd done a few shows, I remember thinking, there's something going on in Marty's personal life he's upset or unhappy about. You know how people sometimes don't want to share that part of their life, but you can still tell something's bothering them—that's the feeling I got from him."[21]

That something was Marty's new home sliding down a hillside. Almost as soon as they moved to the Country Road Estates house, cracks had begun appearing in the foundation and the concrete patio. The porch pulled away, and doors and windows refused to close properly. Janet felt guilty for having convinced her parents to buy the house. "I remember going up the stairs and how lopsided they felt," she says. "Within a month of moving, the window panes had begun to crack." They disconnected the gas and ran hoses across the yard because the water lines pulled apart.[22] Janet had already moved into Coldsnow's apartment when Marty and Marizona purchased a house at 11 Long Valley Road in Brentwood and moved in July 1977.

Marty sued Brooks Custom Homes for $200,000 in damages, asking to have the contract rescinded. The case went to trial in February 1978, and both Marty and Marizona testified. Marty hired a soil engineer who determined the house had been built "on a natural landslide of colluvial soil, or soil which loses its strength to hold foundations when wet." The builder, who had never heard of colluvial soil, conceded, "I would not want to live there."[23]

The Chancery Court rescinded the contract to buy the house, after ruling the developers should have obtained expert advice before building. Marty recovered the amount paid for property taxes but was required to pay rent for the nineteen months his family lived in the house. He won the lawsuit but no award for damages. Real estate agents determined fair rent for the palatial home to be in the $700 to $1,400 range. The judge assigned the higher amount for the first twelve months, because the Robbins family did not complain during that period, and the lower amount for the final seven months. The rental bill came to $21,700.[24]

Marty later said he had paid cash for the house, and he lost $160,000 by the time he won the third appeal. "I wouldn't sue him for his home," he said, pointing out he could have been tougher on the builder. "I'm not that kind of a person. I hope he realizes how lucky he is."[25]

The original court case was decided by the time filming began for the second and final season of *The Marty Robbins Spotlight*. Marty's frustration showed when Emery, who announced and helped produce the show, told Marty his favorite episode on the first season was "the Rex Allen and Rex Allen Jr. western show, where you did all the old western songs." Marty agreed, "I would like to have done more of those. I don't know why we didn't, but it wasn't my fault." The second set of twenty-four shows concluded with "Marty and His Western Show."

"It was done right," Marty said. "It was a good show, but it was not country enough." He said he "had to dress up and wear a tie and everything. I bought forty-five brand-new tailored suits and that cost plenty of money."

Emery asked if it bothered Marty to work with tall people. "No, it doesn't," Marty said. "I'm only five-nine, y'know, and when they put somebody on that's over six feet, I look a lot smaller." Emery reminded him most *Spotlight* guests were filmed sitting down. "Yeah, thank goodness for chairs," Marty said. "I think there's a better way of doing it. They could put me on with somebody my size—let every guest be a girl. Most of the girls are shorter than I am, see."[26]

[20]

The Marty Robbins Band on Tour

In late 1977, Marty took his band to Australia, playing Sydney's Opera House and shows in Perth, Adelaide, Brisbane, Canberra, and Hobart, Tasmania. Del Delamont remembers "lots of famous venues. We played the Palladium in London, we played the famous old theater in Edinburgh, Scotland, we played the Coliseum in Guttenberg, Sweden. Those were landmark years for me. I was so honored to be a part of this great show."[1]

Marty made his third Wembley appearance in March 1978, where he introduced his forty-minute segment by joking, "Next time we come here, it's going to be probably in December, because I heard Mervyn Conn tell some of the people awhile ago it will be a cold day when I work for him again. So I figure it will be December."

His introduction of the band illustrated how he typically used ethnic jabs and poor jokes to entertain his audience:

It's the same bunch, with the exception of one, that I had two years ago. Y'see, we get along real good so we stay together. As far as I'm concerned, they're the best group in the business. On the piano is the Canadian. Which doesn't make him bad—he's one of the colonies. He's not from Quebec, no. Because we don't want any problems, with anybody throwing things at him. No, he is a Canadian, and he's been with us for a couple of years now. A nice hand for him please, Del Delamont. And then Old Gray, here. Now, his wife, I'm sure you're familiar with, Jeanne Pruett.

She got a nice hand and she's not even here. A nice hand for her husband, Mr. Jeanne Pruett. Jack Pruett. And the newest member is back on the drums. He's been with us only since the first of the year, and he is an American, but he speaks very little English. He's a Mexican-American. Well, he's—have you ever heard of a wetback? You haven't. No, that's the ones that, y'know, they come across the border at night, over the Rio Grande. No, he's not one. He's from the state of California, and I think he's a fine drummer. A nice hand for Bill Martinez.

And on the bass, a nice hand for Larry Hunt. And the one on the steel guitar, he's from Tokyo, Japan. He speaks enough English to get by. A nice hand for Katz Kobayashi. And the ones that help me on the cowboy songs, y'know, they've been with me a long time. When you do trio work, y'know, you need three. So that's why I bring them, cuz them and I make three. I hate to say it this way but the shorter of the two, a nice hand please for Don Winters. I hate to say it this way, the heavier of the two, is a very fine singer and a nice guy. A nice hand, please, for Bob Sykes.

Before the introduction, he called attention to the band's tuxedos. "I hope you won't hold that against them," he said, "for not being dressed like regular country acts, that just wear jeans, and sometimes they're dirty. In fact, most of the time they're dirty."[2]

Although said as a joke, he was serious about proper dress. His band's tuxedos were custom made by California designer Nudie, who also designed Marty's costumes. Marty once commented on the industry's desire to upgrade country music's image. "How can you put it on a higher level," he asked, "if you get a shot at national television, and you come down there in a pair of jeans?" He said, "I don't particularly care about dressing up, but I believe there is a time for it, and I believe the awards show is a time when everyone should be dressed."

After watching one awards show, he complained, "I was so disappointed in seeing some of them in jeans, because I don't think it's the right place for it."[3]

At Wembley, he continued with the jokes: "I have a bad cough. Awhile ago I took something to stop my coughing; I took a laxative. Oh, yes, I want to cough. I really want to, but I'm not going to. I'm afraid to. All I can do is go rrr, rrr, and I'm taking a chance then." He then said he'd have to leave immediately after the show for another performance, and he asked his British audience, "You're going to be over there, aren't you? Okay, when I come on the stage, act like you've never seen me before. And just scatter out among the crowd, y'know, everywhere. And go like this to each other and say, isn't he great? Isn't he great? Every time I do a song, you keep that up, see. Hey, I can come back next year, maybe."[4]

He later told an interviewer, "I got through with my part and went back to my dressing room, and they were stomping and yelling. I felt like Presley or the Beatles. There was a roar. They were standing and yelling. That was exciting!"[5]

Marty's new band member on that tour, Bill Martinez, had taken over the drummer slot so his friend Eddy Fox could manage Marty's recording studio. When Fox offered the job, Martinez thought he was lying. He understood it was a serious offer only when his telephone rang and he heard Marty say, "Hey! Don't you believe me?" Martinez marvels at the idea of working for "a gentleman I'd seen on TV and watched in concerts. I remember 'Singing the Blues' and my dad's playing the album, and I'm a kid, ten years old. And to think I'd play with him years down the line."

Martinez had been in Barbara Mandrell's band for three years, with Mandrell occasionally opening shows for Marty. She was not happy to lose her drummer, but Martinez says, "Marty loved the Hispanic people, and of course I'm Hispanic, and I could not resist going with Marty." He arrived with a small drum set that fit into two carrying cases, and Marty repeatedly teased him, "Is that your son's drum set? Are you ever going to buy a grownup one?" After Martinez repeatedly explained he couldn't afford new drums, Marty gave him a blank check and told him to go to a nearby shop and "buy yourself a decent drum set." Martinez says, "I bought this bright blue drum set, and I still have it." His responsibilities grew to include running concessions, which paid a commission, and handling relations with disc jockeys at concerts.[6]

Marty had recently purchased a Silver Eagle touring bus. When he picked up Okie Jones at his house to go inspect the bus, Jones said it "wasn't worth a dime." Marty won him over by saying, "*Anything* can be fixed. And the thing about it, *you* get to fix it." Marty convinced Jones to work for him again, after an eight-year absence.[7]

Martinez disliked driving Barbara Mandrell's bus, and he didn't want to drive Marty's. "You would set up your own equipment," he explains, "then you'd carry it out, and it was my turn to drive at two in the morning. I didn't like it. Marty knew I was a good bus driver. So he told Okie to let Bill drive. I got it up to eighty-five miles an hour and kept swaying it back and forth; I did the worst job I could do." Marty told Okie to "get that damn Mexican out from behind that wheel." Martinez never had to drive again. He loved playing poker and was now able to join the group at the poker table. Marty then hired Randall Edwards, son-in-law of Don Winters, as backup driver.[8]

A sign on the front of the $150,000 Silver Eagle read "Nobody You've Heard Of." The bus contained nine bunks and, unlike most entertainer tour buses, no star's dressing room.[9] The sleeping compartment held Marty's bedroom, two sets of bunks, two closets, and a bathroom. A door separated it from the lounge, which occupied the space behind the driver's seat and shotgun seat. Here travelers ate, watched television, and played poker.

Marty would often come by Martinez's bunk and ask if he was awake. "I was exhausted because I was doing concessions for him, and I was playing a physical instrument," Martinez says. "I'd say, 'yeah, I'm awake,' even though I wasn't. He'd go up front and get his little Martin guitar and start singing. It was Okie Jones driving the bus, and Marty sitting in the shotgun seat and me sitting at the little table, talking and laughing and telling stories. I was honored to be with him."[10]

"There was no one Marty Robbins," Okie Jones says. Marty treated everyone as if they had a special and personal relationship. "You would think you knew him forever, because that's the way he was," Jones explains, "but when it boils down, you never knew Marty." He adds, "He could act the silliest of anybody I ever saw in my life. And just shock me, because I'd been with him for years and never seen that side. If you ever had a relationship with him, any shape, form, or fashion, it was special."[11]

Winters, Kobayashi, Sykes, Pruett, and Martinez were five regulars at the poker table. "We played poker every single night," Martinez says. "Then we'd go in the hotel, go to bed, get up, do sound check about one in the afternoon, come back, sit around the pool, and then do the concert." Whenever Marty joined the game, he placed Martinez to his right. He enjoyed harassing Pruett, the best poker player, and would tell Martinez, "I pay you more than anybody, so when I hit you with my leg, I don't care if you got no pair, you'd better bet." Martinez describes such a game:

> He must have a good hand, and here's that skinny knee kicking me in the side. I have a pair of threes, and I don't want to put twenty dollars down. But I have to; I told him I would. So I put twenty dollars and Jack Pruett goes, "Huh, someone's bluffing here." So Jack says, "Here's twenty and I'll raise you twenty." Katz says, "I'm out." Don Winters is out; Bobby Sykes is out. Marty's kicking me in the leg, so I have to put another twenty to call it. And Marty wins the hand. As he slides money from the table with both arms, he says, "Love it when they cry. Looove it when they cryyyyyy." Before he finishes collecting the money, he says, "Bill, how do you say that in Spanish?" I translate and Marty repeats, "Me gusta cuando llorran." So Jack's looking at him with that evil eye, and I'm out sixty or eighty bucks I didn't want to throw away.[12]

"Marty was a complex soul," says Delamont. "He was a consummate entertainer and a very insecure man. He came across as being confident, but there were many ways he was insecure. He constantly needed accolades from his audiences and his employees. Favorable attention had to come from everyone around him." Delamont adds, "None of us ever liked to sleep alone and rarely did. . . . Wherever there are entertainers, there are groupies."[13]

Don Winters recalls a time the band was "partying and raising hell on the bus and we woke him up. Hell, he wouldn't let any of us sleep for days. Soon as you got in your bunk and dozed off, he'd come by and poke you and tickle you. By the fourth day, he had us dragging."[14]

After Delamont left in late 1978 to get married, Larry Hunt and Bill Martinez reported to Marty they'd seen someone at a Nashville nightclub playing piano and trumpet. Marty called Wayne Jackson, who woke up quickly the morning he heard Marty's voice on the telephone. "I couldn't believe Marty Robbins was calling me," Jackson remembers, "because I'd always loved him and was a fan of his. It was like a dream." When Jackson went to Marty's office, he explained, "I'm not a piano player. I'm a trumpet player—and I play a little piano." Marty gave him two tuxedos and a pair of black patent leather cowboy boots and told him he'd do fine. "Then suddenly I was onstage at the Grand Ole Opry, in a tuxedo, playing piano with Marty Robbins," Jackson recalls. "I watched Larry Hunt's hands, and I would try to match him on the chords. After awhile I learned to play the chords."

Jackson had previously played trumpet for Otis Redding, Stephen Stills, the Doobie Brothers, Rod Stewart, and others before moving to Nashville. Now he adjusted from that lifestyle to a country band. "Instead of flying in a private jet, I was riding in an old bus," he says. "It wasn't a good paying job, but I enjoyed myself. Every show I did with Marty Robbins was like I had the best seat in the house, every night, because he was so wonderful."

Unable to sleep during all-night bus rides, Jackson frequently sat in the front and kept Okie Jones company. "One night Marty came up with his little guitar and sat on the step right beside me and sang," Jackson recalls. "He sang a lot of those western songs. That was his way of exercising his voice and lungs. To think I'm sitting there and Marty Robbins is crooning to me was quite a thrill for me."[15]

Another singer who preserved the western song tradition was Rex Allen Jr. He worked with Marty throughout the 1970s on various package shows. Because both Arizona natives dedicated a section to western music, Allen would go to Marty's bus to decide who would sing which songs. "I always felt Marty Robbins had the most dedicated fans I have ever seen in this industry, second only, perhaps, to the Statler Brothers," Allen says. "Part of the reason I won Most Promising Male Vocalist of the Year award, I feel certain, was because of Marty Robbins fans. They always have been educated to what western music is. So Marty's fans accepted me." On large three- to four-hour package shows, Marty always closed the first half, Allen remembers. Even when he rated headliner status, Marty went on before intermission because he wanted the audience at its peak.

He used his star status—and his temper—to ensure promoters fulfilled their agreements. "I've seen him get mad at promoters," Allen recalls. "I couldn't say anything, but Marty would say, 'Now this is not right. Fix it.' That's something to admire in a performer; he wanted it right." Promoter Smoky Smith considered Marty both "easy to work with" and "particular to the nth degree." He says, "Anything he wanted to have happen, or wanted the show to contain, it was a simple thing to put into work. He had a playful trait, but it didn't interfere with the business of putting the show on. In fact, sometimes it was part of the show."[16]

Marty once explained how problems could result in a poor show. "If the lights aren't right," he said, "and I think they should be right every time, and the sound system should be right every time. As soon as something little happens, the audience can sense you're mad. They think you're being stuck up, and you can't get back on their side." If the first three or four minutes went well, he could relax, but he couldn't recover from a bad start. "I'll get up there and on the first song, the first note, a string will break on my guitar. That's all it takes," he said. His flashy outfits were his way to get the crowd's attention as soon as he walked onstage. "That's why I don't wear jeans," he said. "I design my own clothes and I have Nudie make all my stage clothes. I've worn suits and coats, but I get a lot of response right from the start when I wear a flashy outfit." He had a closet filled with $2,000 suits and fancy boots.

One thing that irritated Marty was to hear anyone announce, "Let's have a nice hand for Marty!" He insisted, "I won't have anybody cranking up my laughter. I want them to clap for me when they want to. That's the only way I can tell when to get off the stage. If they've had enough of me, I'll get off."[17]

"People talk about his singing and his songwriting ability," Allen says, "but Marty Robbins was one of the funniest people on stage I've ever been around. He could make you laugh and then, three minutes later, you're crying. What a wonderful thing to watch a man like that work an audience. I'm glad I lived in a time where I got to see and be educated by someone like Marty Robbins."[18]

"Marty in many ways reminded me of Elvis Presley, because he was always a gentleman," Smith says. "The 'yes sir' and 'yes ma'am' struck a note with me. He was more polite than most of them—actually, all of them. The two of them—I'm putting him with Elvis, because Elvis was a very polite individual."[19]

Marty's western trio changed when Bobby Sykes left at the end of 1978. After more than twenty years of touring he wanted to stay home and concentrate on the booking business. But first he had to find his replacement. One day he answered the telephone at Marty Robbins Enterprises and heard someone say, "We are the Lazy B Wranglers out here in Colorado. We'd like to go on the road in the wintertime and open for Marty." Jeff Chandler quickly learned it took more than singing cowboy songs and calling Information for a telephone number to open Marty's shows. Sykes told him promoters scheduled Marty and then found opening acts. However, Chandler had preceded his call by sending his group's record, and Sykes added, "But—whoever is singing baritone on that record, I would like to talk to him. I'm getting ready to retire from the road. The singer on that record might be a good replacement for me." The baritone was Chandler, and the two men agreed to a Nashville audition at the end of dinner theater season. Chandler and his bride drove there in October 1978.

Chandler met Sykes and Marty, who handed him a guitar and said, "Okay, let's see what you got." Chandler started singing "Tumbling Tumbleweeds," and Marty told him, "That's not bad. Let's try all three of us." They sang two lines before Marty stopped the song and said, "You'll do." After he left the room, Sykes responded to Chandler's request for clarification with, "If he said you'll do, you'll do." Chandler worked construction until the January tour. "I worked for three and a half years on 'you'll do,'" Chandler says in awe. "I was a kid from Little Rock, Arkansas, twenty-three years old, here I was getting on a Silver Eagle bus and driving down the road. For me it was a dream come true."

Back to the routine as before his 1969 heart attack, Marty enjoyed once again being on a bus. "Rarely did he fly," Chandler says. "One time we left New Jersey and had to drive all the way to Reno, Nevada, and he flew. But that was a rare occasion." Chandler believes his boss enjoyed having "a poker table where he could take our money and interact with us."[20]

"I get so excited; I can't get over a good show," Marty said. "That's why I would rather leave one place and drive all night to the next show, because I can't sleep after a good show." Comparing the high of doing a show to the high of racing, he said, "As a race goes on, you settle down, and sometimes the excitement wears off. But on stage it's there for the whole hour and fifteen minutes. I can't go to sleep until three or four in the morning because of that."[21]

Meanwhile, Wayne Jackson continued to play piano as well as trumpet until Marty told him in early 1979, "Son, you really can't play the son of a bitch, can you? I'll get another guy and you just play the trumpet."[22]

Conrad Noddin had been trying to get into Marty's band. He played piano and trumpet for Freddie Hart, whose tours frequently coincided with Marty's. One afternoon Noddin was playing piano backstage and Marty commented on his classical style, saying that was what Janet liked to play. Noddin suggested, "You need another trumpet player in your band. Then you would have that mariachi sound you're known for." He volunteered for the position, but Marty said Hart was his good friend, "and I wouldn't take you away from him." A week later, the Hart group checked into a hotel, and Noddin saw Marty in the lobby. He mentioned their previous conversation and asked, "If I weren't playing anymore for Freddie, would you consider hiring me?" In typical fashion of keeping everyone off guard, Marty answered, "Well, maybe."

Once back in Nashville, Noddin took a chance, quit his job, and called Marty's office. Marty said, "I told you I wasn't going to take you away from

Freddie. He's a friend of mine." When Noddin said he no longer worked for Hart, Marty paused and asked if he had a black suit. He told Noddin to be at the Grand Ole Opry the following evening.

Noddin arrived backstage Saturday night in his black suit, expecting an introductory visit, and Marty said, "Okay, let's go." Noddin asked what he meant. "C'mon. You're going to play piano," Marty said. Noddin recalls the event:

> I'd never played with the band before. I didn't even know all their names. So I march out on stage, and I'm sitting behind the piano, and he starts going through his numbers. Some of them I knew, but then he comes to this one song, and I had no idea what the song was; I'd never heard it in my life. He was playing it, and all of a sudden he turns to me and points, like "Okay," and here the camera comes. It's like oh, my goodness, what's gonna happen here? So I played something, and it seemed to go fine. He didn't look funny or anything. It was being televised nationwide. Everything went okay.

After the Opry segment, Marty gave Noddin the tailor's address and told him to get fitted for his tuxedos. Working in Marty's band, Noddin discovered he could play piano and trumpet at the same time. "I would play the left hand of the piano," he explains, "the bass part and some chords, while I had the trumpet against my lips. I didn't find it terribly hard to do. Some people's brains can do it and some can't; mine just happened to." Marty acknowledged this talent and classical training by gentrifying his name and introducing him as Conrad Nottingham.[23]

During a dinner theater performance, Marty's joking introduction of Noddin went too far and he knew he had hurt his pianist's feelings, but neither man said anything. Back in Nashville the next day, Marty approached Noddin and announced, "Y'know, actually, I'm glad I said that to you." Not knowing what to expect, Noddin asked why. "Well, just so I could apologize," Marty answered, taking off his black leather jacket and giving it to the stunned musician. "I have it to this day," Noddin says. "It was more than an apology. He always wanted to have the upper hand on everything. It was rare that he would come down to our level and just be Martin David Robinson. But he did, right there, and I got to see someone other than Marty Robbins the entertainer."[24]

"Marty was a very imposing figure," Chandler explains. "He wasn't big physically, and he wasn't brawny. But the way he carried himself was intimidating to me. At the time, I thought he was trying to rule us with an iron fist so we'd behave ourselves. I was nervous around him. Now that I look back, I think he was insecure and that was his front. He kept you off guard and never knowing exactly what was going on around him; he kept you at arm's length. He was always joking, but there was always that wall. You knew who the boss was; there was never any question about it. Not so much what he said as the way he behaved."

Chandler only experienced Marty's direct disapproval once. It occurred at the end of "El Paso" during a concert. With three men singing on one microphone, space was too tight for Marty's guitar, and it was Chandler's job to hit the chord after "one little kiss and Feleena," so they could get "goodbye" on perfect pitch. He was daydreaming, unprepared to make a chord. Marty reached over and hit Chandler's guitar with his pick, and it went *brrrannnng.* They finished the show, and Marty made no comment. Chandler returned to the bus with great trepidation. Marty, already there, looked at him and sarcastically asked, "Do you play chords?" "Yes, sir, I do," Chandler replied. Marty said, "Don't do that again!" Chandler sums up the story by saying, "I should have been paying attention, and I wasn't. That was the only time he ever acted like he didn't like what I was doing. Most of the time he ruled by acting intimidating. It worked like a charm."[25]

At the 1979 Wembley festival Marty concluded introductions with, "Look at him—he's not one of us. He was made in Japan. One time for Katz Kobayashi. All right now, this one is part of the trio. We do a lot of cowboy songs. As a trio we're known as Art, Bart and Far—go. A nice hand for Honest Abe, Jeff Chandler. A nice hand, please, for Don Winters."[26]

George Jones recalls that tour: "Not too many people could get real close to Marty. I got to know Marty the best when we traveled to England to the Wembley Festival. I never heard him turn loose so much before, and relax and talk."[27]

Marty's clowning around on stage reached a point where it began to get newspaper attention. As early as 1975 a reviewer had written, "Marty didn't fool around the *whole* time he was on stage, but he fooled around about half the time. It's too bad, because whenever he settled down to business, he was tremendous." Reviewers in 1979 complained about overdoing "showbiz sillies." One reported, "During 'Don't Worry,' a supposedly serious song, Robbins got to laughing and had to stop the song. But he did add, 'I'm sorry,' because he seemed to know he had slipped below his standards." Another complained that music was "almost secondary" to jokes during a dinner theater show in Kansas City. "Several times during the performance," the reviewer wrote, "Robbins seemed on the verge of tying together several songs and getting into some solid vocalizing. But each time, he stopped short and threw out another joke or traded a quip with fans seated near the stage."[28]

"Some people think I take dope or get drunk on stage," Marty told an interviewer. "But I'd *never* do that. It's just that I get so happy on stage sometimes, I get silly. I love it so much."[29] He responded to the attention of those who laughed at his antics, seeming not to realize how many people paid to hear his music rather than his jokes. It also apparently didn't occur to him that making silly faces while posing for photographs created disappointed fans when their pictures were developed.

He ran into a problem trying to entertain Merle Haggard fans during a joint tour when Haggard was hospitalized due to illness. "Some of the Haggard fans apparently decided it would be more fun to heckle than get a refund," a reporter wrote. "Paradoxically, part of the problem resulted from Robbins' excellent rapport with the crowd. He played up to the audience, acting outrageous in his two-piece, bright yellow outfit. He joked, mugged for pictures and encouraged applause." Marty teased, "I'd pay to come to see me anyway. The star of the show is here, baby. The cream always rises to the top." Although Robbins fans expected such self-promotion, the amount of heckling showed Haggard fans didn't appreciate his jokes. More seriously, Marty said, "I know you're disappointed, but don't take it out on me. *I'm* here." Finally, he decided to focus on singing.[30]

The 1978 Haggard/Robbins tour included a swing through Florida, and nineteen-year-old Janet finally saw her father in concert. He never allowed her or Marizona to see him perform. "He talked about how nervous he would get if he thought we were in the audience," Janet explains. She'd moved to Florida the previous year, and when she heard about the upcoming concert, she called his Nashville office for his contact information. She then called him at his hotel and told him to get prepared because she was coming to the show. She later reported to Marizona, "Mama, Daddy is a *great* entertainer."[31]

Bob Eubanks, host of television's *The Newlywed Game,* sponsored a twenty-five-show Haggard/Robbins tour in late 1979. Marty usually did the first half, with Haggard in the headliner spot. "Marty loved the business, loved entertaining, and loved to hear a good singer sing," Chandler states. "He was competitive at the same time, and he didn't like to think there was somebody better than him, but I do know he had a great deal of respect for Merle Haggard." Chandler recalls standing in the wings and watching Haggard and his Strangers perform. "It was a privilege to watch Merle Haggard and Bonnie Owens and the band," he says. "They were so professional." Marty seemed to agree; he sometimes sat in a chair in the wings to watch Haggard's show.[32]

"I have a number of favorite singers," Marty told Ralph Emery, "but for good country singing, Merle Haggard is my favorite. I like Eddy Arnold for his style of singing. I like Gene Autry for his style of singing. I like a lot of different people for different styles of singing, but I guess Merle Haggard, Eddy Arnold, and Gene Autry are the ones I would listen to." He recalled a night during their tour when Haggard's bus stopped, so Marty stopped to see if there were problems. "All they were doing was getting a couple of instruments off one bus to put in the other one," he said, "so I went on his bus and got one of the guitars and we had a little jam session."[33]

[21]

Into the '80s

"I've never had the feeling I had it made," Marty said in 1981. "I never felt like I could get by on what I had. I've always had this fear it could all be taken away." He added, "I've got a long way to go before I can even feel safe. Maybe that's what keeps me going. Besides, I don't like to work. What I'm doing—this is not work for me."[1]

He found a kindred soul in Eddy Arnold, also from an impoverished background, who became Marty's business mentor and partner. "I think he was fortunate that he was befriended by Eddy Arnold very early," Ronny says about his father. "Eddy instilled a lot of business sense in him. He had common sense, and Eddy was able to nurture that in the early '50s. Eddy was instrumental in making him think about what he wanted to do from a business standpoint, not just make it and spend it."

Although Marty and Marizona seldom entertained, Ronny remembers the Arnolds coming to visit at Redwood Drive in the late 1950s. "Daddy would bring all kinds of different Mexican food supplies back from out West, because you couldn't get anything in grocery stores here then," Ronny says. "He would make tacos, enchiladas, refried beans and rice. Eddy and Sally would come over; Little Roy Wiggins would come over." Marty's life had certainly changed since that boozy night a decade earlier when he first heard Arnold's singing and Wiggins's steel guitar. Sometimes teenaged Brenda Lee and her guardian, Charlie Mosley, joined the group.[2] Mosley was Arnold's accountant and later became Marty's accountant and business partner. Marty sold him the micro-midget racetrack in 1963.

Arnold, Mosley, and Martin David Robinson were three of the partners in a real estate investment corporation, The Executive House of Nashville, Inc., in the late 1960s. When asked in 1980 if he'd been in business with Brenda Lee, Marty replied, "Brenda and I—and Eddy Arnold, Charlie Mosley—put in the Iroquois subdivision down in Brentwood. I still do business with Eddy. Eight of us have six hundred acres on the interstate on I-65. I figure anytime Eddy Arnold does business, it's a pretty good venture, because he's a pretty smart man."[3]

In 1968 Marty considered tearing down the old house that served as his office at 713 Eighteenth Avenue South, and he hired an architect to prepare preliminary sketches for a three-story office building. He eventually decided instead to build a one-story addition at the rear of the two-and-a-half-story building. Lucy Coldsnow hired contractors and oversaw the building project, including designing Marty's new executive office. "I decorated it into a rustic western décor," she says. "That was something I did because Marty asked me to. That was just another one of my duties." She chose well. An interviewer described the new office by saying, "The décor of rough-hewn wood walls and a large glass-topped wooden desk befit the Robbins image—strong, sophisticated and very much his own man. The burnt orange, brown and gold color scheme seems to accent his cowboy nature." Marty's large office, to the rear of five other new offices, included a sofa and his piano. He'd previously been located on the second floor near Jim Farmer's office. Coldsnow's office was on the first floor along with the recording studio.[4]

The studio sometimes served as a tool in talent searches. Eddie Crandall brought Mayf Nutter there to record in the early 1960s, after seeing him perform at the WWVA Jamboree in Wheeling, West Virginia. The three songs Nutter recorded in Marty's studio went into Marty's publishing catalog. Later, Nutter started working with Frank Zappa, who wanted Nutter's songs in his company. Zappa asked Marty to sell the song rights and, according to Nutter, "Marty just very kindly said sure."[5]

Although Marty usually used his legal name on real estate documents, he purchased a building from the Nashville Association of Musicians in the name of Marty Robbins in 1978. The building at 1806 Division Street, several doors from Marty's office, became his new recording studio.

Another of Marty's businesses was booking agency Entertainment Exclusive Associates, managed by Louie Dunn. When its workload grew enough to require a secretary in 1974, Lucy Coldsnow interviewed a twenty-year-old woman who had recently moved to Nashville from Baltimore. Dee Henry then worked with Dunn for a year before moving to other employment. She would later marry her idol, Conway Twitty.[6]

In 1979, Marty showed his appreciation to longtime friend Jim Farmer by giving him a bass boat for his thirtieth anniversary as Marty's employee. It was dropped off at Marty's office one afternoon. Marty called Farmer down from his upstairs office and threw him a set of keys. "This is for you," Marty said. "Open the curtain." Farmer looked into the parking lot, where a new bass boat sat on a trailer, complete with depth finders and fishing poles.[7]

While former steel player Farmer ran Marty's publishing companies, former drummer Eddy Fox handled the recording studio, former drummer Louie Dunn managed the booking agency, and former backup singer Bobby Sykes did his personal booking. The issue of who managed Marty remained unclear to everyone except possibly Marty himself. Eddie Crandall, usually referred to as manager, had died of lung cancer in 1972. Bob Hinkle was still somewhere in the picture, and Marty once told Okie Jones he'd made Louie Dunn his manager.

"But I never seen Louie manage him," Jones says. "Bobby would book, and Louie kind of messed around. He didn't do a lot of the work, but he got the money. Bobby was always upset because Louie wouldn't work like he did. Bobby didn't realize there wouldn't be a booking thing for him if it wasn't for Louie." Jones says Marty considered Sykes a great singer, although "he would get aggravated at his drinking. But there at the last, Bobby straightened up." Jones believes Dunn earned his paycheck by being available when Marty wanted him. "I don't know if you know how horrible it is to have to be with a big star like Marty," Jones says. "You just stand back and wait. Because all they want is to talk to him. Louie was on call twenty-four hours a day, seven days a week. Louie was witty, and he kept Marty laughing. The only person he really cared about, I think, was Louie Dunn."[8]

According to Jeff Chandler, Marty "kept Louie as part of his entourage. He liked Louie, and when you were in with Marty, you were in to stay. I always respected that. He was generous and loyal. Louie had his own office. He came to work and kept office hours, but I don't know what he did."[9]

Marty acknowledged his need for attention. "I enjoy being recognized. Absolutely. Sometimes I'll pass people in airports and they'll say, 'Hey, there's Marty Robbins,' and I'll look back and say, 'Where?' I like to play with them. My ears are tuned for Marty Robbins. For some reason, I can hear people whisper 'Marty Robbins' one hundred yards away. I won't even look, see. Finally someone will get up and say, 'Are you who we think you are?' And I'll say, 'You think I'm Marty Robbins. I've been told that three times a day. I wish I was Marty Robbins, but I'm not.' I'll get a conversation going, and I'll say something like, 'He is my favorite singer, though.' Y'know, really building Marty Robbins up! When they finally get ready to walk away, I'll say, 'Hey, I was just kidding. I really am Marty Robbins!'"

On one occasion, Marty could not get out of a situation he created. "We'd played at this small county fair and afterwards we went out on the midway and wandered around and got acquainted with the carnival people," he said. "We were having a big time. It's nice to get to know those people at the carnival because they're in show business, too." Six weeks later, at another fair, he and Winters were walking around the midway when someone yelled, "Hey, Marty Robbins," and he went into his act of looking for Marty Robbins. But it was someone from the previous fair, and he repeatedly asked, "Hey Marty, don't you remember me?" By then, the crowd had grown too large for Marty to admit his identity. "He kept asking me what I was doing there, and I kept telling him I was a farmer who lived nearby," Marty said in recounting the story. The man insisted, "You are Marty Robbins," and Marty denied it. The enraged man started cursing and Marty became concerned about a fistfight. A disc jockey broadcasting from a nearby booth yelled over the air, "Hey, there goes Marty

Robbins!" The real Marty kept looking around to see where Marty Robbins was as he made a quick exit from the area. "That was the only time I've ever let it pass," he stated.[10] As with his clowning on the stage, he seemed oblivious to the feelings of people on the receiving end of his jokes. What mattered to him was his enjoyment, and he apparently thought everyone else enjoyed it as much as he did.

Norman Wade, who looked upon Marty as a father figure, remembers being in the studio one night when the phone rang while Marty was sitting at the desk. Marty picked it up and scolded, "It's ten o'clock at night. Why are you calling here?" His tone quickly turned professional, and he said, "I mean Marty Robbins Studio." Then he put the phone down and commented, "They hung up."

Wade recorded an Eddy Fox song called "Half the Man," and Marty played dobro on the session. When the single was finished, Wade excitedly took it to Marty and asked, "Chief, what do you think?" Marty told him to be quiet so he could listen. When the song ended, Wade again asked, "What do you think?" Marty answered, "Nothing on there very good except that dobro player."[11]

Maintaining his heavy touring schedule, Marty recorded no new albums in 1978. Columbia issued two compilations that year, *The Best of Marty Robbins* and *Greatest Hits, Volume IV*. The title song of Marty's first 1979 album, *The Performer*, sounded like a farewell. "If this night should be the last night we should meet, then let's say goodbye with a song," he'd written. "'Cause there's no way to know when it's our turn to go. Everything's part of life's plan." The song concluded with, "Life's been worth living."

August 1979 brought another western album, *All-Around Cowboy*, mostly a collection of Marty's previously unreleased songs. He wrote the title track about Larry Mahan, five-time Professional Rodeo Cowboys Association World All-Around Champion during the years 1966–70. "I wrote it about Larry Mahan and released it," Marty told Ralph Emery, "and six weeks later his wife released him. The song had nothing to do with it, y'know, but it was kind of funny. His wife's a very pretty girl named Linda. She's a blonde. Blonde little filly." When Emery asked about Mahan's reaction to the song, Marty said, "Larry liked it. He got a big kick out of it."[12]

The horse pictured with Marty on the album was twenty-year-old The Brute, made famous in Marty's 1964 song, "The Cowboy in a Continental Suit." Marty said, "Every time I get on him, he tries to throw me off. I grab leather, mane, hide, anything I can get hold of. I'll ride him until he gets tired of bucking. It's kind of a job to go out and get him, because he's not gonna come to me unless I've got a sack of corn, and he runs from me. Then after I saddle and ride him, then I've gotta rub him down and give him a little more corn. Y'know, for a fifteen minute ride, you've got to spend a couple hours, and it's not hardly worth it."[13]

"All-Around Cowboy," with Marty's "The Dreamer" on the flipside, only charted in *Billboard*'s top twenty. The album contained "The Ballad of a Small Man," which Marty had recorded twice and waited for years to release as a single. "I couldn't get the people at Columbia to go along with me," he explained. "Being they're the ones out in the field looking and watching and listening, they gave it a fair trial—not on the air—they played it for some program directors and they didn't feel like it was the song. Of course, that's not a real good gauge. That's one of many, I suppose." Marty got the song idea from reading a story about a short Texas Ranger in *True West* magazine. Emery told him, "I've often wondered if you wrote this song about the small man because of your height." Marty replied, "Yeah, because I think the small man's always the underdog, y'know." He said he wrote "Big Iron" and "Mr. Shorty" from "The Ballad of a Small Man" but recorded them first. He also wrote and published, in the 1960s, a western paperback novel titled *The Small Man*.[14]

On February 3, 1980, Marty joined with entertainers such as Frank Sinatra and Dean Martin to celebrate Ronald Reagan's sixty-ninth birthday. Republican backers, realizing Governor Reagan's age would be an issue in his Presidential campaign, confronted the matter directly by hosting a gigantic birthday celebration. Although Marty's band didn't participate, he did take Conrad and Alisa Noddin along to Los Angeles. "Marty wanted me to write some arrangements for the house band," Noddin recalls. "I have a degree in music, and so I found out what instruments were going to be there, and I wrote some arrangements for him. Wives *never, ever* got to travel with him. But he made an exception in that case. I guess because he was kindhearted in many ways."[15] The Noddins enjoyed their evening backstage with the celebrities.

Marty's popularity was evident when the prestigious fan-voted *Music City News* award nominations were announced in April. Faron Young had established the magazine in 1963 to provide fans with news about the country music industry, and he started a fan-voted awards show during Ernest Tubb's Midnite Jamboree in 1967. By 1980, several years after Young sold the magazine, the awards show had grown enough to be broadcast live on syndicated television. Marty was nominated in nine of fifteen categories—almost everything except female artist and bluegrass group. His nominations included those of musician and comedy act, as well as single of the year for "All-Around Cowboy" and album of the year for *All-Around Cowboy*.[16]

During the 14th Annual *Music City News* Awards show at the Opry House on June 9, 1980, he won the Songwriter and Male Artist awards. Accepting the second award, he told the audience, "Larry Gatlin and I were talking about these awards backstage and he said he thought I must have bought that Songwriter of the Year award. I said he had this mixed up with one of those other shows." Backstage, he continued his dig at the Country Music Association (CMA) by saying, "This is the only award in the world that means anything to me because I know it's from the people who go out and buy my records, come to my shows. It didn't come from some big-shot organization and from some board of directors."[17]

Marty's lack of support for his industry's major association emphasized his outsider status in Nashville. The fact that he never received a CMA award may have been either the cause or effect of his attitude. "I have nothing against the CMA, the people," he said, "it's just that I do not agree with them. So if I don't agree with them, I think I would be a hypocrite if I would take part in it." He told an interviewer, "They think, 'What can we do to help CMA?' not the industry." Referring to his two number one hits and number one album in 1976, he implied his lack of membership resulted in his lack of award nominations. "I don't belong to the CMA," he said. "I don't think you should have to. I don't think that should matter."[18]

Never one to mince words, he also expressed political opinions. "Every now and then, especially around election year, he would get off on a tangent and talk about politics," Chandler recalls. "Sometimes he would go on a little bit too long. Sometimes the audience would get a little restless. They'd say, c'mon, sing, sing, and he'd get back to it."[19] That happened in Ohio when he was urging his audience to get involved in politics, and someone shouted, "We need more entertainment on the stage!" Marty frowned at him and replied, "You don't need more entertainment from the stage; you need a lot less entertainment from Washington, D.C." The crowd applauded. He worried about the United States losing the world's respect and becoming a second-rate power. He said, "You can't have respect unless you have strength, y'see," and he saw his role as trying to get people to vote.

Marty gave one of his Vietnam-era compositions, "Song of the Patriot," to Columbia label mate Johnny Cash to record. Marty sang harmony on the lines,

"And when I see Old Glory burnin'," my blood begins to churnin' and I could do some fightin' of my own." He felt the song wasn't strong enough for what he wanted to say. He liked the Charlie Daniels song, "In America." Marty said, "Mine is the song of the patriot. Charlie's is more like the song for the fighter."[20]

His relationship with Columbia also brought out the fighter in Marty. He and Billy Sherrill would have heated arguments, driving Marty to say, "Sherrill, the only thing you ever wrote was your name at the bottom of somebody else's song."[21] Marty told an interviewer in 1981, "Now I'm not bragging, but I know more about the music business—and you can print this—than anybody who's in the business. I don't care if it's the president of Columbia Records or Billy Sherrill or who it is. I know what a good record is, and I know how to make a good record. But I can't sell that record if it's not out in the record store." *The Greatest Hits of Marty Robbins*, issued in 1977 for television sales, illustrated his point. "K-Tel leased an album of mine from Columbia and sold about four hundred thousand of them real quick," he said. "So I know that's the way to do it. But Columbia Records is not set up for mail order business."

Marty liked experimenting with different styles of songs on his albums. "I don't want to get in a rut," he said. "I can try one or two songs of the new type of music on an album, but I'll guarantee you, I'll get a bunch of letters saying, 'You shouldn't have tried that!' I've got to satisfy the people who have been buying records from me all these years, and I've also got to get Columbia Records interested enough in me that they will try and sell my product."[22]

"I like to handle the production end of it," he said. "Produce it myself and then sell the finished album to the record company for a certain price, plus royalties." That is what he did with his only album of 1980. He recorded and produced *With Love, Marty Robbins* in his Division Street studio. Released in June, with the title a theme rather than a song, it contained four songs by band members Winters and Noddin and only one written by Marty. Columbia released two singles from the album. Marty's reticence in talking about his family contrasted sharply with the emotion he poured into his songs. When Emery asked if the first single, "She's Made of Faith," was written for Marizona, Marty replied, "Well, you get inspired to write about certain people, certain things."[23] The song referred to a woman "strong enough for me to lean upon" and declared, "Sometimes it's hard to face a new day. When she looks at me and smiles I know I've found a way."

"He wanted to do his own thing when he did *With Love, Marty Robbins*, so he did that at his own studio," Noddin says. "I don't think it was up to par with some of the others he had done, because when you get a top-notch producer, they're geared to do one thing and do it well. I think everything was spread a little too thin. It could have been a quality product, but a record is an accumulative thing. It depends on who plays on it, who's engineering it, who mixes it, and where you have it mastered."[24]

Showing his insecurities, Marty told Emery, "I'm not what you call a professional writer, although I've written a lot of songs, I imagine around five hundred. I think, if there's such a thing as being an inspirational writer, that's what I am, because I have to be inspired, and then it comes very easy. But if I have to sit and work on a song, I don't do that, because no one's going to record it anyway. Well, let's face it, no one records my songs. I have to do them myself."

The album's second single, "One Man's Trash," came from Don Winters and Don Winters Jr. When Emery asked about the recording, Marty said, "I would like to forget it." Then he explained he'd tried a new arrangement as an experiment. He said sales had been dropping for four years, and each succeeding love song sold fewer copies, as well as ranking lower in the charts. Those statistics told him his audience was "getting tired of me singing love songs," and it was time to try something different. However, he said, "I knew the first night it was played on WSM that I had made a *big* mistake." He realized "One Man's Trash" wasn't the kind of song his fans wanted to hear him sing. "I think the song is a good song. I'm not ashamed of the job I did, not ashamed of the record," he told Emery. "The only way it's a mistake is that it's not going to sell." Emery commented, "I think you are the first person I've ever heard sit here and openly criticize his own record." Marty repeated, "It's a good song, but it is not a Marty Robbins song."[25] It peaked at number seventy-two on *Billboard.*

Regardless of how his songs performed on the charts, his live shows thrilled his audiences. A reporter described his entrance on a West Virginia stage: "Out pops Robbins from behind the huge stage speakers, resplendent in a tailored, expensive looking pale yellow suit that plays background to a riotous garden of Mexican-style embroidered flowers. His boots match, flowers and all. The crowd yells. Marty yells back. The singer poses. He preens. He struts like a peacock, and suddenly stops to mug a crazy face. The crowd keeps applauding, and Robbins struts again, all the time making his way to center stage. His small Martin magically appears in his hands." Later in the concert, the reporter wrote, "His wits are rapier sharp, and his clowning just fringes on being excessive. But just about the time he seems to have dropped off the edge of common sense he is grounded again, in music." Marty acknowledged after the show, as he often did, that even though his clowning irritated people who were serious about music, and he didn't want to offend anyone, he couldn't resist having fun.[26]

Whether his fan mail addressed the subject is unknown. By 1980 Marty no longer had an official fan club. Peggy Ann Munson, who started the club in 1952, handled it for more than two decades until health problems prevented her from continuing. "So rather than have someone else take it over," Marty said, "it's a group of people who call themselves Marty's Army." Carol Hutson, Marty's secretary, handled his mail. Hired first by Jeanne Pruett, she then worked in the booking agency with Sykes and Dunn until Marty asked her to work for him, on what she calls "the fan side of Marty." She placed all fan mail on his desk, unopened. "I read them and I put on the outside of the envelope what I want her to say, and she types them up, because people could not read my writing, see," Marty told Emery. "I want people to know I read all the letters. Every letter I get I read." He frequently received letters without a street address, and one envelope said, "Marty Robbins, Super Singing Star, Nashville, Tennessee."[27]

Hutson typed letters and placed them with photographs and addressed envelopes on Marty's desk. "He signed *everything* that went out of this office," she says. "So if anyone received an autographed photo or letter from Marty it was signed by him. I always thought highly of him for taking the time to do this. Sometimes fans may have to wait a month due to his touring schedule, but he would eventually sit down at his desk and sign everything."[28]

Emery always inquired about Marty's health. "I get a physical once a year," Marty said in 1979, "and I check up on my doctor. Sometimes he's overweight, and I put him on a diet, y'know, and I get him back down where he belongs." Marty weighed 145 pounds, and when Emery asked if he worked out, Marty replied, "I jog every morning. I guess it's about fifteen feet into the bathroom. I jog into the bathroom and back to the bedroom, and that's about it."[29]

[22]

NASCAR—Phase Two

Following Marty's wrecks at Charlotte in 1974 and Daytona and Talladega in 1975, articles carried headlines such as "Marty Robbins Gives Up Racing!" He told reporters he had retired permanently from NASCAR. "I've had the prayers of a lot of people going out on that race track with me," *Country Song Roundup* quoted him as saying, "and the Lord's always stuck by me. I don't believe He's deserting me now, but He may be trying to tell me something. If He is, I got the message loud and clear."[1]

While Marty struggled to subordinate his racing passion to his singing livelihood, Cotton Owens rebuilt the car in his Spartanburg garage. He painted it again in attention-getting purple and fluorescent yellow. Owens says the colorful car and Marty's purple helmet with musical notes were "Marty's way of bringing show business and racing together for his fans, many of whom were the same, and showing fellow drivers he raced purely for fun."[2]

Although it would be 1977 before Marty raced the car again, he told Ralph Emery in 1976, "I have a car. I intend to try it out sometime this year. It's just that I have been working quite a lot this summer and spring, and I have been booked at the time that—certain tracks I wanted to run—so I haven't been able to run." He said he planned to race in November at Atlanta and maybe Ontario, California. Emery touched a sore spot with, "How many cars have you had?" Marty responded, "Why do you ask *that?*" Emery got himself deeper in trouble by saying, "Well, I know you have hit a few walls." Marty complained, "That's the only thing they can say about Marty Robbins in racing. He hits walls. And you know, I've only hit a wall once." Emery mentioned Talladega and was rebuffed with, "No, I didn't hit a wall in Talladega. The only wall I hit was in Charlotte."[3]

Being selected as pace car driver for the 1976 Indianapolis 500 somewhat assuaged Marty's need for a racing life. Former Indy 500 winners usually filled that role, although actor James Garner drove the previous year. "When it was first suggested to me that I was being considered, I didn't think I had much of a chance of being selected," Marty told an interviewer. "It's something that is really big to do." He spent a week in Indianapolis, with Bob Hinkle at his side, attending various functions but performing no concerts, and he rode in the festival parade on Saturday. Marty had never before appeared in front of a crowd as large as four hundred thousand people, which made driving the pace car in the famous race even more thrilling.

At the signal, "Gentlemen, start your engines," he climbed into the 1976 Buick Century Custom coupe. With a former Indy winner in the passenger seat, Marty led thirty-three drivers on the parade lap. The speed of forty miles an hour allowed engines to warm up while drivers took one more look at the track. Then came the pace lap. Marty steadily increased speed while racers behind him stayed three abreast and evenly aligned. At the end of this second lap, Marty pulled off. "I was probably going one hundred miles per hour when I left the track to pull into the pit apron," he said. "It was a pretty big thrill." He received accolades for getting the race off to a safe and smooth start. It began better than it ended; the race was called for rain at the halfway point.[4]

In October Marty ran a late model stock car race at I-70 Speedway near Kansas City, driving Freddie Fryar's 1974 Chevrolet Camaro, with Fryar as relief driver. Marty's return to NASCAR was delayed when he blew an engine during time trials at Atlanta's Dixie 500 in November.[5] Finally, two years after his Talladega wreck, he once again raced his number 42 Dodge, finishing thirteenth at Michigan International Speedway in June 1977. Transmission failure knocked him out of the Talladega 500 in August.

The Nashville Speedway, formerly Fairgrounds Speedway, occasionally honored Marty. There had been a "Marty Robbins Night" in 1974 and 1975, and the "Marty Robbins World Open 500" race in 1977 featured out-of-town drivers. "It's a different type of sportsman than they run right here in Nashville," Marty explained. "They run less pounds per cubic inch, and they're a little faster." Because Marty wasn't in Nashville during qualification, he planned to share the race with Freddie Fryar, whose car had qualified. Fryar would drive 125 laps, Marty would drive the second quarter, Fryar the third, and Marty would finish the race. "The car lasted five laps," Marty said. "I didn't even get to race."[6]

His only race of 1978 brought him an eighteenth place finish at Talladega. By then, Owens had turned the 1974 Charger into a 1978 Magnum to keep up with NASCAR requirements. Features included a padded dash and adjustable bucket seat. Air flowed through a hole in the firewall and under an aluminum footrest to keep Marty's feet from burning. Owens also dipped the steering wheel in a rubberized softening solution to protect Marty's hands against blisters. "His hands were tender because he didn't drive regularly," Owens says, "and a lot of times he had to go pick his guitar soon after he raced." A plate on the dash read "Marty Robbins Special."[7]

Marty's three 1979 NASCAR starts resulted in blown engines, two in Michigan and one at Talladega. When Emery asked how much money went out the window each time an engine blew up, Marty responded, "The way I buy engines it costs maybe $4,500; a good engine costs $10,000 to 12,000." He explained, "I don't spend that much time racing, so I can't afford to spend that much money, y'know."[8]

The June race at Michigan International Speedway was Marty's last as number 42. Knowing Kyle Petty planned to become the third generation of racing Pettys, Marty magnanimously offered the number that had identified his purple-and-yellow car for nine years. This allowed Kyle to run his grandfather's number, which Lee Petty had chosen in NASCAR's infancy. Richard Petty, in his autobiography, recalls saying, "We can bring Daddy's Number 42 out of retirement. He'd like Kyle usin' it."[9] It was a strange comment to be made while the number graced what was possibly NASCAR's most photographed race car.

Marty's Magnum used number 36 at Talladega in August and then carried number 6 through the following year. Marty raced twice at Talladega in 1980, with one engine failure and one thirteenth place finish. Because his car didn't qualify at the Firecracker 400 in Daytona Beach, he drove someone else's car, but engine problems took him out. He burned his leg from leaning against the hot gearshift. "I was having so much fun I wasn't realizing it was burning for a while, y'know," he said. "It turned into a big, big blister about three inches long and an inch wide." Emery reminded Marty of his heart surgery ten years earlier and asked if his racing scared his doctor. "No, because he knows I'm in good shape, see," Marty answered. "I have to pass a real stiff physical in order to race."[10]

At Charlotte in October 1980, his car didn't qualify, and he drove one owned by Benny Parsons. Marty was on his way to a top ten finish when the right front wheel broke off coming into a turn. He couldn't get the car to turn left. "I had about one half second to realize I was gonna hit that guard rail," he explained later, "and I thought what if part of that guard rail gets inside this car. That's the only time I have ever been scared."[11]

Danger of another type lay around the corner.

[23]

Super Legend

New Year's Day, 1981, after returning home from a three-show New Year's Eve performance in Evansville, Indiana, Marty experienced chest pains. "I thought it was just an extra bad case of indigestion," he said later, "because I've had a heart attack, and it was *nothing* like the one I had in '69."[1] He waited from Thursday until Monday to call Doctor Ewers for an appointment. "I told him I had a little pain in my chest, and he said come on over," Marty remembered. "I said I was planning on coming over tomorrow, and he said get on over here right now." It was almost five o'clock on January 5, and Marty was leaving his office to go home. Instead, he drove to the doctor's office.

"I had on a big cowboy hat, a straw hat, I had on boots and jeans and a big jacket like real cowboys wear, y'know," Marty recalled. The doctor checked him and called an ambulance. Marty thought he was kidding until ambulance attendants rolled in a stretcher. "Doctor Ewers," Marty said, "I'm not dressed for the hospital." The doctor insisted he get in the ambulance. Marty said later, "So I went out of there on my back, but I still had my boots on. I had that hat lying across, and I felt real silly, a little embarrassed, y'know."[2]

The ambulance took him to St. Thomas Hospital where he'd had triple by-pass surgery eleven years earlier. He was placed in a special care unit, diagnosed with a mild heart attack, and listed in serious but stable condition. A hospital spokesman said on Wednesday, "When I saw him this afternoon he was joking with his doctor and had his guitar in bed with him." A spokesman said the damage wouldn't be known until doctors ran an arteriogram. Evelyn Lamb, Marty's secretary, reported that Marty called the office frequently. "He laughs a lot and says he's bored," she said.[3] Doctors determined no surgery would be required.

The following week Marty called Ralph Emery's WSM radio show from the hospital. Broadcasting live, Emery said, "I've been getting various reports on you—that you were improving, that you were bored, and that you wanted to get out of the hospital." Marty answered, "Yeah, I'd like to get out. But you have to do what the doctors tell you to do. I think I'm getting out Saturday. But if it's not Saturday, then I'll wait till Monday." He said he'd cancelled his January and February personal appearances.

Marty told Emery he had written one song and started another, "Jumper Cable Man," which he would finish when in the mood. "I'm gonna play around with that thing, 'cause it's really cute," he said.[4] The double entendre song referred to working on a car and a woman's emotions: "I've got a reputation I believe is hard to beat; I know what wires to work with when your battery needs some heat."

The song idea occurred to him when a nurse taking his pulse asked a man who was cleaning nearby, "Henry, can you jump me off?" Marty had never heard that term, and even though he was drowsy with medication, the comment caught his attention, and he came alert enough to see what would happen next. The man asked, "What's the matter—battery dead?" Marty realized the nurse referred to jumper cables, which he called booster cables. "Out in the west," Marty explained to Emery, "if you wanted somebody to help you get your car started, you say, 'Can you give me a boost?'" He added, "I thought that's a good title and a good idea for a song." He never saw that nurse again, but he sang the song for several others, "and they got a big kick out of it."[5]

During the interview, Emery asked, "Have you heard a lot from Marty's Army?" Marty said he'd received three or four hundred pounds of mail, and calls came from "Ireland. London. Canada. All over the world, really." The most unusual card arrived from El Paso, Texas. Measuring four feet by eight feet and weighing one hundred pounds, the sheet of wood showed El Paso's location on an outline of Texas, with a note that read, "Get Well Marty!!" KHEY Radio displayed the card at a shopping mall for fans to sign and then shipped it to Marty's office.[6]

When Emery referred to Marty as a superstar, Marty corrected him with, "super legend." He said, "There's already superstars, so I started calling myself a super legend, and I even get some mail, 'Super Legend Marty Robbins.'" In later interviews, Emery would introduce his friend as "Mr. Teardrop, Old Golden Throat, and Super Legend, Marty Robbins." He'd started calling Marty "Old Golden Throat" more than a decade earlier, in response to Marty's dislike of "Mr. Teardrop."[7]

Emery asked if Doctor Ewers fussed at Marty about driving race cars, and Marty said, "Well, yeah, a bit, but I won't do that anymore. I don't think I'd put the other drivers under that much of a strain. I don't think they could do their best with me out there now." He said he quit in 1975 after his three consecutive crashes because not having a car was a good time to quit. "Now is a good time to quit, too," he said, "because I do have a car, but I don't have a car that's legal to run on NASCAR tracks. So probably what I'll do is find me a little dirt track car someplace, maybe go out into Arkansas and Missouri, y'know, race a little half-mile track and have a good time. I do like it an awful lot and I get to meet a lot of people that way."[8]

Marty was discharged January 17, 1981, and sent home to rest for two months. A newspaper photo showed him standing at the hospital's front entrance, waving his little Martin guitar in one hand and his hat in the other. Two weeks later he told a reporter he was eating properly and following doctor's orders. He said he did some singing and writing and that his favorite television programs were afternoon reruns of *Wonder Woman*. He admitted, "What really caused [the heart attack] was not doing what they told me to do for the past ten years. I did up to about a year and a half ago. For the past year—I love milk so much—I would take a quart of milk and mix it with a pint of whipping cream, and then I would put that on cereal, with a lot of sugar. I would eat four or five bowls a day. And I would eat eggs, y'know. That just irritated the problem I already had."[9]

Columbia released a new single during his hospital stay. Marty had written "Completely Out of Love" for George Jones. "I sang it to George when we were over in England, sang it to his manager," Marty said, "and they didn't go for it too much. So I thought Merle Haggard might like the song, but I sang it for him, and he didn't care for it. So I put it in the album because I thought it was a good song, y'see. Well, it came off better than any song in the album, so we released it."[10]

It stalled at forty-seven on *Billboard* and was the only single from *Everything I've Always Wanted,* an album completed before Marty's heart attack and released in late January. Eddie Kilroy, who previously worked with Faron Young at MCA, produced it. "I needed a change because I wasn't satisfied with the way I was going with Columbia," Marty said. "Most every song, to me, was beginning to sound alike. Billy Sherrill—I like him, and he's one of the best producers to ever come to Nashville, but I wanted another sound. I wanted to go back more country—and we did." Kilroy remembers Marty "as a complete professional and a joy to work with." He asked if Marty would consider rerecording "I'll Go On Alone," and Marty agreed. Kilroy had first heard the song as a ten-year-old in Texas—and now he was producing it. His second thrill came from having one of his own compositions on the album. When Kilroy protested, "Marty, you don't have to do that song," Marty said he recorded "The Woman In My Bed" because he liked it.[11]

Another cut was Marty's tribute to his childhood idol, "Gene Autry, My Hero." Marty first saw Autry in person during the singing cowboy's visit to Marty's high school. Don Law introduced them in 1952 at Columbia's studio in Hollywood. Their paths crossed occasionally in later years in Nashville. They'd enjoyed a forty-five minute visit at the Cowboy Hall of Fame in Oklahoma City in April 1979 when Marty was presented with the Golden Trustee Award in appreciation of his cowboy songs. "I told him how I felt about him, that he was my favorite singer, and I always prayed to be a singing cowboy," Marty stated. "And he said, 'Marty, you're my favorite singer, too.' That really thrilled me." Marty asked permission to write a song about Autry, and he sent him "Gene Autry, My Hero" before he put it on the album. "He loved it so much," Marty said. "He played it for different people and he called me back three times and told me how much they liked it. That's the way I feel about him, and I'm glad I have a hero."[12]

His sidemen worried how they would support their families without a touring schedule. At $200 a show and ten shows per month, they normally made $2,000. After the heart attack, they expected Marty to be off the road for six months or so, and they would have to find other employment. "We were back at work the next month," Chandler marvels. "He did not slow down. He probably should have taken the year off. But he couldn't be still." Even during two months of cancelled shows, Marty paid his band. "He put us on salary because he didn't want to lose us," Martinez says.[13]

While Marty recuperated in early 1981, he hosted reporter Bob Allen at his office and his farm during an interview for *Hustler* magazine. "I can look around and see what I've already done in this business," Marty told Allen. "I don't have to go in the Hall of Fame to be remembered. I could make personal appearances for the next twenty years off of what I've already done, even if I never recorded again. It may sound like I'm bragging, but it's a fact. I don't want to stop making records, though. I want them to be in the home. When I'm gone, fifty years from now, they'll still [be playing my records], if they don't wear 'em out before then." He emphasized, "I'm more interested in looking ahead at what I'm going to do than I am at looking back at what I've already done. I still want to write a song that's better than 'El Paso.'"

Marty said he didn't like doing interviews or going to radio stations during the day while on tour, and added, "I'm kind of hard to get along with right before a show." He said, "I hate to go on last. I want to play the audience first." He wanted his audiences to think his show was the best they'd ever seen. "Every time I go out there," he said, "I do my very best I can to make them say that."[14]

After receiving medical clearance to perform again, he and his band left from his office early on March 6, 1981, for a show date in Saginaw, Michigan. "Members of his band are kissing their wives goodbye and climbing sleepily onto the bus," wrote Allen, who rode along for the weekend. "The Silver Eagle pulls out of Nashville and rolls northward."[15]

"Man, I'm glad to be back out here," Marty told Allen. "I've been waiting for this. I've been traveling for so long that when I stop for awhile, it makes me a little nervous. Maybe I needed the rest, I don't know. But I didn't want it." He added, "I don't know what it's going to feel like tonight. I guess this is the longest I've gone in my life without singing. Even when I was a little kid I sang almost every day. After I had that heart attack in 1969, I used to sing three or four hours a day. We lived out on the farm then. My wife would go to bed around eleven, and I would go to the other side of the house where the piano was and she couldn't hear me, and I would play from eleven until four. I used to know at least a thousand songs by heart."[16]

He returned to the Opry the following Saturday and headed off to Great Britain a month later for his fifth Wembley appearance. After his opening songs, he said, "We're only allowed a few minutes on stage, so all the talking I'm going to do is right now, and I want to introduce the band, very quickly. There they are!" Then he explained, "We had a long tour lined up, see, but I had a—I know I look real healthy and all that, but you know I had a heart attack January the first, and the doctor didn't want me to come this far away from home, see, so I said to him, 'Would it be all right if I went to Wembley?' He said, 'Well for one day, it would be all right.' And tonight we're here."[17]

"I was cooling off, y'see, and the records weren't selling real good," he joked to an interviewer, "and I needed a little publicity. So the attack came, letters came, now the crowd has improved. So it'll be another ten years before I'll have the same thing."[18]

On May 11, a day before Jeff Chandler's wife was due to give birth to their first child, Marty and the band left on a three-week tour. They drove to New Jersey for two days at a dinner theater and then across the country for two weeks in Reno, Nevada. Chandler called Nancy daily. Marty said, "If she goes into labor, I'll fly you home to be there." They returned to Nashville on May 31, and Chandler's daughter was born the following day. "Marty was very generous," Chandler says. "If you needed something, he'd give it to you. If you needed to borrow money, he made sure he got it back, but he didn't ask any questions; he'd give it to you."

Marty headlined at a Fourth of July picnic hosted by President and Nancy Reagan on the south lawn of the White House. "He was very competitive," Chandler says. "He didn't like to think somebody else was the star of the show, even the President of the United States." Ronny remembers listening to the performance on the radio. He thought the White House crowd appeared to be enjoying the show but not excited about it. Marty's comments were "going over everybody's heads because they weren't listening," Ronny says. "I could tell it bothered him." Okie Jones says Marty appeared to be comparing himself with Reagan, even competing with the president, and coming across as self-conscious without the presence of his fans. Ronny says, "When he didn't have his fans there, or when he felt it wasn't going right, he got insecure real quick. Once he got tense like that on stage, it was hard for him to get it back. He'd just as soon cut it short and get out."[19]

His insecurities came to the forefront when an interviewer wondered at what point in his career Marty realized he was a success and could relax in the confidence of having it made. Marty answered, "I don't know. I haven't found that yet." The reporter asked, "Have you got everything you've always wanted?" Marty said, "No. I want security. I don't have it yet. I feel as long as I can [perform], I have security. So I'm gonna keep doing it. Also, I love the business. I do 110 to 130 days a year." He added, "I know what it is to be without and I know what it feels to have a little something, and I don't feel I have enough to feel comfortable about it."[20]

Being unable to race also bothered him. "Now that I've said I wouldn't do it anymore," he commented, "a lot of people have told me they're glad, because they were worried about me. I know I could pass the physical, but I would feel the other drivers wouldn't feel safe, because when you say heart attack, that's serious. My wife never did like it. And everybody that worked with me didn't like it." In the spring of 1981, he said, "I don't even like to go to races, because I want to be in them so bad. I couldn't even watch the Daytona 500 this year, because I wanted to be there so bad."[21]

He remembered a decade earlier when a doctor told him he would never race again. "In fact, he said 'You will live a quiet life,'" Marty recalled. "I said, 'Hey, no way I'll live a quiet life.' I didn't think it was up to him to tell me I was going to have to live a quiet life. So I prayed and I prayed and I said make me strong enough, God, and let me race again because he does not have the right to tell me that. And even if he had the right, he shouldn't have told me that. It tears the spirit down, y'know. How can you think you're going to get better if the doctor says you're not? So I took physicals and all that I had to take to prove I was capable of running races."

After the 1981 heart attack, his concern was mostly for other drivers. "They're all good friends of mine," he said. "I don't get in the way. I find somebody as slow as I am and I chase him all day long. And have a good time, y'know."[22] But, by August he couldn't take it any longer. Although his 1978 Dodge Magnum was obsolete for NASCAR's Winston Cup, he ran it in the ARCA 500 at Talladega.

September brought the release of his second 1981 album. "I don't have anything to do with titling albums," Marty said. "I didn't come up with *The Legend*. What I wanted was *Super Legend*. But they didn't go along with it, so it's just *The Legend*." Although it became a Columbia album, Marty recorded it in his studio with his band.

Neither of two singles from *The Legend* charted well. "Jumper Cable Man" came first. "The public didn't accept it like I thought they would," Marty said. "I guess they're used to hearing cowboy songs or love songs. But it goes over well at personal appearances." Some radio stations played it; others considered it not Marty Robbins music. "I think I did the song just like I was an experienced rock 'n' roll singer," he commented. "I think the musicians did a great job on it, and I think it was, y'know, it was a pretty decent record. But radio stations didn't, ah, just didn't dig it."

The second single was an old Sons of the Pioneers hit called "Teardrops in My Heart." Marty played guitar and sang all three parts, trying to duplicate the original sound. "It didn't come off quite like I wanted it to, but I was satisfied," he said. "It's not urban cowboy, it's not trail-driving cowboy, but it's cowboy music. Your trail-driving stuff is like 'Cool Water' and 'Tumbling Tumbleweeds.' Urban cowboy music is like for your rodeo cowboys. And there's a difference in rodeo cowboys and ranch cowboys. There's quite a big difference."[23]

Always happy to give his opinions on anything from cowboys to clothing, he discussed a variety of subjects with reporter Stacy Harris when she interviewed him for *Country Song Roundup*. Harris remembers initially wondering why he stared out his office window instead of making eye contact. Then she realized it was shyness, not rudeness, causing him to act so unlike his normal backstage behavior at the Opry. Finally, he relaxed and even sang a few songs for her.[24] After discussing cowboys and cowboy attire, he told her how he designed his stage outfits. "When I see what a woman likes, then I take parts of different things until I get them all together the way I like them," he said. "When I can satisfy a woman with a color on stage, then—sure—it will satisfy a man." He used both Nudie and Italian designer Anthony Gasbari to make his clothing, and he said he wouldn't wear a suit that looked like it might belong to someone else.

He compared designing clothes to recording songs, saying he demonstrated to the musicians what music he wanted on each record. "Then I expect them to do better, 'cause that's their job," he said, "to do better than I can do, as far as playing a musical instrument. So I'm proud of all the music that's on my records, because part of it is me—like I'm proud of my clothes. Part of the clothes is me."[25]

Marty also mentioned his plans for building a mail-order organization to market his records. With the lack of promotion by Columbia (sometimes referred to as CBS) Records and the possibility his contract might not be renewed, he had to rely on himself. He told Harris he was compiling a mailing list from his former fan club, his fan mail, and current album sales requests. He said he'd collected thirty thousand names over seven or eight years. "In five years I will have the address of every Marty Robbins fan in the world," he predicted.[26]

Another venue for fans was the Marty Robbins Gift Shop at 1806 Division Street, in the same building as the recording studio. "I had some room up front and didn't know what to do with it," Marty said. "It was wasted space, and I said I'll put some gifts in it and my albums. Carol Hutson is in charge. It's been doing quite well. In fact, I think I'm gonna make a bigger one. Then I would have other people's T-shirts and other people's records."

Emery asked how many fans were in Marty's Army, and Marty replied, "I don't know, but there can never be enough. I never, never, ever get over saying thanks to the people that have bought my records over the years. I appreciate and love the people that have made life easy for me. There could have been a time where a man or woman might have said, 'Can I have this album or shall I buy something else I need, or shall I wait till next year for that and get Marty's album?' I'm sure that's happened. So the people are faithful followers of Marty Robbins."[27]

His faithful followers in Beaumont, Texas, cheered his appearance in October. A reviewer described him as "very slender in a bright blue leisure suit with colored decorations and sequins." Katz Kobayashi was "the standout instrumentalist of the night, although he never showed more emotion than a sphinx as his fingers flew effortlessly over the frets." Marty told the crowd he had experienced three heart attacks, but he didn't sweat little things in life, and he'd weather seven or eight more if he had to. The crowd responded with applause.[28]

Emery, later that month, mentioned how people worried about Marty and often asked how he could race with a bad heart. "I don't have a bad heart," Marty insisted. "I have a good heart, or I wouldn't be alive. I have a cholesterol problem, see. So I have to stay on a strict diet to keep the cholesterol count down." Emery asked, as he had ten months earlier, what Marty's doctor said about his racing. "Doctors naturally wouldn't want anybody to race," Marty said. "You're their patient, and their reputation is at stake, y'see, so they don't want you doing anything. Racing doesn't get me any more excited than a good hot stage show." He responded to Emery's "So obviously you haven't given up racing" comment with, "Oh, no. I'll wait till next year. I want to get me the best deal I can get on a car. Mine is too big this year; they've downsized the cars so I can't run. But if I can pass the physical, and I don't see any reason why I can't pass the physical, see, because there is nothing wrong with my heart."[29]

[24]

No Plans of Quitting Any Time Soon

"Women just drooled over him," Wayne Jackson says about Marty. "Sometimes we'd have to sit on the bus for two or three hours while he would be sitting on the side of the stage after a show. He would shake every man's hand and kiss every woman on the cheek. And they all thought they knew him personally. He was the epitome of how to treat fans. You treat them with love and kindness because they're the reason you got the Cadillac and the farm. He knew that in a supreme manner."[1]

To improve his shows, Marty made an attempt to cut up less on stage. "I wouldn't want somebody doing that to a song that was a favorite of mine," he acknowledged. "If I was to go and watch Kenny Rogers or Barbara Mandrell and one of the songs they did was my favorite, and they did something funny, it would take away because when I get listening I get involved with that song, y'know, and I don't want somebody pulling funnies." Still, he admitted, "Sometimes I do a ballad and have a little fun with it, but I know that's the wrong thing to do, y'know. Make funny faces to people that's taking pictures or, y'know, have a big time. But I know I shouldn't *do* that, y'see, with a pretty song."[2]

He also changed his negative attitude about membership in the Country Music Association. He joined after the 1980 CMA awards show because it pleased him when Barbara Mandrell was named Entertainer of the Year and George Jones won the Male Vocalist award. "Some of the things I don't agree with them," he said, "but I think, y'know, they did something right."[3]

As Marty prepared for a heavy year of touring, the road became too grueling for some band members. When Wayne Jackson left at the beginning of 1982, Marty's team searched for a replacement. Eddy Fox was sitting at the desk in the foyer of Marty's recording studio when he saw an unhappy man come out of the studio, which had been rented for a session. He asked what was wrong, and Jim Hannaford replied, "I came down here to audition, and I came right away, and these guys have already hired someone." He said he played keyboards and piano, and Fox asked, "You don't happen to play trumpet, do you?" Hannaford acknowledged playing trumpet and French horn in high school. "I may have a job for you with Marty Robbins," Fox said. "Get a trumpet and come back tomorrow, and let's talk."

Hannaford went directly to a pawn shop on Lower Broadway and bought a trumpet for $35. Not having played one in years, he practiced all night and returned to the studio the next afternoon. "I've already heard about your piano playing," Fox said. "Let me see if you can blow that horn." Fortunately for Hannaford, Fox chose "El Paso City," with only two trumpet licks, and Hannaford followed the record. Fox then took him across the street to meet the boss. Marty said, "Get him some tapes and have him start learning the show, and we'll get the band together." When Hannaford took the tapes home, as he remembers, "I heard Wayne Jackson wailing on that trumpet, and I said, 'Oh, me, I made a mistake.' I went back down there and I said, 'I'm not really a trumpet player. I cannot play like that.'" Marty told him, "That's okay, just take your time, learn your parts."

During rehearsal, it became obvious he could not play the first trumpet part. "Conrad was playing second trumpet," Hannaford recalls. "On the trumpet songs, he'd pick up his horn from the piano bench and play the second trumpet line. So he took over the first trumpet part, and I played second trumpet." There were only six or seven trumpet songs in the show, which didn't give Hannaford much to do, especially since he couldn't take solos. Marty purchased an electronic keyboard synthesizer for Hannaford to play orchestral strings on non-trumpet songs. That didn't last long, because Marty didn't like the sound and didn't think it was "country."[4]

Next to leave the road in 1982 was Katz Kobayashi. After giving notice, he stayed until the end of February. When Wayne Hobbs arrived for an audition, Marty said, "Meet me over at the studio. I want to hear you play." Hobbs expected the whole band to be there, but it was only Marty with his guitar. "He started singing Hawaiian music, and I think we took a liking to each other right off the bat," Hobbs says. Marty asked how he knew all those songs, and Hobbs explained he'd recently returned from five years in Hawaii where he played Hawaiian steel guitar and worked with Don Ho. He said he began playing acoustic guitar and singing Marty Robbins songs at age four, and he learned to play steel guitar from his steel guitarist father.

"Marty was the highlight of my career," Hobbs states. "It was a thrill to be sitting up there on stage, just to listen to him sing. That was the honor." He reminisces, "Marty used to sometimes take out a little lap steel and play Hawaiian music or older country sounds of the '40s and '50s. Probably his favorite instrument was the steel guitar."[5]

Marty and his band joined a package of American artists for a European tour in April. Following a show in Sweden, they performed at the Silk Cut Festival in Wembley, England, Marty's sixth appearance there. After singing "You Gave Me a Mountain," Marty told his audience, "The only reason I did that song is because it was written by one of the greatest writers living. I wrote it. I ain't kidding you. I wrote the song, and a guy by the name of Presley recorded that song, see. To me, he was the greatest rock and roll singer that has ever lived or will ever be." Then Marty said, "When he was first getting started, y'see, he had this song and it didn't do too much for him. But I liked that song real well, and I said to myself, 'Hey!' I said, 'What?' I said, 'You ought to do that song.'" Marty sang "That's All Right," which hadn't charted for Elvis Presley in 1954 but had been a number seven hit for Marty in 1955.[6]

They concluded with dates in Holland, Germany, Switzerland, and then back to England. "All through England and Europe they loved him," Jeff Chandler remembers. "We did shows in Germany and Holland and places where they didn't speak English. I don't know how they understood a thing, but they loved country music."

Chandler was next to leave Marty and the demanding tours. He had given his notice before going to Europe. "My daughter was about a year old," he says, "and I decided I didn't want to be on the road all my life." He moved his family to Ruidoso, New Mexico, to open a dinner theater with a friend.[7] Bobby Sykes temporarily rejoined the group, and they headed to Canada the first week of May.

Conrad Noddin left at the end of May. "We were playing a lot of gigs, and it was starting to wear on me, being gone so much," he says. He talked with Marty about running the recording studio, and he recommended an upgraded mixing board to draw people to record in a higher class studio. Marty's attorney disapproved of the expensive idea, and Noddin found other employment. Jim Hannaford says, "After Conrad left, there went the trumpet. We didn't use trumpet anymore, and I moved over on piano and played strictly piano."[8]

June brought the famous International Country Music Fan Fair to Nashville—an event started in 1972 to keep fans from overrunning the CMA disc jockey convention. Marty signed autographs at the CBS (Columbia) Records booth, and he hosted a "Marty Party" at the Opryland Hotel. "All of those people were rabid fans," says former WSM disc jockey Chuck Morgan. "There would be legions of Marty fans, asking for autographs and pictures. I never saw him refuse anybody."[9]

The week opened with the sixteenth annual *Music City News* awards show, televised live from the Opry House on June 7, 1982. Marty was nominated in six of fourteen categories, and he won as Male Artist of the Year, with Barbara Mandrell his counterpart as Female Artist. The Marty Robbins Band, current reigning Band of the Year from 1981, received its third consecutive nomination.

When Marty accepted the Male Artist award, he told the audience, "I'm glad I hung around." He explained on Ralph Emery's radio show a week after Fan Fair, "I won that award two years ago, see. I didn't think I was gonna win anything, so I wanted to go someplace and watch the show. There's no place to sit. You couldn't watch it from the wings; I couldn't go out in the audience." When Emery asked why he couldn't sit in the audience, Marty said, "Because you go in the audience, you sign autographs. And that messes up the show. I wouldn't want somebody to do that to me."

He illustrated his point by describing little county fairs where he took a break to let Don Winters and Bobby Sykes sing. "Somebody will try to get an autograph from me if I'm standing on that stage," he said. "I say I can't do it, y'see. I've had it done to me, and I'm sure they didn't mean anything by it, but it wasn't too professional. . . . I don't care how big you are; you don't do anything to get the attention of the crowd while somebody is trying to entertain . . . I always say, 'Not while he's singing.'"

Concerning his awards show attire, Marty said, "I wanted to look good. I felt good. I was surprised when I got the award. It's like a race. I never make a plan in case I win, because I don't think I'm gonna win." About his nomination for Comedy Act of the Year, he joked, "Now if I win that, I don't know what I'll do. Here I've been trying to sing for all these years, and wind up as a comedian. I think they're trying to tell me that's why I haven't had any number ones in the last six years."[10]

The 1982 Fan Fair included an event called All-American Country games, with three teams of singers competing in sporting events at the Vanderbilt University Stadium. Barbara Mandrell was captain of Marty's team. Temperatures hovered close to one hundred degrees, and everyone felt hot and tired. "It was all we could do to put forth all this physical energy," Mandrell remembers. Because of Marty's heart condition, she placed him in the soccer competition, with the expectation he would "only do a little bit, in and out, in and out, and not be in it that long." She was wrong. "He was in there the whole time," she says, "fighting, going, doing, kicking. He wanted to win. He loved it, every minute of it." She reminisces, "Of all the things we had in common, this was the most special thing to me. Marty Robbins was a tremendous competitor."[11] Their team won the gold medal.

Marty described several events: "They had the softball throw, the high jump, the bicycle race. And they had a big ol' ball called earth ball. That thing was about six foot high, and they had three members from each team, so that made nine people out there, pushing that ball, trying to get it into three different goals. I tripped over somebody, and then somebody tripped over me, and then somebody tripped over him, and his knee hit me in the back of the head right behind the ear."

Marty's long warm-up pants prevented him from participating in one event. "I was gonna take them off but I didn't have on the little short pants underneath, and so I wouldn't run the fifty-yard dash with heavy pants on," he told Emery. He'd forgotten to put on his jogging shorts, which were in the locker room. "I'm just so glad I checked," he said.

Emery's interview questions covered a variety of topics, and when he suggested, "Marizona has rarely ever been seen," Marty joked, "I can't help it if she don't have any money." He called her a very shy person and "a very fine lady." Emery asked if she ever attended his concerts, and Marty answered, "She has seen me in about four or five shows, I guess, all my life." Janet insists Marty's protectiveness, rather than Marizona's lack of interest, kept her from his shows. "I'm sure she would like to have felt more included, but at the same time, it wasn't her world and she wasn't comfortable in it," Janet says. "She had a whole other world with her church friends and activities."[12]

Thinking back to his youth in Glendale, Marty told Emery, "I have had so many people say to me, remember when you brought your guitar to school and would sing for us? I never took my guitar to school because I didn't have one. I never did sing for anybody when I was in high school. . . . I didn't have any ambition to be a singer. I didn't want to be a singer until—well, I did in a way, but I *really* wanted to be one after I got out of the Navy." About a vocation, he said, "I never did think that far ahead. I knew I didn't like school. My thoughts were always, how can I get out of going to school?"[13]

How much he'd achieved over the years showed when the Country Music Association announced finalists for October's Country Music Hall of Fame induction. Marty, as a first-time nominee, would be competing with four other men in the active performer category, including Little Jimmy Dickens, whom Marty credited with getting him his Columbia contract. The others chosen by an anonymous panel of two hundred electors were comedian Whitey Ford, known as the Duke of Paducah, country music pioneer Bradley Kincaid, and Floyd Tillman of "Slippin' Around" fame. "I don't believe I deserve it yet," Marty said. "I can wait fifteen more years because I'm going to be here fifteen more years, y'know." He wanted Dickens to win.[14]

Considering the CMA's previous lack of acknowledgment, this nomination was especially surprising. In spite of Marty's Grammy awards, his selection as the Academy of Country Music's Man of the Decade, his numerous fan-voted *Music City News* awards, and his tremendous impact as a songwriter, performer, and recording artist, his only CMA award nominations occurred in 1970. He didn't win those, and he was never acknowledged as an entertainer.

The announcement came on July 3, the day Marty qualified in his new Buick for his first race in 1982, Daytona's Firecracker 400. Because his Dodge Magnum had become obsolete by NASCAR rules, he purchased a Buick from Junior Johnson, who built an engine for it. Cotton Owens continued to maintain and store Marty's car. Marty explained to an interviewer why he used old-fashioned pit boards instead of radios for communicating with his pit crew. "If I don't use ear plugs," he said, "my ears ring for three or four days, and I can't have that happening when I've got a date coming up in the next couple of days." During the Independence Day race, the engine blew on the forty-fifth lap. Marty tried again in August, at Michigan International Speedway, but qualified thirty-seventh of thirty-six spots and didn't get to race.[15]

Marty's one album of 1982 was finally released in August, six months after recording the songs. Its title, *Come Back To Me*, referred to a line in "Lover, Lover," the only song on the album written by Marty. "I don't know where they got that title for the album," Marty said, "but if you listen to that song, I got it. They're all love songs, so the title of the album does fit." Marty finished writing "Lover, Lover" at the last recording session, and he showed it to his new Columbia producer, Bob Montgomery, who chose it to replace one of the other songs.[16]

Marty started recording with Montgomery at the suggestion of Rick Blackman, head of Columbia Records, in an attempt to improve sales and radio plays. "The story songs I had done were not being accepted by the public or the radio stations," explained Marty as his reason for trying a "brand new" style of music.[17] He told Montgomery to "find the songs and tell me when to come to the studio. I don't want anything to do with it. You mix it and you do everything." Montgomery changed Marty's style of phrasing and helped him find a more commercial sound.

Montgomery selected "Some Memories Just Won't Die," which became Marty's favorite song on the album. "It wasn't at first," he said, "but the more I listened to it the more I thought it didn't sound like me, y'know. I guess that's been my problem for the past five or six years. I've been cutting songs that fit Marty Robbins, y'know, and somehow people were not buying them. So this song is not the average-type song Marty Robbins does. It's a love song, but it's not arranged the way I would do it. I phrased differently on this. I had to learn to sing again. I thought I knew it all, and all the time I didn't know anything."

"Some Memories Just Won't Die," with "Lover, Lover" on the flipside, reached number ten on *Billboard*. "When we do it on the stage, they start applauding," Marty said. "I don't like to do a song on the stage that isn't a good seller. If they don't start asking for it, I never bother to even sing the new singles, but they started asking for this one. Before we ever started doing it, see, so we had to learn it." The record's success led Marty to admit, "I think that proved, y'know, to me, that I was wrong. There's been times when I was right, and so, I can take the responsibility of being wrong once in a while, just as well as—I like to get the credit, though, when I'm right."

Marty's efforts to duplicate a record on stage came through in his concern about releasing "Praying for Rain" as a single. "If this comes out to be a hit, it will be the end of me," he told Emery. "I would hate to have a hit and then not be able to do it on the stage." He'd recorded it with a rhythm track only, and Montgomery overdubbed with violins and other instruments. "It is gonna be hard to do," he said. "We don't want to deal with all that trouble. It's got some little funky sounds in it."[18] However, the second single from the *Come Back To Me* album was "Tie Your Dreams To Mine." Released in August, it didn't reach the top twenty.

Marty continued a strenuous touring schedule of ten to fifteen one-nighters each month. During an Iowa fair date, he visited with Larry Jordon, whose youthful interview had been a near disaster years earlier. "I was directed through a labyrinth to the tiniest little cubicle," Jordan recalls about his visit to the bus, "where Marty sat on the other side of a small table. He had aged a lot but his skin was tanned and lined like leather. He still had a firm handshake and a friendly smile."[19]

Bobby Sykes wanted to get off the road. Wayne Hobbs, an Ohio native, called several of his Ohio buddies and invited them to come to Nashville to audition. Mike Cutright and Gary Adams, longtime friends, showed up at Marty's office at the same time without knowing the other would be there. "We kind of laughed about it, and we auditioned for him," Adams says, "and he was undecided because he only wanted to hire one. He couldn't make up his mind so he wound up hiring both of us." According to Hobbs, "Marty felt like Mike Cutright's voice blended a bit more than Gary's did, but Marty loved the way Gary played guitar. So he hired him." Marty might have been thinking about updating his sound. According to Bill Martinez, the two new guitar players "were playing little rock things. They were kinda changing Marty's style."[20]

The two Ohio residents planned to keep their homes and commute as required. Cutright agreed to meet Marty's group in Portsmouth, Ohio, on September 1 for two shows at Southern Ohio College. He planned to shadow Sykes during the eight-day tour. But Sykes became ill between shows and was rushed to a nearby hospital. Cutright recalls, "Having been a Marty Robbins fan since

I was a little boy, I pretty much knew his songs, and they shoved me in a show uniform that was too small and I had to do the second show." When he went to Nashville, he received properly fitting uniforms.

Cutright, the youngest band member, compared working with Marty to "being with a favorite uncle on a permanent paid vacation," and he sometimes served as Marty's good luck charm during poker games. "He'd make me get out of my bunk and come sit across the aisle from him," Cutright recalls. "He'd put his foot over on me, if it was a big pot. I'd be all groggy-headed, wanting to go back to sleep, and I'd have to sit there and be his little lucky charm."

Marty enjoyed playing with remote-controlled cars. Cutright remembers sitting in the office, doing paperwork, and looking up to see a little race car coming at him. "He loved life and loved to mess with people," Cutright says. "You couldn't see him, but the car would be banging into your feet. If you were walking, he'd try to trip you up. He'd be back in his office laughing his butt off. He would do the same thing to the girls in the office."[21]

Adams remembers leaving his car at Shoney's Restaurant when it refused to start. He walked three blocks to Marty's office, and Marty insisted on taking a look. The two men walked to Shoney's, and Marty crawled under the car. Customers in the restaurant, realizing who it was, came out and swamped him.

What impressed Adams most, however, was Marty's love of music. "He was a true musician," Adams says. "The rest of them just did it for a living, as far as I was concerned. But Marty loved it. He'd set there and sing an hour before he'd go on stage. I never seen anybody that liked music as well as he did, besides me. And he not only played piano, he played pretty good lap-type steel guitar, Hawaiian style." Adams especially appreciated Marty being a nondrinker. At the end of each show date they immediately drove to the next location. Adams thinks Marty did that to "keep shenanigans down. If you wasn't staying over, you didn't get in trouble."[22]

"He was a fanatic about being on time," Hobbs recalls. "If you didn't hear the bus, sometimes it started pulling out without you. Of course, they never left anybody behind, but they wanted you to know you needed to be there on time. He was a kindhearted person, too." Hobbs recalls an incident where a security person at a concert chastised a fan for taking a picture. Marty made a joke out of it because he didn't want to embarrass anybody. He told the security person, "Hey, don't talk to my people like that. Those are my fans. They come to see me. They can take all the pictures they want." He grabbed the camera and took his own picture.[23]

Cutright and Adams roomed together, and Adams remembers Marty's late-night visits. "He would take the strongest sleeping medication he could get his hands on, and it would knock him out for about an hour, and he'd be up again," Adams explains. "We'd hear him come shuffling down the hallway at three or four o'clock in the morning, and see if anybody was awake so he could talk to them. If he'd hear us in there laughing or talking, he'd knock on the door. We'd sit and talk and laugh."[24]

One of Jim Hannaford's fondest memories of Marty occurred in a Chicago nightclub dressing room. He wanted his hair to turn under in back, but it was flipping up, and Marty said, "Here, let me help you with your hair." Not having a blow dryer, Marty used a hairbrush to turn Hannaford's hair under, and he started breathing on it to provide moisture to hold it in place. Hannaford marvels, "I thought, here I am, all these thousands of fans wanting just to touch Marty Robbins, and he is fixing my hair. It was a profound moment for me."[25]

During the televised presentation of the CMA awards at the Opry House on October 11, 1982, Marty sang "Some Memories Just Won't Die." When time came to announce new Hall of Fame members, host Barbara Mandrell introduced Eddy Arnold. "Well, my good people," Arnold said, "it's really a joy for me to be a part of country music's biggest night of the year, and especially to be able to escort this particular fellow into the Hall of Fame. And I can't keep it a secret any longer. Marty Robbins, come up here." Arnold stated, "Believe it or not, this young man has been a singer, a composer, musician, and an actor for more than thirty years. His country songs were being played on pop stations before anyone ever invented the word crossover. He's written more than five hundred songs, including the one that put El Paso on the map. . . . Welcome to the Hall of Fame, Marty."[26]

"It means quite a lot, naturally, because everybody's not going to be in the Hall of Fame," Marty said later. "But I don't believe I deserve it yet, because there's three other people I think who deserve it before I get it. One is Little Jimmy Dickens. The other is Webb Piece, and one is Carl Smith." He added, "In fact, I was a little embarrassed and ashamed to take it the other night. I walked by Little Jimmy when he was sitting there, y'know, and I wished so much—if my name hadn't been on it, I would have given it to him." Still, he said, "I'm glad I have mine now. It wouldn't bother me to wait . . . but I don't run the operation, so I thought I better take it. They might not nominate me ten years from now or five years from now. So I went up and got it."[27]

He said in another interview, "I thought, y'know, to me, it was a little too soon for me because I don't have plans of quitting any time soon, and I'm still pretty active in the business, and I still do 120 show dates a year because I love it, y'know, and turn down probably 220 show dates a year."[28]

The 1982 CMA awards show was also a big night for WSM's Chuck Morgan, named Country Music Deejay of the Year. Morgan had replaced Ralph Emery on the all-night radio show where he inherited Marty's prank phone calls and late-night visits. Morgan remembers seeing Marty as they both headed to an after party. Marty said, "Hey, man, you and me, the same year! What do you think?" Morgan replied, "It's fitting, Marty. It's perfect."

When WSM had started a nationwide show several years earlier, to be delivered by satellite, Morgan had invited Marty to the grand opening. "He didn't feel comfortable with this," Morgan says. "Suddenly we'd gone from just being on WSM to a hundred stations across the country." Marty refused to appear on the network show until he listened to it several times. Then, Morgan says, "Once he started coming by the network show, it was like old times."[29]

"Ranger Doug" Green of the group Riders in the Sky recalls an evening with Marty and Ricky Skaggs on Morgan's show. "We all sang 'Red River Valley,' which was a cool trio and one of the highlights of my career," he says. "The Riders hadn't been going very long. Ricky sang tenor, and Marty sang lead, and I sang baritone. I'll never forget it."[30]

In spite of accolades, Marty still struggled with his lifelong insecurities, as evidenced by his comments in a mid-1982 interview:

> I go out to WBAP in Fort Worth sometimes and sit in with Bill Mack, y'know, just requests over the phone. I had a real good time with Ralph, y'know, because it was nothing but request night, y'know. I still do it once in a while now with Chuck Morgan. They don't have a piano in the studio now, but I usually take my guitar when I go to visit with him. It's a lot of fun to do that, and I think the people get a kick out of it, because, whether they like my singing or not, y'know, they might like me as a friend, y'know, after they hear the show. It's not really a show, y'know, it's just getting together with somebody.[31]

Four days after the CMA awards, Marty and his band left on a ten-day tour of Canada and the Northwest. His back bothered him the entire tour. Shortly before leaving Nashville, he'd strained it picking up his motorcycle. "All through this Canadian tour, in the middle of our show," Cutright recalls, "Don Winters had a ten-minute yodeling segment, and Marty and I would leave the stage, and he would do exercises to try and alleviate his back troubles." He would be either flushed or pale, and he'd answer Cutright's questions of concern by blaming the motorcycle. "He'd even lay across a chair, belly-down," Cutright says, "and have me put my thumb in a certain spot and rub, so he could finish the show." If Marty worried about his heart, he didn't say so.[32]

Racing still occupied his thoughts. He'd intended to run two races in 1982, but he hadn't been able to start at Michigan. So he decided to try the Atlanta Journal 500 in early November. Racing was an expensive hobby for both Marty and Cotton Owens, and Owens wanted to quit. "He said if I'd go to one more race with him, it would mean more than his induction into the Country Music Hall of Fame," Owens said in a magazine interview. "How could I refuse?" They got the car ready, and Marty easily qualified at the Atlanta track. "All of us were proud of that," Owens stated, "because competition had gotten so stiff it was hard for a nonregular to get in." Marty was knocked out of the race when another car hit him after eighty-nine laps.[33]

"I like competition," Marty said later, "and I like to be as close to it as I can, without getting so involved I forget I'm not a professional driver. . . . I'm a good amateur. I don't want to get too deep into it because I'll forget I'm in the music business, and that's how I make my living, and that's what I really love, also. Racing is show business to me also."[34]

On November 18, Marty spoke via satellite with Charlie Cooke on KLAC Radio's *Talking Country* show in Los Angeles. He said his new single, the title song from Clint Eastwood's new movie, *Honkytonk Man,* would be released in a few days. "That's the only thing I have left this year," he said. "Then I'm starting a new album, and we'll have it completed in another couple weeks and a single will come out of that sometime after the first of the year." When asked if he ever thought of recording a duet, he joked, "Well, if I could think of somebody that would sing with me, I'd ask 'em. But I can't think of anybody."

During the interview, he told Cooke, "I have been near death six times in my life, and really should have been taken away, but God decided it's not my time to go. Maybe he might have something for me to do. . . . In the wrecks I've had, up to 180 miles an hour, y'know, with the automobile completely wiped out, I've had enough time to say, 'Not yet, God,' and I'm thankful he didn't take me at the time. I believe he's gonna take care of me, and when it's time for me to go, I will be the way he wants me to be."[35]

[25]

"I'll Be Drifting Home"

Marty wrapped up his 1982 touring with a post-Thanksgiving weekend in Pennsylvania and a quick trip to Cincinnati, while holding a recording session between them. On the evening of November 30, he recorded five songs, telling producer Bob Montgomery he thought those songs were even stronger than the previous album. They planned to record the remaining songs Friday, after Marty's return from Cincinnati. Montgomery observed Marty as being tired but in great spirits and excited about "making the best record he could possibly make." Marty's bus left at 10:00 PM for a show twelve hours later.[1]

Marty and his band performed December 1 for 1,700 members of the American Bus Tour Association at the Cincinnati Convention Center. Mike Cutright and Gary Adams met their bandmates at the venue, where Marty greeted Adams by saying, "I recorded your song last night. I did a good job on it. You're gonna like it." He planned to put "Baby, That's Love" on the album.

Both Adams and Cutright remember the Cincinnati show as "a strange day." The piano was out of tune, the band was out of tune, and there were problems with sound and lighting. "I was the sound check guy, and the monitor man was argumentative," Cutright says, "and it was a bad day all around. It made Marty kind of mad."[2]

Jack Pruett thinks Marty was uncomfortable because he didn't have his fans in the audience. The convention crowd didn't care who was onstage. Pruett says, "I couldn't get in tune, and when one's out, everybody's out. Knowing he was all uptight kinda tightened up everything else. . . . All I remember about that show was hoping we could get ourselves in tune. There ain't nothin' worse than an out-of-tune band."[3]

"That was probably the shortest show we ever did," says Wayne Hobbs. Marty usually sang for an hour and a half to more than two hours. Hobbs remembers beginning in the normal way, with "Ribbon of Darkness" followed by "White Sport Coat" and then a medley. The band was surprised when Marty turned around and cued "Some Memories Just Won't Die" as his next song. He usually sang his current hit later in the show. "We all looked at each other like, boy, that's way out of place," Hobbs says. "I think we did one more song after that, and then he turns around and says, '"El Paso," Bandy.'" They really wondered then, as Pruett kicked off the final song. "People were looking at us like, wow, that was a short show," Hobbs recalls. "I would say we did about thirty minutes. And that's nothing for Marty; he just starts getting warmed up by then. But he didn't say anything to nobody. He didn't let on like he felt bad. He did look like he obviously needed sleep. We took it that he was tired, because he was up all night doing his last album."[4]

They gathered on the bus and briefly discussed upcoming plans before heading back to Nashville. Marty was scheduled for the Saturday night Opry, which would be the Opry debut for Cutright and Adams. The pair would drive to Nashville, and Marty told them to take their belongings off the bus, because he planned to put it in the shop and have it redone. He was taking a six-week Christmas break, and they also talked of a trip to Australia. Hobbs remembers Marty saying he planned to make a second movie with Clint Eastwood and would limit his show dates mostly to the Opry for the next six months. Marty promised to put his band on salary and give everyone a raise. "Everything was looking so great for the following year," Hobbs says, "so everybody left that day thinking, it's going to be a great year." As Hobbs walked off the bus to spend a few days with his parents, Marty told him, "Wayne, my boy, I'll see you Saturday night."[5]

Back home Marty called Cotton Owens, who said the Dodge Magnum was almost ready to deliver. NASCAR's Bill France had asked Marty to exhibit it at the International Motorsports Hall of Fame and Museum in Talladega. "That's what I thought he was calling me for," Owens remembers. He asked what else was on Marty's mind, and received the response, "Oh, I just called to see how you're doing, and wanted to chat a little bit."[6]

The next morning, Marty woke with chest pains so severe that Marizona called an ambulance. She called Ronny, saying, "I think Daddy's having another heart attack." Ronny arrived at St. Thomas Hospital the same time as the ambulance. "Dad, in his usual bull-headed way, was helping the EMS guys transfer him from gurney to gurney, saying he was fine," he remembers. "A little while later when they wheeled him into surgery was the last time I saw him conscious."[7]

Marty was admitted at 11:32 AM on Thursday, December 2 and taken into surgery less than two hours later. A clot in a coronary artery had shut off blood flow to part of his heart muscle. After an initial arteriogram, Marty was briefly wheeled out to allow Marizona and Ronny to talk to him. "Just long enough to say everything's going to be all right," Ronny remembers. "I could tell he was hurting, but with him being so alert, I didn't comprehend this was going to be the last one. I told him I loved him and he said, 'Take care of everything.' That spooked me."[8]

A twelve-person surgical team performed a quadruple bypass in the midst of Marty's ongoing heart attack. During the eight-and-a-half-hour operation, his three bypass grafts from thirteen years earlier were repaired and a fourth one added. Cardiologist Harry Lee Page told reporters the amount of damage couldn't yet be determined, but he hoped Marty would be able to resume most normal activities, and he estimated a two-week hospital stay. The hospital reported Marty's condition on Friday as "critical but stable."[9]

Members of Marty's band represented their boss at the premier of Clint Eastwood's new movie, *Honkytonk Man,* held on Thursday night, two weeks before its release to theaters.[10] Eastwood played a dying singer during the Great Depression, with Marty appearing as a guitarist on a recording session in the movie. Marty's recording of the title song was scheduled for release as a single on December 17.

Marty's heartbeat deteriorated Friday night to the extent that electric shock was required to restore its rhythm. His condition was downgraded to "critical" on Saturday and "extremely critical" on Sunday. Drugs, along with a device that pumped blood between heartbeats, kept his vital signs stable. The balloon pump had been inserted into his artery before surgery to lighten the workload on his heart. "We would have hoped to have gotten him off the balloon by this time," Page stated Monday. He warned listeners Marty might have physical limitations that would affect his career. Hospital officials reported he could respond to questions but was heavily sedated.[11]

Lamar Jackson, St. Thomas public affairs director, explained in a press conference that Marty had been given a ten percent chance of survival prior to Thursday's surgery. When he came through surgery and appeared to be improving on Friday, they increased the odds to fifty-fifty. By Monday, however, doctors refused to speculate. "It's minute-to-minute and wait-and-see," Jackson said. Doctor William Ewers, Marty's longtime personal physician, said, "I thought he was going to make it, but all the odds are pulling against him now. Only time will tell."[12]

Janet arrived from her home in California and joined Marizona and Ronny at the hospital, where they took turns visiting Marty's bedside. She remembers rubbing her father's swollen feet as she talked to him, sensing he could hear even if he couldn't respond.[13] Calls came from around the world, the hospital held regular press conferences, and national networks reported Marty's condition on morning and evening newscasts. "The phones never stopped ringing," says Sandy Daens about the Marty Robbins Enterprises office. "Fans would call, friends, everybody was calling. Fans would call sometimes several times a day, trying to get updates on him. It was hard because we knew how serious it was, but we still had to project an upbeat image." Daily updates came from the hospital. "I don't think it was ever said he was not expected to live," Daens states. "There were occasional improvements that made us get our hopes up, but we still knew it was really, really bad."

When Daens moved from Florida earlier in the year, the nineteen-year-old fan volunteered to update scrapbooks and photo albums on display in Marty's gift shop. Marty then hired her to help Carol Hutson run the gift shop. She enjoyed Marty's serious moments. "We could talk heart to heart," she reminisces, "and he'd tell me about his hopes, fears, dreams. . . . He had his piano there, and sometimes he would practice songs for a show. But my favorite memories were when he got that little guitar out."[14]

An ABC Information Network news report late Monday evening announced, "Hospital officials say Robbins continues to show no improvement in his heart function and his kidneys are said to be beginning to fail. They also say, though, that barring any unforeseen developments, he should live through the night."[15]

With Marty's heart unable to pump enough blood to move fluids through his kidneys, doctors inserted a tube into his abdomen on Tuesday to remove fluid buildup. "There continues to be no improvement in cardiac function," Jackson announced. "Things have continued to go downhill." The flood of calls to the hospital switchboard began to include offers of kidney donations. One woman even offered to donate her heart.[16]

The news of failing kidneys, Ronny recalls, "was the first time I realized this may not turn out the way it always had in the past." He spent much of his time on the telephone in the waiting room. "I remember doing some interviews with Channel Four about the third or fourth day," he says. "I know I talked with Ralph Emery on the air a couple of times. Johnny Cash came by one night, probably one o'clock in the morning."[17]

Although Marty's heart still couldn't beat without assistance, the aorta would be damaged if the balloon pump wasn't removed soon, so doctors planned to reduce the pumping rate to see how the heart responded. This may have led to a misperception about Marty's condition. When Cutright called the office for an update, the overly optimistic Evelyn Lamb told him Marty was improving and would soon be off life support. She thought he might enjoy a visit. Cutright decided to drive to Nashville the following week, after completing a performance commitment in Dayton.[18]

Mamie Minotto, Marty's twin sister, arrived from Arizona on Tuesday. By Wednesday morning, in addition to the balloon pump and heavy sedation, a respirator was helping Marty breathe and a dialysis machine worked to remove excess fluids. Ronny was on his way out of the hospital at six in the evening, to go home for his first shower in three days, when a nurse stopped him. Whatever her words, the look on her face told him not to leave. "I realized then that this is not good," he says.[19]

"I remember feeling like he was either hanging on or—something wasn't right," Janet recalls. "I felt unsettled by it." She had been praying all week for her father's survival. That evening she went into the little hospital chapel and prayed if it was in his best interest to leave, she didn't want to hold him back. She left the chapel, walked to the elevator, and pushed the button. When the doors opened, Janet saw her mother inside the elevator. Marizona was crying because she had just been informed of Marty's death and was on her way to his room.[20]

Martin David Robinson died of cardiac arrest at 11:15 PM on Wednesday, December 8, 1982.

"His heart just stopped beating," Lamar Jackson told the press. When Chuck Morgan received the news during his all-night WSM radio show, he announced in shock that Marty had passed away. "We just kind of shut down operations and let people call in and tell Marty Robbins stories," Morgan recalls about that night. Cutright was driving home from Dayton to Chillicothe, Ohio, in the early hours of Thursday morning when he turned the dial to WSM Radio and heard Morgan say, "Marty Robbins's ravaged heart gave up on him." Cutright pulled off the road and turned up the radio. "I sat in that cold, snowy cornfield and bawled for an hour and a half," he says.[21]

Jackson gave ten interviews from his home that night, including two with callers in Birmingham, England, and Brisbane, Australia. He estimated hospital personnel conducted more than a thousand telephone interviews during the last week of Marty's life.[22]

When Ronny and Janet were leaving the hospital to go to their mother's house, a pay telephone rang as they walked down the hall. Something compelled Janet in her shock to pick it up. The caller was crying and screaming that Marty Robbins had died. Janet put the receiver back on the hook without a word.[23]

Marty often used a drifter theme in his songs and movies. A cowboy in "The Dreamer" sings, "But I want to see Mother—tomorrow I start driftin' home." The race car driver in "Twentieth Century Drifter" says his wife prays "that come Monday mornin,' I'll be driftin' home."

The drifter had finally made it home.

[26]

Some Memories Just Won't Die

A cold steady rain fell in Nashville on Saturday morning, December 11, 1982. Mourners began filling the Woodlawn Funeral Home two hours before the eleven o'clock funeral service. The Woodlawn Chapel of Roses held three hundred people, and more than a thousand crowded other rooms and hallways. They competed for space with elaborate flower arrangements that lined the hallways and filled the rooms. Marty Robbins music played softly over the speaker system. Before the service, fans were allowed to enter the chapel and pass by the closed casket covered with pink flowers.

A floral arrangement behind the casket formed a white sport coat with a pink carnation, and a guitar made from brown-colored daisies stood nearby.

Willie Nelson sent a map of Texas, made of white carnations with gold letters spelling out "El Paso" across its length. A checkered NASCAR flag of black and white carnations came from Bobby Allison. An arrangement of autumn flowers contained an open Bible.[1]

"I remember having such a sense of respect from people who were there," Janet says, "of seeing the smile on people's faces when certain songs would come on, and people would just kind of glow. I was really appreciative of that."

A childhood friend asked Janet if she remembered sending a cassette tape to her father. She told him she'd bought a tape recorder and recorded several songs for him when she moved to California two years earlier. "I got brave," she said, "and I wrote a song." Marty never told her he received the tape. The friend said, "I walked into your dad's office one day, and he said, 'I've got something to play for you.'" Marty played the tape and then said, "That's my daughter. She's so talented I don't even know how to tell her." And he never did.[2]

Public visitation had been held the day before, with private viewings on Thursday and Friday evenings. Marizona and her children were present but numb. After Marty's death late Wednesday evening, it was the early hours of the next morning by the time they gathered his belongings and went home. They met at Woodlawn at nine o'clock Thursday morning to make arrangements. Expecting a huge crowd, they chose not to have the funeral in a church with a procession across town to the cemetery. A service at a funeral home with an adjoining cemetery allowed people to walk to the burial site.

Ralph Emery arrived shortly after they did, following his early morning television show. Ronny had briefly watched the show, seeing Emery so broken up he could hardly talk. "He stayed with me until about four o'clock that afternoon," Ronny recalls. "I picked the casket out while Mama and Janet were doing other arrangements, and we walked up to the site to the available plots. He didn't make any decisions; he was just there to talk to. I've always thanked him, and I used to try to do it on the air, but he would cut me off. He didn't want any praise, but it meant a lot to me that he did that."[3]

Carol Hutson arrived at the Marty Robbins Enterprises office Thursday morning to find a beautiful pink carnation wreath on the door, placed by a local florist. "It was eerie walking into that building," she says. "I did still feel his presence there.[4]

"We had visitation for two days straight," Ronny says. "I think I talked to probably five [thousand] to eight thousand people over a two-day period." Eddy and Sally Arnold attended Thursday night's viewing, as did many friends of Ronny and Janet. Most of Marty's industry associates mixed with the public on Friday. Marty lay in a silver casket in front of plum-colored curtains in the small parlor. He wore a black suit with white pinstripes and an open-collared ruffled shirt. A reporter on Friday noted that Janet "gently stroked the arm of her father's jacket while looking into his face." A fan who never met Marty stated, "In his songs he made you feel like you were part of his family." A woman from Los Angeles told Ronny, "I had to come when I heard about his death."[5]

Jeff and Nancy Chandler arrived from New Mexico and went to the funeral home Friday afternoon. "There were a lot of fans we'd seen over the years, but there wasn't anybody from the band," Chandler says. "I was looking for them, to go through this process with them. That night was a private viewing for friends and family, and that's where I saw everybody again." When Roy Acuff came into the room, Chandler remembers, "Roy completely broke down, just sobbing, because he loved Marty. And Marty loved him."[6]

During Saturday morning's funeral, the pastor giving the eulogy said Marty "mended thousands of broken hearts each year, as he sang the songs that touched the very soul of America." The choir from the Foursquare Gospel Church, where Marty and Marizona normally attended services, sang several hymns, and Brenda Lee sang "One Day at a Time." Five black limousines carried the family through the cold, blowing rain to the Woodlawn Memorial Park hillside for a private graveside service.[7]

"A sad day and the weather matched the mood," Sandy Daens says. "Fans flew in from out of state. I was amazed at how many people who didn't live in the area attended."[8]

Pallbearers, all wearing pink carnations, were Don Winters and Bobby Sykes, Jim Farmer and Jack Pruett, Ralph Emery and Chuck Morgan, Eddy Arnold and Dr. Ewers, along with Ronny's friend Morris Mashburn, and Okie Jones, who carried his beloved chief one last time.

* * *

Marty's career continued after his death. "Honkytonk Man," issued on schedule as a single, entered *Billboard*'s country chart on Christmas Day and peaked at number ten. Columbia released a single in February, "Change Of Heart" backed with Jay Dee Hoag's "Devil in a Cowboy Hat." Hoag had last seen Marty at a show in Seattle where Marty asked, "Have you written any more tunes, Hoag? Sing me something you've written lately." Hoag sang "Devil in a Cowboy Hat," and Marty told him to send a tape of the song. "He did a scratch vocal, I think, before he did the Atlanta race," Hoag explains, "[and] my record got to be on his last album."[9]

Bob Montgomery chose several previously recorded songs to finish the album begun in November. Because "Some Memories Just Won't Die" had become a catchphrase to represent Marty's life, Montgomery placed it on its second consecutive album and made it the title track. *Some Memories Just Won't Die* was released in April 1983. "What If I Said I Love You" was Marty's last single release, with the B side his recording of Gary Adams's "Baby That's Love." Montgomery included "Honkytonk Man" on the album.

The *Pen Friends* newsletter for Marty's Army encouraged fans to acquire the January issue of *Music City News* and vote for Marty for the 1983 awards. On June 6, 1983, during the seventeenth annual fan-voted *Music City News* awards presentation, "Some Memories Just Won't Die" was named Single of the Year, and *Come Back To Me* won Album of the Year. For the third time in four years, Marty Robbins was honored as Male Vocalist of the Year.[10]

Sandy Daens eventually took over *Pen Friends*, which she published until 2003. She says, "I made a promise to Marty before he died—one of his biggest fears was to be forgotten—and I promised him I would do everything in my power to see he wasn't forgotten. I put many years of my life into dealing with fans and radio stations and providing materials for all kinds of research projects on Marty." She remembers a television show called *The Life and Times of Marty Robbins*, for which camera crews came to her house to film parts of her collection.[11]

In 2008, the Country Music Hall of Fame and Museum presented a yearlong exhibition called *Marty Robbins: Among My Souvenirs*. The Friends of Marty Robbins Gift Shop and Museum holds an annual celebration in Willcox, Arizona, and tribute shows routinely play around the nation. The racing world hasn't forgotten Marty either. He was elected to the Fairgrounds Speedway Hall of Fame in Nashville in 2009.

Forty years after the Academy of Country Music named Marty Robbins its first Man of the Decade, it honored him in September 2010 with the Cliffie Stone Pioneer Award.

Some memories just won't die.

The End

Appendix: Band Members

Steel guitar

Jack Evins (early 1953)
Joe Vincent (June 1953–December 1954)
Jim Farmer (1955–59)
Pete Drake (1960)
Bill Johnson (September 1960–late 1961; early 1964–July 1974)
Don Powell (July 1974–December 1974)
Katsuhiko "Katz" Kobayashi (January 1975–February 1982)
Wayne Hobbs (March 1982–end)

Upright bass (approximate dates)

Floyd "Lightnin'" Chance (January 1953–55)
Lester Wilburn (1956)
Hillous Butrum (1955–60)
Howard "Cedric Rainwater" Watts (1960)
Henry Dorrough (1961–70)

Electric bass

Larry Hunt (1970–end)

Drums

Buddy Harmon (1957)
Louie Dunn (1957–66)
Buddy Rogers (1967–68)
Eddy Fox (1969–77)
Bill Martinez (1978–end)

Lead guitar

None (1953–55)
Joe Wright (December 1955–late 1956)
Jack Pruett (late 1956–end)

Second lead guitar

John "Jay Dee" Hoag (January–November 1975)

Gary Adams (September 1982–end)

Rhythm guitar

Ray Edenton (January 1953–late 1955)

Hillous Butrum (late 1955–58)

Lee Emerson (1956–57) (opened shows)

Bobby Sykes (August 1958–59, 1961–78, June–September 1982)

Jimmy Selph (1960–61)

Jeff Chandler (January 1979–May 1982)

Mike Cutright (September 1982–end)

Fiddle

Don Slayman (1953 or 1954)

Don Haggard (1953 or 1954)

Earl White (1955–56)

Grover "Shorty" Lavender (approx. 1956)

Ken McDuffy (1974)

Piano

Floyd Cramer (approx. 1957)

Joe Babcock (1961–65)

Bobby Braddock (1966)

Del Delamont (December 1975–late 1978)

Wayne Jackson (January–March 1979)

Conrad Noddin (April 1979–May 1982)

Jim Hannaford (February 1982–end)

Trumpet

Del Delamont (1975–78)

Wayne Jackson (1979–February 1982)

Conrad Noddin (April 1979–May 1982)

Jim Hannaford (February–May 1982)

Banjo

Haskel McCormick (December 1973–December 1974)

Harmony

> Glaser Brothers (1958–60) (opened shows)
> Joe Babcock (January 1959–65)
> Bobby Sykes (August 1958–59, 1961–78, June–September 1982)
> Jeff Chandler (January 1979–May 1982)
> Mike Cutright (September 1982–end)
> Don Winters (September 1960–end)

Original Teardrops band—December 1955

> Joe Wright   lead guitar
> Earl White   fiddle/rhythm guitar
> Hillous Butrum   upright bass
> Jim Farmer   steel guitar

Final Marty Robbins Band—December 1982

> Jack Pruett   lead guitar
> Larry Hunt   bass guitar
> Jim Hannaford   keyboard
> Wayne Hobbs   steel guitar
> Bill Martinez   drums
> Mike Cutright   rhythm guitar/harmony
> Gary Adams   rhythm/lead guitar
> Don Winters   harmony

Notes

Chapter 1. In the Hall of Fame

1. Country Music Association awards show, October 11, 1982, video excerpt in *Marty Robbins: Super Legend* (1989).
2. Bill Anderson, email to author, November 4, 2009.
3. Charlie Louvin, telephone interview with author, November 14, 2006.
4. Michael Erlewine, Vladimir Bogdanov, Chris Woodstra, and Stephen Thomas Erlewine, ed., *All Music Guide to Country* (San Francisco: Miller Freeman Books, 1997), 398.
5. Louie Roberts, telephone interview with author, December 11, 2006.
6. Bobby Allison, telephone interview with author, November 10, 2006; James Hylton, telephone interview with author, March 6, 2007.
7. Cotton Owens, telephone interview with author, December 7, 2006.
8. Al Reinert, "What Makes Marty Robbins Race Against Richard Petty?" *Country Music*, October 1973.
9. Marty Robbins, *Miller and Company*, with host Dan Miller, TNN, 1981.
10. Marty Robbins, *The Ralph Emery Show*, WSM Radio, October 26, 1981.

Chapter 2. Child of the Arizona Desert

1. Lillie Robinson Nevitt, "Mom's Book," unpublished manuscript.
2. Andrew Means, *Some Memories: Growing Up with Marty Robbins* (Booklocker .com, 2007), 32–34.
3. Ibid., 41.
4. Nevitt, "Mom's Book"; and Means, *Some Memories*, 45.
5. Nevitt, "Mom's Book."
6. Means, *Some Memories*, 49.
7. Nevitt, "Mom's Book."
8. Ibid.
9. Ibid.; *Fifteenth Census of the United States: 1930 Population Schedule*, April 21, 1930.
10. Nevitt, "Mom's Book."

11. Means, *Some Memories*, 17, 71, 58.
12. Ibid., 50; Ann Todd, letter in Marty Robbins fan club newsletter, "The Drifter," Fall/Winter 1971; "Marty Robbins 75th Birthday Tribute," hosted by Eddie Stubbs, WSM Radio, Nashville, September 26, 2000.
13. Nevitt, "Mom's Book"; Means, *Some Memories*, 59.
14. Marty Robbins, *The Ralph Emery Show,* WSM Radio, December 20, 1979, September 16, 1976; Means, *Some Memories*, 60.
15. Nevitt, "Mom's Book"; Means, *Some Memories*, 55.
16. Nevitt, "Mom's Book"; Means, *Some Memories*, 57–58.
17. Ibid; Means, *Some Memories*, 63; Marty Robbins, *Miller and Company,* with host Dan Miller, TNN, 1981.
18. Nevitt, "Mom's Book"; Means, *Some Memories*, 63, 64.
19. Nevitt, "Mom's Book"; Means, *Some Memories*, 21.
20. Means, *Some Memories*, 17–19.
21. Ibid., 56.
22. Marty Robbins, *The Ralph Emery Show,* December 16, 1977.
23. Nevitt, "Mom's Book"; Means, *Some Memories*, 71, 73.
24. Means, *Some Memories*, 88–89.
25. Ibid., 75; Nevitt, "Mom's Book."
26. Nevitt, "Mom's Book"; Marty Robbins, interview with Bob Allen, Nashville, February 12, 1981; Marty Robbins, interview, Country Music Foundation Oral History Project, Nashville, November 26, 1975.
27. Earl Romine, telephone interview with author, November 11, 2008.
28. Means, *Some Memories*, 76–77, 26.
29. Ibid., 84.

Chapter 3. A Drifter

1. Marty Robbins, *Miller and Company,* with host Dan Miller, TNN, 1981.
2. Marty Robbins, guest of Bill Mack, WBAP Radio, Fort Worth, TX, February 11, 1982.
3. Marty Robbins, *Miller and Company*; Marty Robbins, guest of Bill Mack.
4. Marty Robbins, "Gene Autry My Hero," BMI Work #459610, Mariposa Music Inc.
5. Andrew Means, *Some Memories: Growing Up with Marty Robbins* (Booklocker .com, Inc., 2007), 90.
6. Marty Robbins, *The Ralph Emery Show,* WSM Radio, August 12, 1980; Marty Robbins, interview with Bob Allen, Nashville, February 12, 1981.
7. Marty Robbins, *The Ralph Emery Show,* December 17, 20, 1979; Marty Robbins, *Miller and Company*; Linda Cornett, "Marty Robbins: Something Unique in Country," *The Record Delta,* June 4, 1980.

8. Means, *Some Memories*, 97; Marty Robbins, *The Ralph Emery Show*, August 14, 1980; Manuel Martinez, telephone interview with author, October 31, 2008.

9. Marty Robbins, interview, Country Music Foundation Oral History Project, Nashville, November 26, 1975.

10. Stella Rodriguez, conversation with author, Glendale, AZ, October 1, 2008; Marty Robbins, *Talking Country*, with Charlie Cooke, KLAC Radio, Los Angeles, November 18, 1982; Martinez, telephone interview with author, October 31, 2008.

11. Marty Robbins, interview with Bill Black, *Country Sounds*, Radio Clyde, Glasgow, Scotland, 1978; Marty Robbins, interview with Bob Allen, February 12, 1981.

12. Means, *Some Memories*, 97–98.

13. Marty Robbins, interview with Bob Allen, February 12, 1981.

14. Marty Robbins, *The Ralph Emery Show*, September 21, 1973.

15. Marty Robbins, interview with Bob Allen, February 12, 1981.

16. Means, *Some Memories*, 102–3.

17. Marty Robbins, *Miller and Company*; Marty Robbins, *The Ralph Emery Show*, September 13, 1976.

18. Marty Robbins, interview with Bob Allen, February 12, 1981.

19. Marty Robbins, guest of Bill Mack, February 11, 1982.

20. Mamie Robinson-Minotto, *Marty Robbins: Photographic Journal of Marty's Family—A Private Collection*, 1985, 17; USS *Crescent City* (APA 21) ship's log, "Remarks," p. 525, September 28, 1943.

21. CINCPACFLT, *Ship to Shore Movement: General Instructions for Transports, Cargo Vessels, and Landing Craft of Amphibious Forces*, January 1943, para. 201, 1103-d-1, 306-i-1, 412; Marty Robbins, *The Ralph Emery Show*, October 30, 1981.

22. USS *Crescent City* (APA 21), "Operational Remarks (War Diary)," p. 567, October 19, 1943; p. 599, November 1, 1943; ship's log, "Administrative Remarks," p. 295, November 1, 1943.

23. Marty Robbins, *Miller and Company*.

24. USS *Crescent City* (APA 21) ship's log, "Administrative Remarks," p. 295, November 1, 1943.

25. Marty Robbins, *Miller and Company*.

26. USS *Crescent City* (APA 21) ship's log, "Administrative Remarks," p. 295, November 1, 1943.

27. James H. Belote and William M. Belote, *Titans of the Seas* (New York: Harper & Row, 1975), 190, 227; Ronny Robbins, email to author, November 15, 2006; Marty Robbins, *Miller and Company*.

28. Martin D. Robinson, letter, "Readers Letters," *Glendale Herald*, approx. March 1944.

29. Marty Robbins, *The Ralph Emery Show,* October 30, 1981; Jack Pruett, telephone interview with author, November 5, 2006.

30. Marty Robbins, *The Ralph Emery Show,* September 15, 1976, December 14, 1977; Marty Robbins, *Talking Country.*

31. "Mother's Interest Lies With Sons In Service," *Glendale Herald,* September 1944.

32. Bill Davenport, telephone interview with author, November 11, 2006.

33. Johnny "K" (Koval), "Mini-View: Marty Robbins," *Country Song Roundup,* July 1974; "Young Navy Man Terminates Leave," *Glendale Herald,* September 1945.

34. Don Winters, "NASCAR's Own Balladeer," *Stock Cars '73,* 1973, 85; Marty Robbins, *The Ralph Emery Show,* December 20, 1979.

35. Marty Robbins, guest of Bill Mack, February 11, 1982; Marty Robbins, *The Ralph Emery Show,* September 14, 1976; interview with Bob Allen, February 12, 1981.

36. Marty Robbins, *The Ralph Emery Show,* September 17, 1973, August 14, 1980.

Chapter 4. Music and Marizona

1. Marty Robbins, *The Ralph Emery Show,* WSM Radio, September 14–16, 1976, August 13, 1980, and December 15, 1977.

2. William L. Turner and Gayla Pankey, *Face To Face With Country* (Branson, MO: Branson Publishing Company, 1994), 197; Marty Robbins, *The Ralph Emery Show,* December 15, 1977, August 14, 1980.

3. Marty Robbins, *Miller and Company,* with host Dan Miller, TNN, 1981.

4. Marty Robbins, *The Ralph Emery Show,* August 14, 1980, June 16, 1982; interview with Bob Allen, Nashville, February 12, 1981.

5. Marty Robbins, *The Ralph Emery Show,* September 16, 1976, June 16, 1982.

6. Andrew Means, *Some Memories: Growing Up with Marty Robbins* (Booklocker .com, Inc., 2007), 110–11.

7. Marty Robbins, interview with Bob Allen, February 12, 1981.

8. Means, *Some Memories,* 111; Judy Myers, "A Talk With Marty Robbins," *Country Songs Roundup,* June 1969, 9.

9. Marty Robbins, interview with Bob Allen, February 12, 1981; Marty Robbins, *The Ralph Emery Show,* September 18, 1973.

10. Marty Robbins, interview with Bob Allen, February 12, 1981.

11. Frankie Starr, unpublished personal audio recording, 1985.

12. Marty Robbins, *The Ralph Emery Show,* September 16, 1976.

13. Marty Robbins, guest of Bill Mack, WBAP Radio, Fort Worth, TX, 1976.

14. Marty Robbins, *Miller and Company.*

15. Frankie Starr, interview with John P. Dixon in Phoenix, AZ, in "The Frankie Starr Story," *Elevator Boogie: Frankie Starr* (Germany: Bear Family Records, 1996); John P. Dixon, telephone conversation with author, December 11, 2008.

16. Marty Robbins, *The Ralph Emery Show*, August 11, 1980, December 20, 1979.

17. Marizona Robinson, interview, video excerpt in *Marty Robbins: Super Legend*, VHS, Marty Robbins, Inc., 1989.

18. Marizona Robinson, "Marty Robbins 75th Birthday Tribute," hosted by Eddie Stubbs, WSM Radio, Nashville, September 26, 2000.

19. Marty Robbins, *The Ralph Emery Show*, December 20, 1979; Marizona Robinson, "Marty Robbins 75th Birthday Tribute."

20. Means, *Some Memories*, 120.

21. Marizona Robinson, "Marty Robbins 75th Birthday Tribute"; Marty Robbins, *The Ralph Emery Show*, September 18, 1973; Frankie Starr, unpublished personal audio recording, 1985.

22. Marizona Robinson, "Marty Robbins 75th Birthday Tribute."

23. Means, *Some Memories*, 120.

24. Marty Robbins, guest of Bill Mack, and interview with Bob Allen, February 12, 1981.

25. Marizona Robinson, "Marty Robbins 75th Birthday Tribute."

26. Bill Hickman, telephone interview with author, October 15, 2008.

27. Marty Robbins, interview with Bob Allen, February 12, 1981.

28. Ibid.

Chapter 5. On Columbia Records

1. Marty Robbins, interview, Country Music Foundation Oral History Project, Nashville, November 26, 1975.

2. Marizona Robinson, "Marty Robbins 75th Birthday Tribute," hosted by Eddie Stubbs, WSM Radio, September 26, 2000.

3. Andrew Means, *Some Memories: Growing Up with Marty Robbins* (Booklocker.com, Inc., 2007), 101–2.

4. Frankie Starr, interview with John P. Dixon in Phoenix, AZ, in "The Frankie Starr Story," *Elevator Boogie: Frankie Starr* (Germany: Bear Family Records, 1996); Means, *Some Memories*, 114; Colin Escott, *Marty Robbins Country 1951–1958* (Germany: Bear Family Records GMBH, 1991), 5; Marty Robbins, interview with Bob Allen, Nashville, February 12, 1981; Marty Robbins, *The Ralph Emery Show*, WSM Radio, September 18, 1973.

5. Betty Sexton Shalley, telephone interview with author, November 12, 2008.

6. Marty Robbins, *The Ralph Emery Show*, August 14, 1980; interview with Bob Allen.

7. Marty Robbins, interview with Bob Allen; interview with Susan Scott, "Top Country-Western Singer Marty Robbins Tells *Tattler* How Prayer Saved Son's Life," *National Tattler*, June 1975; and interview with Bill Black, *Country Sounds*, Radio Clyde, Glasgow, Scotland, 1978.

8. Joan Dew, "Marty Robbins Made a Deal With God," *Country Music*, November 1976, 22; Marty Robbins, interview with Bill Black, *Country Sounds*.

9. Marty Robbins, *The Ralph Emery Show*, December 21, 1979, October 29, 1981.

10. Little Jimmy Dickens, *The Ralph Emery Show*, WSM Radio, date unknown; Marty Robbins, interview with Bob Allen.; Marty Robbins, *The Ralph Emery Show*, August 14, 1980.

11. Marty Robbins, guest of Bill Mack, WBAP Radio, Fort Worth, TX, 1976.

12. *Marty Robbins Live Classics*, Track 1, Country Music Hall of Fame Classics Collection, audio CD (Audium Records, 2001).

13. Bill Hickman, telephone interview with author, October 15, 2008; Escott, *Marty Robbins Country 1951–1958*, 8.

14. Marty Robbins, interview with Bob Allen.

15. Peggy Ann Munson, "The 'Robbin' Sings," publication unknown, Fall 1954.

16. Bob Powel, "Bob Powel Interviews Marty Robbins," *Country Music People*, January 1973, 18.

17. Charlie Walker, telephone interview with author, September 22, 2006.

18. Alan Cackett, "Marty Robbins in Depth: Part One—Early Days," *Country Music People*, March 1975, 18; Joel Whitburn, *Top Country Singles 1944–2001*, 5th ed. (Menomonee Falls, WI: Record Research, 2002), 296; "On the Spot: Marty Robbins," *Cowboy Songs*, January 1956; "BAM Deep South Jamboree," http://www.hillbilly-music.com/programs/story/index.php?prog=580.

19. Whitburn, *Top Country Singles 1944–2001*, 269.

20. Eddie Kilroy, telephone interview with author, July 27, 2008; Johnny Bush, telephone interview with author, July 14, 2008.

21. Johnny "K" (Koval), "Mini-View: Marty Robbins," *Country Song Roundup*, July 1974.

22. Marty Robbins, guest of Bill Mack, 1976.

23. Marty Robbins, interview, Country Music Foundation Oral History Project, Nashville, November 26, 1975; Ralph Emery, with Tom Carter, *More Memories* (New York: Berkley Books, 1995), 15.

24. Marizona Robinson, interview, video excerpt shown in *Marty Robbins: Super Legend*, VHS, Marty Robbins, Inc., 1989; Shalley, telephone interview.

Chapter 6. Mr. Teardrop

1. Marty Robbins, interview with Bob Allen, Nashville, February 12, 1981.

2. "Celebrating 20th Opry Year," *Nashville Banner*, January 30, 1973; Little Jimmy Dickens, *The Ralph Emery Show*, WSM Radio, date unknown; "Artist of the Month—Marty Robbins," *Hillbilly and Cowboy Hit Parade*, Fall 1953; Joel

Whitburn, *Top Country Singles 1944–2001*, 5th ed. (Menomonee Falls, WI: Record Research, 2002), 296.

3. Ray Edenton, telephone interview with author, September 20, 2006; Floyd "Lightnin'" Chance, interview with Doug Green for Country Music Foundation Oral History Project, Nashville, March 4, 1975; Jack Evins, telephone interview with author, June 5, 2007; *The Hank Williams Appreciation Society International*, http://www.angelfire.com/me2/kulacoco/lum.txt.

4. Marty Robbins, interview with Bob Allen, February 12, 1981.

5. Edenton, telephone interview.

6. Evins, telephone interview.

7. Marty Robbins, *The Ralph Emery Show*, WSM Radio, June 16, 1982; Ralph Emery, with Tom Carter, *More Memories* (New York: Berkley Books, 1995), 15.

8. Marty Robbins, interview with Bob Allen, February 12, 1981; Charlie Walker, telephone interview with author, September 22, 2006.

9. Colin Escott, *Marty Robbins Country 1951–1958* (Germany: Bear Family Records GMBH, 1991), 10; Evins, telephone interview.

10. Joe Vincent, interviews with author, September 18, 2006, January 6, 2000, Marty Robbins band reunion, Nashville, July 18, 2009.

11. Marty Robbins, guest of Bill Mack, WBAP Radio, Fort Worth, TX, 1976; Marty Robbins, interview, Country Music Foundation Oral History Project, Nashville, November 26, 1975.

12. Vincent, telephone interview.

13. Earl White, Ronny Robbins, Marty Robbins band reunion, Nashville, July 18, 2009.

14. Edenton, telephone interview; Bill Hickman, telephone interview with author, October 15, 2008.

15. Vincent, interviews with author, Marty Robbins band reunion; Escott, *Marty Robbins Country 1951–1958*, 10.

16. Frankie Starr, unpublished personal tape recording, 1985.

17. Alanna Nash, "Marty Robbins: Silly on Stage; Serious in the Office," *Louisville Courier Journal*, February 26, 1978.

18. Escott, *Marty Robbins Country 1951–1958*, 12; Edenton, telephone interview.

19. "On the Spot—Marty Robbins," *Cowboy Songs*, January 1956.

20. Lee Cotton, *Did Elvis Sing in Your Hometown?* (Sacramento, CA: High Sierra Books, 1995), 83–84; Rose Maddox, interview with John Rumble, Country Music Foundation Oral History Project, Nashville, January 25, 1985.

21. Edenton, telephone interview; Buddy Holly Center, City of Lubbock, www.buddyhollycenter.org.

22. Edenton, telephone interview.

23. Marty Robbins, interview with Ruud Hermans, *KRO Countrytime,* October 1982; "Artist of the Month—Marty Robbins," *Hillbilly and Cowboy Hit Parade,* Fall 1953; Marty Robbins, interview with Ruud Hermans.

24. Joe Wright, telephone interview with author, December 8, 2006; Hillous Butrum, telephone interview with author, January 18, 2002.

25. Joe Wright, telephone interview with author, July 28, 2009; Earl White, Marty Robbins band reunion, Nashville, July 18, 2009.

26. Wright, telephone interview with author, December 8, 2006; Earl White, telephone interview with author, September 12, 2008.

27. Wright, telephone interviews, December 8, 2006, July 28, 2009.

28. Wright, telephone interview, December 8, 2006; White, Marty Robbins band reunion.

29. Marty Robbins band reunion.

30. Faron Young, *Country Style: Nashville Special,* November 1971; "On the Spot—Marty Robbins," *Cowboy Songs,* January 1956; Marty Robbins, interview with Ruud Hermans.

31. Wright, telephone interview, December 8, 2006; Marty Robbins, *The Ralph Emery Show,* June 15, 1982.

32. White, telephone interview, email to author, August 10, 2009; Wright, telephone interview, July 28, 2009.

33. White, telephone interview with author, September 12, 2008.

34. Goldie Hill Smith, telephone interview with author, May 22, 2003.

35. Albert C. Gannaway, producer and director, *Raiders of Old California,* Republic Pictures (Albert C. Gannaway Production, 1957); Faron Young, cohost, *Country Standard Time,* TNN, May 1990; *Marty Robbins: Super Legend,* VHS, Marty Robbins, Inc., 1989; Ralph Emery, with Patsi Bale Cox, *50 Years Down a Country Road* (New York: William Morrow, 2000), 117.

36. Otto Kitsinger, *Webb the Wondering "Boy" Pierce 1951–1958* (Germany: Bear Family Records GMBH, 1990), 32; Albert C. Gannaway, director, *Buffalo Gun,* Republic Pictures (Albert C. Gannaway Production, 1957).

37. Charlie Lamb, "Charlie's Column," *Country Music Reporter,* August 18, 1956.

38. "The Man With A 'Heart': Marty Robbins," *Cowboy Songs,* June 1958, 13; Don Roy and Richard Weize, "Marty Robbins: The Discography 1951–1958," *Marty Robbins Country 1951–1958* (Germany: Bear Family Records GMBH, 1991), 38.

39. Wright, telephone interviews, December 8, 2006, July 28, 2009.

40. Jack Pruett, telephone interview with author, November 5, 2006.

41. Ralph Emery, with Tom Carter, *Memories: The Autobiography of Ralph Emery*

(New York: Macmillan, 1991), 106–7. Page references are to 1992 Large Print edition (Boston: G.K. Hall, 1992); Marty Robbins, *Miller and Company,* with host Dan Miller, TNN, 1981.

Chapter 7. Singing the Blues in a White Sport Coat

1. Ben A. Green, "Country Music for Everybody," *Nashville Banner,* November 22, 1956.
2. Ben A. Green, "Millions Hear Melvin's Love Songs But . . . He Hasn't A Girl Friend," *Country and Western Jamboree,* May 1957; Ben A. Green, "Marty Robbins Almost Gave Away 'Singing The Blues' That Won Him Triple Crown," *Nashville Banner,* January 13, 1957.
3. Green, "Millions Hear Melvin's Love Songs."
4. "No 'Blues' For Marty Robbins," *Folk and Country Songs,* January 1957; Joel Whitburn, *Top Country Singles 1944–2001,* 5th ed. (Menomonee Falls, WI: Record Research, 2002), 296.
5. Don Roy and Richard Weize, "Marty Robbins: The Discography 1951–1958," *Marty Robbins Country 1951–1958* (Germany: Bear Family Records GMBH, 1991), 38; Ken Nelson, telephone conversation with author, December 14, 2003; Donnie Jennings, "Marty Robbins Discography and Career Information Thru 1990," 22, unpublished. Copy provided to author by Bill Johnson, October 2006.
6. Roy and Weize, "Discography 1951–1958," 38; "The Billboard Tenth Annual Disk Jockey Poll," *Billboard,* November 11, 1957.
7. Marty Robbins, interview, Country Music Foundation Oral History Project, Nashville, November 26, 1975.
8. Marty Robbins, *The Ralph Emery Show,* WSM Radio, October 28, 1981, June 17, 1982.
9. Joe Wright, telephone interview with author, December 8, 2006.
10. "Robbins Given Royal Treatment in New York Stay," *Country Music Reporter,* February 2, 1957; Roy and Weize, "Discography 1951–1958," 38.
11. Marty Robbins, Country Music Foundation Oral History Project.
12. "Robbins Named Top Artist in Deejay Poll," *Country Music Reporter,* March 2, 1957.
13. "'Golden Guitars' To Price, Robbins Highlight Opry," *Nashville Banner,* April 6, 1957.
14. Jerry Bailey, "The Singing Sheriff Shoots from the Hip," *Country Music,* November 1974; Ralph Emery, with Tom Carter, *Memories: The Autobiography of Ralph Emery* (New York: Macmillan, 1991), 127–28. Page references are to 1992 Large Print edition (Boston: G.K. Hall, 1992).

15. Ren Grevatt, "Country & Western Field Hops Fences, Covering the Nation," *Billboard,* March 23, 1957.

16. Mitch Miller, interview with John Rumble, Country Music Foundation Oral History Project, Nashville, February 24, 1983; "Marty 'Sports' a Hit," *Country Song Roundup,* October 1957.

17. Marty Robbins, *The Ralph Emery Show,* September 15, 1976, June 14, 17, 1982.

18. Joe Wright, telephone interview, December 18, 2006, email to author, September 8, 2008; Earl White, email to author, August 10, 2009, telephone interview with author, September 12, 2008.

19. Jack Pruett, telephone interview with author, November 5, 2006.

20. Joe Wright, telephone interview, December 18, 2006.

21. Lee-Mart Agency advertisement, *The Music Reporter,* August 31, 1957; Emerson-Shucher Agency advertisement, *The Music Reporter,* October 28, 1957.

22. Hal Willis, telephone interview with author, December 21, 2007.

23. Jim Glaser, email to author, September 11, 2009.

24. "Robbins Heads Three Firms In New Trade Twist," *The Music Reporter,* August 17, 1957.

25. Jim Glaser, telephone interview with author, February 20, 2007, email to author, September 11, 2009.

26. Roy and Weize, "Discography 1951–1958," 40.

27. Marty Robbins, *Marty Robbins at "Town Hall Party"* DVD, BVD 20007 (Germany: Bear Family Records, 2003), October 3, 1959; Marty Robbins, guest of Bill Mack, WBAP Radio, Fort Worth, TX, February 11, 1982; Marty Robbins, *The Ralph Emery Show,* August 14, 1980, October 27, 1981.

28. Jennings, "Marty Robbins Discography and Career Information Thru 1990," 1–9.

29. Roy and Weize, "Discography 1951–1958," 40; and Whitburn, *Top Country Singles 1944–2001,* 296.

30. Bill Maples, "Marty Robbins Fired by Opry," *Nashville Tennessean,* March 3, 1958.

31. Ibid.; "Marty Robbins, Opry Part," *Nashville Banner,* March 3, 1958.

32. Bill Maples, "Marty, the Opry Together Again!" *Nashville Tennessean,* March 7, 1958; Maples, "Marty Robbins Fired by Opry."

33. Joe Wright, telephone interview, December 18, 2006.

34. "Marty Robbins Signs With Denny Bureau," *The Music Reporter,* June 2, 1958; "Robbins Gains Strength; Nashville Hub of Indies," *The Music Reporter,* June 30, 1958; photo caption, *The Music Reporter,* July 14, 1958.

35. "Marty Robbins, Opry Part"; Marty Robbins band reunion, Nashville, July 18, 2009.

36. Roy and Weize, "Discography 1951–1958," 42.

Chapter 8. Gunfighter Ballads and Trail Songs

1. Craig Havighurst, *Air Castle of the South: WSM and the Making of Music City* (Urbana: University of Illinois Press, 2007), 203.

2. Jim Glaser, telephone interview with author, February 20, 2007; U.S. Bureau of the Census, *U.S. Census of Housing, 1960, Vol III, City Blocks* (Washington DC: U.S. Government Printing Office, 1961), http://www2.census.gov/prod2/decennial/documents/41994949v3p14ch4.pdf.

3. Colin Escott, *Marty Robbins Country 1951–1958* (Germany: Bear Family Records GMBH, 1991), 32.

4. Bobby Sykes, interview with Alan Potter, Nashville, date unknown.

5. Joe Babcock, telephone interview with author, November 9, 2006.

6. Glaser, telephone interview.

7. Ronny Robbins, email to author, October 14, 2009.

8. Joe Babcock, Marty Robbins band reunion, Nashville, July 18, 2009, telephone interview, November 9, 2006.

9. Marty Robbins, interview with Johnny Bond, *Marty Robbins at "Town Hall Party"* DVD, BVD 20007 (Germany: Bear Family Records, 2003), February 21, 1959.

10. Marty Robbins, *The Ralph Emery Show,* WSM Radio, December 16, 1977, December 19, 1979.

11. Marty Robbins, interview, Country Music Foundation Oral History Project, Nashville, November 26, 1975; Marty Robbins, guest of Bill Mack, WBAP Radio, Fort Worth, TX, date unknown; Marty Robbins, *The Ralph Emery Show,* September 15, 1976.

12. Marty Robbins, *Talking Country,* with host Charlie Cooke, KLAC Radio, Los Angeles, November 18, 1982.

13. Marty Robbins, *The Ralph Emery Show,* December 16, 1977; and Glaser, telephone interview.

14. Barbara J. Pruett, *Marty Robbins: Fast Cars and Country Music* (Metuchen, N.J.: Scarecrow Press, 1990), 111; Glaser, telephone interview.

15. Pruett, *Fast Cars and Country Music,* 111–12.

16. Ibid., 110.

17. Joe Babcock, telephone interviews with author, November 9, 2006, February 21, 2008.

18. Glaser, telephone interview.

19. Babcock, telephone interview with author, February 21, 2008.

20. Hal Willis, telephone interview with author, December 21, 2007.

21. Marty Robbins, *The Ralph Emery Show,* December 16, 1977; Country Clippings, *The Music Reporter,* September 7, 1959.

22. Doug Green, telephone interview with author, June 4, 2007.

23. Marty Robbins, *Talking Country.*

24. Joe Wright, telephone interview with author, July 28, 2009.

25. Marty Robbins, *The Ralph Emery Show,* September 13, 1976.

26. Marty Robbins, *Talking Country.*

27. Marty Robbins, *The Ralph Emery Show,* September 15, 1976, December 18, 1979.

28. Marty Robbins, *Talking Country;* Marty Robbins, *The Ralph Emery Show,* September 16, 1976.

29. Marty Robbins, *The Ralph Emery Show,* October 28, 1981.

30. Bill Anderson, email to author, October 28, 2009.

31. Glaser, telephone interview.

32. Babcock, telephone interview with author, November 9, 2006.

33. *Music City News,* September 1966; Babcock, telephone interview, November 9, 2006; Okie Jones, telephone interview with author, May 25, 2007; Pruett, *Fast Cars and Country Music,* 63.

34. Bill Johnson, telephone conversation with author, November 17, 2006; "Marty Robbins 75th Birthday Tribute," hosted by Eddie Stubbs, WSM Radio, Nashville, September 26, 2000.

35. Babcock, telephone interview, November 9, 2006.

36. Marty Robbins, *The Ralph Emery Show,* December 14, 1977.

37. Pruett, *Fast Cars and Country Music,* 63–64; Marty Robbins, interview with Bob Allen, Nashville, February 12, 1981.

38. Marty Robbins, Country Music Foundation Oral History Project; Marty Robbins, guest of Bill Mack, WBAP Radio, Fort Worth, TX, date unknown.

39. Joe Wright, telephone interview, July 28, 2009.

40. Marty Robbins, *The Ralph Emery Show,* December 18, 1979; Johnson, telephone conversation, November 17, 2006.

41. Marty Robbins, Country Music Foundation Oral History Project.

42. Johnson, telephone conversation, November 17, 2006.

43. Jack Pruett, telephone interview with author, November 5, 2006; Johnson, telephone conversation, November 17, 2006.

44. Marty Robbins band reunion, Nashville; Babcock, telephone interviews with author, November 9, 2006, February 21, 2008.

45. Joel Whitburn, *Top Country Singles 1944–2001,* 5th ed. (Menomonee Falls, WI: Record Research, 2002), 296.

46. Grammy.com, http://www.grammy.com/nominees/search?artist=Marty+ Robbins&title=El+Paso&year=1960&genre=All; Marty Robbins, *The Ralph Emery Show,* August 14, 1980.

47. Don Winters, "NASCAR's Own Balladeer," *Stock Cars '73,* 1973.

Chapter 9. Early 1960s

1. Don Stauffer, "Evolution of midget racing," *Motorsport,* May 16, 2000; "Sport: The Micro Midgets," *Time,* February 15, 1954; Ellyn Trigg, "Hobbies of the Stars: Tracking Marty Robbins," *Music City News,* August 1963.

2. Ronny Robbins, telephone interview with author, February 11, 2010.

3. "Marty Robbins Unhurt In Crash, *Nashville Banner,* August 22, 1960, *Nashville Tennessean,* August 22, 1960.

4. Joe Babcock, telephone interview with author, November 9, 2006, and Marty Robbins band reunion, Nashville, July 18, 2009.

5. Okie Jones, telephone interview with author, May 25, 2007.

6. Country Clippings, *The Music Reporter,* September 12, 1960.

7. Johnny Seay, telephone interview with author, January 8, 2007.

8. Norman Wade, telephone interview with author, January 25, 2007.

9. Okie Jones, telephone interview with author.

10. Seay, telephone interview with author.

11. Jim Glaser, telephone interview with author, February 20, 2007.

12. Babcock, email to author, October 31, 2009.

13. Babcock, telephone interview, November 9, 2006.

14. Ben A. Green, "Marty Robbins Almost Gave Away 'Singing The Blues' That Won Him Triple Crown," *Nashville Banner,* January 13, 1957; Madeleine Jones, email to author, October 24, 2009; Glaser, telephone interview.

15. Babcock, telephone interview, November 9, 2006; Okie Jones, telephone interview.

16. Madeleine Jones, email; Marty Robbins band reunion.

17. Babcock, telephone interview, November 9, 2006.

18. Marty Robbins band reunion; Earl White, email to author, October 14, 2009.

19. Babcock, telephone interview, November 9, 2006; Jack Pruett, telephone interview with author, November 5, 2006.

20. Babcock, telephone interview, November 9, 2006; Bill Johnson, telephone conversation with author, November 17, 2006; Jack Pruett, Marty Robbins band reunion, Nashville, July 18, 2009; Barbara J. Pruett, *Marty Robbins: Fast Cars and Country Music* (Metuchen, NJ: Scarecrow Press, 1990), 72.

21. Babcock, telephone interview, email to author, February 23, 2008, and Marty Robbins band reunion, July 18, 2009; Ronny Robbins, *Marty Robbins: Super Legend,* VHS, Marty Robbins, Inc., 1989.

22. Johnson, telephone conversation, November 17, 2006.

23. Ellis Nassour, *Honky Tonk Angel: The Intimate Story of Patsy Cline* (St. Martin's Paperbacks, 1994), 275; Jack Pruett, telephone interview; Phil Sullivan, "Opry Pulls Full House In Carnegie Hall," *Nashville Tennessean,* November 20, 1961.

24. Leo Jackson, telephone interview with author, January 11, 2008.

25. Johnson, telephone conversation, November 17, 2006.

Chapter 10. Cowboy in a Continental Suit

1. Marty Robbins, interview with Bob Allen, Nashville, February 12, 1981; Lee Iacocca, with William Novak, *Iacocca: An Autobiography* (New York: Bantam Books, 1984), 71.

2. Marty Robbins, interview with Bob Allen, February 12, March 6, 1981; Personal Exemptions and Individual Income Tax Rates, 1913–2002, http://www.irs.gov/pub/irs-soi/02inpetr.pdf; Ronny Robbins, Marty Robbins band reunion, Nashville, July 18, 2009.

3. Marty Robbins, *The Ralph Emery Show,* WSM Radio, December 15, 1977, August 14, 1980; Marty Robbins, interview, Country Music Foundation Oral History Project, Nashville, November 26, 1975.

4. "Marty Robbins 75th Birthday Tribute," hosted by Eddie Stubbs, WSM Radio, Nashville, September 26, 2000.

5. Joe Babcock, telephone interview with author, November 9, 2006.

6. Okie Jones, telephone interview with author, May 25, 2007; "Marty Robbins 75th Birthday Tribute."

7. Marty Robbins, *The Ralph Emery Show,* September 17, 19, 1973; "Marty Robbins 75th Birthday Tribute."

8. Janet Robinson, telephone interview with author, February 7, 2010.

9. Marty Robbins, interview with Bob Allen, February 12, 1981.

10. Ronny Robbins, Marty Robbins band reunion; Highland Rim Speedway, http://www.highlandrim.com/; Don Winters, "NASCAR's Own Balladeer," *Stock Cars '73,* 1973; Marty Robbins, interview with Bob Allen, February 12, 1981; Ellyn Trigg, "Hobbies of the Stars: Tracking Marty Robbins," *Music City News,* August 1963.

11. Marty Robbins, *The Ralph Emery Show,* December 18, 1979; Ronny Robbins, Marty Robbins band reunion; Ralph Emery, with Tom Carter, *More Memories* (New York: Berkley Books, 1995), 48.

12. Marty Robbins, *The Ralph Emery Show,* December 18, 1979.

13. Jean Shepard, interview with Robert MacMillan, Radio Nevis, December 3, 1995.

14. Marty Robbins, *The Ralph Emery Show,* September 14, 1976, December 20, 1979.

15. *Ballad of a Gunfighter,* Bill Ward Production (Parade Pictures: 1964).

16. Marty Robbins, *The Ralph Emery Show,* June 17, 1982, August 12, 1980.

17. Marty Robbins band reunion.

18. "Robbins Seeks No Limelight," *Nashville Banner,* November 5, 1964.

19. "Marty Robbins: "The Night I Knew I Was Going To Die," *Country Music Stars,* Fall 1964.

20. Emery, *More Memories,* 51; Janet Robinson, telephone interview with author, February 7, 2010.

21. Okie Jones, telephone interview with author, November 15, 2009; Emery, *More Memories,* 50.

22. Okie Jones, telephone interview, November 15, 2009; Larry Jordan, email to author, May 28, 2007; Janet Robinson, telephone interview.

23. Emery, *More Memories,* 51; Okie Jones, telephone interview, November 15, 2009.

Chapter 11. Still More Gunfighter Ballads and Trail Songs

1. Marty Robbins, interview, Country Music Foundation Oral History Project, Nashville, November 26, 1975; Marty Robbins, *The Ralph Emery Show,* WSM Radio, June 14, 1982.

2. Colin Escott, *Marty Robbins Country 1960–1966* (Germany: Bear Family Records GMBH, 1995), 29; *Marty Robbins: Super Legend,* VHS, Marty Robbins, Inc., 1989.

3. "Marty Robbins 75th Birthday Tribute," hosted by Eddie Stubbs, WSM Radio, Nashville, September 26, 2000.

4. Joe Babcock, telephone interview with author, November 9, 2006.

5. Bobby Braddock, telephone interview with author, November 11, 2006.

6. Marty Robbins, *The Ralph Emery Show,* April 15, 1982.

7. Escott, *Marty Robbins Country 1960–1966,* 10; "Marty Robbins 75th Birthday Tribute"; Braddock, telephone interview.

8. Marty Robbins, *Miller and Company,* with host Dan Miller, TNN, 1981; Braddock, telephone interview; Robert Hinkle, telephone interview with author, October 19, 2009; William Greenburg, "Marty Robbins Tapes TV Series, 'The Drifter,'" *Nashville Tennessean,* December 9, 1965.

9. Hinkle, telephone interview; Braddock, telephone interview.

10. Hinkle, telephone interview; Ronny Robbins, Marty Robbins band reunion, Nashville, July 18, 2009; Braddock, telephone interview; Judy Myers, "A Talk With Marty Robbins," *Country Songs Roundup,* June 1969.

11. Marty Robbins, *The Ralph Emery Show,* September 15, 1976; Marty Robbins, interview with Ruud Hermans, *KRO Countrytime,* October 1982.

12. Marty Robbins, Country Music Foundation Oral History Project.

13. "Robbins Tops Goldwater Entertainers," *Nashville Banner,* September 12, 1964; "Nixon Fete Slates Acuff, Robbins," *Nashville Banner,* February 3, 1966; Braddock, telephone interview.

14. "Columbia Says No To Marty Robbins!" *Georgia World of Country Music,* October 1966, 1.

15. Bob Powel, "Bob Powel Interviews Marty Robbins," *Country Music People,* January 1973, 18.

16. Ibid.; "Columbia Says No To Marty Robbins!"; R. Serge Denisoff and Richard A. Peterson, *The Sounds of Social Change: Studies in Popular Culture* (Chicago: Rand McNally, 1972), 89.

17. Janet Robinson, telephone interview with author, February 7, 2010; Ronny Robbins, telephone interview with author, February 11, 2010.

18. Janet Robinson, telephone interview.

19. Okie Jones, telephone interview with author, May 25, 2007.

20. "Marty Robbins 75th Birthday Tribute"; Okie Jones, telephone interview with author, May 25, 2007.

21. "Marty Robbins 75th Birthday Tribute."

22. Marty Robbins, *The Ralph Emery Show,* September 17, 1976, December 17, 1979; "Marty Robbins 75th Birthday Tribute."

23. Marty Robbins, *The Ralph Emery Show,* December 15, 1977; "Marty Robbins 75th Birthday Tribute."

24. Marty Robbins, *The Ralph Emery Show,* October 28, 1981, June 16, 1982.

25. "Marty Robbins 75th Birthday Tribute"; Ronny Robbins, *The Ralph Emery Show,* September 20, 1973; Marty Robbins, *The Ralph Emery Show,* September 19, 1973; *Marty Robbins: Super Legend,* VHS, Marty Robbins, Inc., 1989.

26. Ronny Robbins, telephone interview; Marty Robbins, *The Ralph Emery Show,* September 19, 1973.

27. Ronny Robbins, telephone interview, Marty Robbins band reunion, Nashville, July 18, 2009.

Chapter 12. From Dirt Track to NASCAR

1. Tom Powell, "So It's a Mountain! . . . Marty Robbins Tries To Climb It!" *Tennessean,* February 23, 1969; "Bobby Ball," Find a Grave, http://www.findagrave.com/cgi-bin/fg.cgi?page=gr&GRid=1569.

2. Don Winters, "NASCAR's Own Balladeer," *Stock Cars '73,* 1973.

3. Ronny Robbins, email to author, December 7, 2009; Winters, "NASCAR's Own Balladeer"; Marty Robbins, interview, Country Music Foundation Oral History Project, Nashville, November 26, 1975.

4. "Marty Robbins," Racing Reference Info, http://racing-reference.info/driver/ Marty_Robbins; Marty Robbins, interview with Bob Allen, Nashville, February 12, 1981.

5. *Road To Nashville,* Robert Patrick Productions, released by Crown International Pictures, 1966.

6. Mildred Harper, telephone interview with author, January 10, 2008.

7. Kathy Carroll, "Red Carpet Greets Stars At Premiere," *Nashville Banner,* June 17, 1967; Kathy Sawyer, "Premiere Attracts 3,000 Here," *Tennessean,* June 17, 1967.

8. Eddie Allison, telephone interview with author, November 10, 2006; Bobby Allison, telephone interview with author, November 10, 2006.

9. Joan Dew, "Marty Robbins Made a Deal With God," *Country Music,* November 1976.

10. E. W. "Bud" Wendell, telephone interview with author, November 25, 2009; Bob Powel, "Bob Powel Interviews Marty Robbins," *Country Music People,* January 1973.

11. Wendell, telephone interview; Susan Scott, "Marty Robbins & His Hobby Cars," *Stock Car Racing,* September 1975.

12. Wendell, telephone interview.

13. Lucy Coldsnow Smith, telephone interview with author, November 12, 2009.

14. Marty Robbins, *The Ralph Emery Show,* WSM Radio, September 18, 1973, September 17, 1976.

15. Louie Roberts, telephone interview with author, December 11, 2006.

16. Wendell, telephone interview; "Marty Robbins 75th Birthday Tribute," hosted by Eddie Stubbs, WSM Radio, Nashville, September 26, 2000.

17. Marty Robbins, *The Ralph Emery Show,* September 15, 1976.

18. Marty Robbins, *The Ralph Emery Show,* September 16, 1976, December 20, 1979, October 29, 1981.

19. Johnny Bush, telephone interview with author, July 14, 2008.

20. Judy Myers, "A Talk With Marty Robbins," *Country Songs Roundup,* June 1969; Powell, "So It's a Mountain!"; Winters, "NASCAR's Own Balladeer."

Chapter 13. A Hot Dog Ready to Pop

1. Bobby Braddock, telephone interview with author, November 11, 2006.

2. Buddy Rogers, telephone interview with author, October 30, 2006; Okie Jones, telephone interview with author, May 25, 2007.

3. Rogers, email to author, January 13, 2010, telephone interview with author.

4. Larry L. King, "The Grand Ole Opry," *Harper's Magazine,* July 1968; Stacy Harris, "Marty Robbins Interview, *Country Song Roundup,* July 1977.

5. Robert Hinkle with Mike Farris, *Call Me Lucky: A Texan in Hollywood* (Norman: University of Oklahoma Press, 2009), 227–29; Lucy Coldsnow Smith, email to author, December 13, 2009; Hinkle, telephone interview with author, October 19, 2009.

6. Okie Jones, telephone interview.

7. Larry Jordan, email to author, May 28, 2007.

8. Mildred Harper, telephone interview with author, January 10, 2008.

9. Ronny Robbins, telephone interview with author, February 11, 2010.

10. Madeleine Jones, email to author, December 11, 2009.

11. Bill Johnson, telephone interview with author, September 26, 2006; Okie Jones, telephone interview.

12. Marty Robbins, *Miller and Company,* with host Dan Miller, TNN, 1981.

13. Okie Jones, telephone interview; Johnson, telephone interview.

14. Marty Robbins, *Miller and Company.*

15. Okie Jones, telephone interview.

16. Johnson, telephone interview; *Marty Robbins: Super Legend,* VHS, Marty Robbins, Inc., 1989.

17. Okie Jones, telephone interview; Johnson, telephone interview.

18. Marty Robbins, interview with Bob Allen, Nashville, February 12, 1981.

19. Okie Jones, telephone interview.

20. "Opry Star Robbins To Return Tomorrow," *Tennessean,* August 15, 1969.

21. Marty Robbins, interview with Bob Allen.

22. "Marty Robbins Back in Nashville," *Tennessean,* August 18, 1965; Marty Robbins, *Miller and Company*; Johnson, telephone interview.

23. Okie Jones, telephone interview; *Music City News,* September 1969; Johnson, telephone interview.

24. Okie Jones, telephone interview.

25. Madeleine Jones, email to author, December 11, 2009; Ronny Robbins, telephone interview.

26. Marty Robbins, *The Ralph Emery Show,* WSM Radio, December 18, 1979.

Chapter 14. "I Want To Race Again"

1. Marty Robbins, *The Ralph Emery Show,* WSM Radio, June 18, 1982; Madeleine Jones, email to author, December 11, 2009; Marty Robbins, *Talking Country,* with host Charlie Cooke, KLAC Radio, Los Angeles, November 18, 1982.

2. "Marty Robbins 75th Birthday Tribute," hosted by Eddie Stubbs, WSM Radio, Nashville, September 26, 2000.

3. Marty Robbins, *The Ralph Emery Show,* September 16, 1976.

4. Marty Robbins, interview with Bob Allen, Nashville, February 12, 1981; Jack Hurst, "Singer Marty Robbins' Unique Heart Artery Operation Successful," *Tennessean,* January 28, 1970.

5. Marty Robbins, interview with Bob Allen.

6. Red O'Donnell, "Marty Has Short Walk At Hospital," *Nashville Banner,* February 3, 1970.

7. Jack Hurst, "Robbins Considers Heart Operation," *Tennessean,* January 24, 1970; Red O'Donnell, "Robbins makes Plea For Prayers," *Nashville Banner,* January 27, 1970.

8. "Robbins Heart Surgery Gave National Coverage To Our Cardiac Program," *St. Thomas Scope,* March 1970; Hurst, "Singer Marty Robbins' Unique Heart Artery Operation Successful"; Red O'Donnell, "Marty Robbins Said In Satisfactory Condition," *Nashville Banner,* January 28, 1970.

9. "Robbins Heart Surgery Gave National Coverage To Our Cardiac Program."

10. Marty Robbins, *The Ralph Emery Show,* September 21, 1973.

11. *Marty Robbins: Super Legend,* VHS, Marty Robbins, Inc., 1989.

12. Marty Robbins, interview with Bob Allen.

13. "Robbins Shaves Self, Sits in Chair," *Tennessean,* January 30, 1970; "Recuperating Robbins Gets Private Room," *Nashville Banner,* January 31, 1970; O'Donnell, "Marty Has Short Walk At Hospital."

14. Lucy Coldsnow Smith, telephone interview with author, November 12, 2009.

15. Red O'Donnell, "Marty Will Go Home Tuesday," *Nashville Banner,* February 9, 1970.

16. Okie Jones, telephone interview with author, May 25, 2007; Bill Johnson, telephone interview with author, September 26, 2006.

17. "Robbins Heart Surgery Gave National Coverage To Our Cardiac Program."

18. Marty Robbins, interview with Bob Allen.

19. Jerry Thompson, "They Stayed On and On For Marty," *Tennessean,* March 30, 1970; Betty Kight, letter to Peggy Ann Munson, *Marty Robbins Club Magazine,* September 1972.

20. Thompson, "They Stayed On and On For Marty."

21. "Marty In Person—Returns To Ovations," *Country Hot-Line News,* May 1970.

22. Geoff Lane, "El Paso To Phoenix," *Country Music People,* September 1971.

23. Bob Myers, "Racing Saved His Life," *Charlotte News,* July 3, 1970.

Chapter 15. Back in the Groove

1. Louise Mayer, "Tour To Music City," *The Drifter: The Official Marty Robbins Fan Club Magazine,* November/December 1970.
2. Jackie Knar, "Marty Robbins at the Fremont," *The Drifter: The Official Marty Robbins Fan Club Magazine,* November/December 1970.
3. Marty Robbins, letter to fans, *The Drifter: The Official Marty Robbins Fan Club Magazine,* November/December 1970.
4. Peggy Ann Munson, "Let's Chat," *The Drifter: The Official Marty Robbins Fan Club Magazine,* September 1969.
5. Ralph Emery, with Patsi Bale Cox, *50 Years Down a Country Road* (New York: William Morrow, 2000), 155–56.
6. Louise Mayer, "Simu-Cast," *The Drifter: The Official Marty Robbins Fan Club Magazine,* November/December 1970; Country Music Association, Past Winners, "Marty Robbins," http://www.cmaawards.com/past-winners/ArtistDetail.aspx?artistId=405.
7. Lucy Coldsnow Smith, telephone interview with author, November 12, 2009.
8. "13th Annual Grammy Awards," *Washington Post,* March 18, 1971; Robert Hinkle, telephone interview with author, October 19, 2009.
9. Jeannie Moody, "Marty at the Fremont," *The Drifter: The Official Marty Robbins Fan Club Magazine,* Fall/Winter 1971.
10. Louise Mayer, "Fans Meet In Music City To Celebrate Marty's Birthday"; Doris Fjelstad, letter to Peggy Ann Munson; both in *The Drifter: The Official Marty Robbins Fan Club Magazine,* Fall/Winter 1971.
11. Marty Robbins, letter, *The Drifter: The Official Marty Robbins Fan Club Magazine,* Fall/Winter 1971.
12. Marty Robbins, *The Ralph Emery Show,* WSM Radio, September 16, 1976.
13. Marty Robbins, interview with Bob Allen, Nashville, February 12, 1981.
14. Hinkle, telephone interview; Lucy Coldsnow Smith, telephone interview with author, November 12, 2009.
15. Hinkle, telephone interview.
16. "Marty Gets a Decca Welcome," *Nashville Banner,* June 28, 1972; Jack Hurst, "Marty Robbins To Star in Westerns, *Tennessean,* June 28, 1972.
17. Joel Whitburn, *Top Country Singles 1944–2001,* 5th ed. (Menomonee Falls, WI: Record Research, 2002), 297.
18. Hinkle, telephone interview.
19. Lucy Coldsnow Smith, telephone interview.
20. Dan Cotterman, "Return of the Singing Cowboy," *Horse & Rider,* May 1973, 33.

21. Marty Robbins, *The Ralph Emery Show,* September 18, 1973.

22. Marty Robbins, guest of Bill Mack, WBAP Radio, Fort Worth, TX, 1976.

23. D. J. Mathews, "Star of 'the Drifter' Is Also Down-to-Earth Humorist," *Apache Sentinel,* August 3, 1972.

24. Barbara J. Pruett, *Marty Robbins: Fast Cars and Country Music* (Metuchen, NJ: Scarecrow Press, 1990), 118; Hinkle, telephone interview.

25. Louise Mayer, "Fan's Eye View," *The Drifter: The Official Marty Robbins Fan Club Magazine,* September 1972.

26. Doris Fjelstad, "The Marty Robbins show—Anderson, Indiana," *The Drifter: The Official Marty Robbins Fan Club Magazine,* September 1972; Mayer, "Fan's Eye View."

27. Marty Robbins, letter to fans, *The Drifter: The Official Marty Robbins Fan Club Magazine,* September 1972.

Chapter 16. NASCAR 42

1. Ronny Robbins, email to author, August 5, 2009; Richard Petty, with William Neely, *King Richard I: The Autobiography of America's Greatest Auto Racer* (New York: MacMillan Publishing: 1986), 66.

2. Marty Robbins, letter to fans, *The Drifter: The Official Marty Robbins Fan Club Magazine,* November/December 1970.

3. Ronny Robbins, email to author, December 4, 2009; Don Winters, "NASCAR's Own Balladeer," *Stock Cars '73,* 1973, 93; James Hylton, telephone interview with author, March 6, 2007.

4. Winters, "NASCAR's Own Balladeer," 93.

5. Bobby Allison, telephone interview with author, November 10, 2006; Susan Scott, "Marty Robbins & His Hobby Cars," *Stock Car Racing,* September 1975, 17.

6. Edith Hanes, "Marty at the 1971 Races," *The Drifter: The Official Marty Robbins Fan Club Magazine,* Fall/Winter 1971; Petty, *King Richard I,* 221; Don Winters, "NASCAR's Own Balladeer," 94.

7. Eddie Allison, telephone interview with author, November 10, 2006.

8. William Burt, *The American Stock Car* (St. Paul, MN: MBI Publishing, 2001), 86, 88; Cotton Owens, telephone interview with author, December 7, 2006.

9. Eddie Allison, telephone interview.

10. Petty, *King Richard I,* 220–21.

11. Marty Robbins, interview with Bill Black for Radio Clyde, Glasgow, Scotland, May 1975.

12. Burt, *The American Stock Car,* 84; Eddie Allison, telephone interview; Bobby

Allison, telephone interview with author, November 10, 2006; Charlie Wright, telephone interview with author, November 14, 2006.

13. Marty Robbins, *The Ralph Emery Show,* WSM Radio, June 14, 1982; interview at Talladega, August 3, 1980, shown in *Marty Robbins: Super Legend,* VHS, Marty Robbins, Inc., 1989.

14. Eddie Allison, telephone interview; Bobby Allison, telephone interview; Kim Chapin, "Start This Story With a Song," *Sports Illustrated,* October 8, 1973, 87–88.

15. Marty Robbins, interview at Talladega.

16. Bobby Allison, telephone interview; Eddie Allison, telephone interview.

17. Bobby Allison, telephone interview.

18. Gene Granger, "Marty Just Likes It," *Southern Motor Sports Journal,* May 26, 1972; "Marty Robbins: I'll Keep Racing," *Country Hot-Line News,* July 1972.

19. Wright, telephone interview.

20. Fred Meade, "Robbins Is Hit in Racing Circles, and Country Music Circles," *Florence Morning News,* September 1972.

21. Marty Robbins, *The Ralph Emery Show,* September 19, 1973; "Marty Robbins at the Nugget: Is This the Real Marty?" *The Drifter: The Official Marty Robbins Fan Club Magazine,* October 1973; Buncie Nappier, letter, *The Drifter: The Official Marty Robbins Fan Club Magazine,* October 1973.

22. Marty Robbins, *The Ralph Emery Show,* December 21, 1979.

23. Marty Robbins, *The Ralph Emery Show,* September 20, 1973; Johnny "K" (Koval), "Mini-View: Marty Robbins," *Country Song Roundup,* July 1974.

24. Becky Ashby, letter, *The Drifter: The Official Marty Robbins Fan Club Magazine,* October 1973; Dottie Pelascini, letter, *The Drifter: The Official Marty Robbins Fan Club Magazine,* October 1973.

25. "Marty Honored in Franklin," *Tennessean,* March 4, 1973.

26. Marty Robbins, *The Ralph Emery Show,* September 17–21, 1973.

27. Marty Robbins, letter, *The Drifter: The Official Marty Robbins Fan Club Magazine,* October 1973.

28. Marty Robbins, and Ronny Robbins, *The Ralph Emery Show,* WSM Radio, September 17–21, 1973.

29. Marty Robbins, interview with Bill Black for Radio Clyde, Glasgow, Scotland, May 1975.

Chapter 17. Twentieth Century Drifter

1. Marty Robbins, *The Ralph Emery Show,* WSM Radio, September 19, 1973.

2. Kim Chapin, "Start This Story With a Song," *Sports Illustrated,* October 8, 1973, 88.

3. Marty Robbins, guest of Bill Mack, WBAP Radio, Fort Worth, TX, Summer 1973; Marty Robbins, telephone interview with Ralph Emery, January 1981.

4. Bob Myers, "Marty's Magnum," *Circle Track,* January 1985, 64–65; Chapin, "Start This Story With a Song," 82–83; Marty Robbins, *Talking Country,* with host Charlie Cooke, KLAC Radio, Los Angeles, November 18, 1982.

5. Marty Robbins, interview with Bob Allen, Nashville, February 12, 1981; Marty Robbins, *The Ralph Emery Show,* September 19, 1973; Steve Waid, "Texas Motor Speedway Not Lone Star State's First, Nor Fastest, NASCAR Track," April 1, 2009, http://www.texasworldspeedway.com/about-tws/news/9-nascar-at-texas-world-speedway.html.

6. Marty Robbins, *The Ralph Emery Show,* September 19, 1973.

7. Cotton Owens, telephone interview with author, December 7, 2006.

8. Lucy Coldsnow Smith, telephone interview with author, November 12, 2009.

9. Glen Wood, telephone interview with author, November 14, 2006.

10. UltimateRacingHistory.com, http://www.ultimateracinghistory.com/racelist2.php?uniqid=4889; Susan Scott, "Marty Robbins, Racing Driver, Part 2," *Country Song Roundup,* March 1975, 18.

11. UltimateRacingHistory.com; Myers, "Marty's Magnum," 64; "His Anthem: Roar of the Engines Provides a Backup for Marty Robbins," *Detroit Free Press,* August 21, 1982; Owens, telephone interview.

12. Scott, "Marty Robbins, Racing Driver, Part 2," 17.

13. "Pearson Takes 500, Marty Robbins Hurt," *Washington Post,* October 7, 1974.

14. Marty Robbins, interview with Bob Allen.

15. Richard Childress, telephone interview with author, December 15, 2009, and video excerpt shown in *Marty Robbins: Super Legend,* VHS, Marty Robbins, Inc., 1989; Scott, "Marty Robbins, Racing Driver, Part 2," 16.

16. Joan Dew, "Marty Robbins Made a Deal With God," *Country Music,* November 1976, 24; Marty Robbins, interview with Bob Allen.

17. Scott, "Marty Robbins, Racing Driver, Part 2," 16.

18. Childress, telephone interview.

19. Darrell Waltrip, video excerpt shown in *Marty Robbins: Super Legend,* VHS, Marty Robbins, Inc., 1989.

20. Dew, "Marty Robbins Made a Deal With God," 24; Susan Scott, "Marty Robbins & His Hobby Cars," *Stock Car Racing,* September 1975, 17.

21. Scott, "Marty Robbins & His Hobby Cars," 15.

22. Susan Scott, "Marty Robbins Gives Up Racing!" *Country Song Roundup,* November 1975, 9; Marty Robbins, interview with Bob Allen.

23. Marty Robbins, interview with Bill Black for Radio Clyde, Glasgow, Scotland, May 1975; Scott, "Marty Robbins Gives Up Racing!" 9–10; Marty Robbins, *The Ralph Emery Show,* September 16, 1976.

24. Marty Robbins, interview with Bob Allen.

25. James Hylton, telephone interview with author, March 6, 2007.

26. Jack Pruett, telephone interview with author, November 5, 2006.

27. Marty Robbins, interview with Bill Black.

28. Marty Robbins, *The Ralph Emery Show,* September 16, 1976.

29. Marty Robbins, interview, Country Music Foundation Oral History Project, Nashville, November 26, 1975.

Chapter 18. Return to the Road

1. Ryman Auditorium website, "History," http://www.ryman.com.

2. Patrick Carr, "Nashville's Biggest Weekend: Farewell To The Ryman, Hello To Opryland," *Country Music,* 1974, reprinted in *The Drifter: The Official Marty Robbins Fan Club Magazine,* June 1974.

3. Haskel McCormick, telephone interview with author, April 29, 2008; Bill Johnson, telephone interview with author, November 17, 2006.

4. Marty Robbins, interview with Bill Black for Radio Clyde, Glasgow, Scotland, May 1975.

5. Don Powell, telephone interview with author, April 29, 2008; McCormick, telephone interview.

6. Dottie Pelascini, letter to Peggy Ann Munson, *The Drifter: The Official Marty Robbins Fan Club Magazine,* June 1974.

7. Johnson, telephone interview with author, September 26, 2006; Powell, telephone interview.

8. McCormick, telephone interview; Powell, telephone interview.

9. Powell, telephone interview; Susan Scott, "Marty Robbins, Racing Driver, Part 2," *Country Song Roundup,* March 1975, 16; McCormick, telephone interview.

10. Robert Hinkle, telephone interview with author, October 19, 2009; Lucy Coldsnow Smith, telephone interview with author, November 12, 2009; Ronny Robbins, Marty Robbins band reunion, Nashville, July 18, 2009.

11. Powell, telephone interview.

12. John "Jay Dee" Hoag, telephone interview with author, December 28, 2009.

13. Marty Robbins, live performance at International Festival of Country Music, Wembley, England, March 29, 1975.

14. Marty Robbins, interview with Bill Black.

15. Ibid.

16. Stacy Harris, "Marty Robbins Interview," *Country Song Roundup,* July 1977, 15.

17. Ibid., 46; Hinkle, telephone interview.

18. Lucy Coldsnow Smith, telephone interview.

19. Hoag, telephone interview.

20. Scott Lindley, email to Friends of Marty Robbins, July 14, 2008.

21. Marty Robbins, *The Ralph Emery Show,* WSM Radio, September 17, 1976.

22. Diane Jordan, telephone interview with author, May 24, 2007.

23. Harris, "Marty Robbins Interview," 15; Marty Robbins, interview with Bob Allen, Nashville, February 12, 1981.

24. David Lyons, "Wouldn't Live In Robbins' Home, Builder Says," *Nashville Banner,* February 8, 1978; Janet Robinson, telephone interview with author, February 7, 2010.

Chapter 19. Back on Columbia Records and in the Spotlight

1. Colin Escott, *Marty Robbins Country 1960–1966* (Germany: Bear Family Records GMBH, 1995), 10; "Barry Sadler Sentenced in Shooting Death," *Free Lance-Star,* May 9, 1980.

2. Stacy Harris, "Marty Robbins Interview," *Country Song Roundup,* July 1977, 15.

3. Marty Robbins, live performance at International Festival of Country Music, Wembley, England, April 18, 1976; Tom Rogers, "Dolly, Marty Win Honors," *Tennessean,* April 19, 1976.

4. John "Jay Dee" Hoag, telephone interview with author, December 28, 2009; Maurice "Del" Delamont, telephone interview with author, December 29, 2009.

5. Marty Robbins, *The Ralph Emery Show,* WSM Radio, September 13, 17, 1976, December 13, 1977, October 30, 1981; Delamont, telephone interview.

6. Janet Robinson, email to author, February 8, 2010; Lucy Coldsnow Smith, telephone interview with author, November 12, 2009.

7. Janet Robinson, telephone interview with author, February 7, 2010.

8. Stacy Harris, "Marty Robbins Interview," 15.

9. Barbara Funkhouser, "Country-Western Star To Tout EP In Film," *El Paso Times,* June 17, 1976; Marty Robbins, *The Ralph Emery Show,* September 13, 1976.

10. Barbara Funkhouser and Debbie Normann, "Robbins' Crowd Small, Warm," *El Paso Times,* July 3, 1976; Marty Robbins, *The Ralph Emery Show,* September 13, 1976; Hoag, telephone interview.

11. Marty Robbins, *The Ralph Emery Show,* September 13, 17, 1976; Marty Robbins, *Talking Country,* with host Charlie Cooke, KLAC Radio, Los Angeles, November 18, 1982.

12. Lucy Coldsnow Smith, telephone interview.

13. Joel Whitburn, *Top Country Singles 1944–2001,* 5th ed. (Menomonee Falls, WI: Record Research, 2002), 297.

14. Marty Robbins, *The Ralph Emery Show,* December 12, 1977.

15. Timothy "Timmy" Tappan, telephone interview with author, September 11,

2008; Delamont, telephone interview; "Blue & White Checkered Grand: A New Guinness Record," *Music Trades*, Englewood, NJ, April 1977.

16. Marty Robbins, interview with Bob Allen, Nashville, February 12, 1981; Marty Robbins, *The Ralph Emery Show*, December 12, 1977.

17. Tappan, telephone interview.

18. Delamont, telephone interview.

19. Marty Robbins, interview with Rodger Beard, Gibson County (Indiana) Fairgrounds, July 1982.

20. Alanna Nash, "Marty Robbins: Silly on Stage; Serious in the Office," *Louisville Courier Journal*, February 26, 1978; Marty Robbins, interview with Bob Allen.

21. Tappan, telephone interview.

22. David Lyons, "Wouldn't Live In Robbins' Home, Builder Says," *Nashville Banner*, February 8, 1978; Janet Robinson, telephone interview; "Singer Marty Robbins' House Said Sliding Down Hill; $200,000 Asked," *Nashville Banner*, October 20, 1977.

23. "Sliding Home Case To Be Decided In 3 Weeks," *Nashville Banner*, February 13, 1978; Lyons, "Wouldn't Live In Robbins' Home."

24. Ralph Dawson, "Robbins Pleased Over Court Ruling on Home," *Tennessean*, March 4, 1978, "Robbins Must Pay Rent for Living In 'Sliding House,'" *Tennessean*, May 9, 1978.

25. Marty Robbins, interview with Bob Allen.

26. Marty Robbins, *The Ralph Emery Show*, December 12–15, 1977; interview with Bob Allen.

Chapter 20. The Marty Robbins Band on Tour

1. Maurice "Del" Delamont, telephone interview with author, December 29, 2009.

2. Marty Robbins, live performance at International Festival of Country Music, Wembley, England, March 26, 1978.

3. Marty Robbins, *The Ralph Emery Show*, WSM Radio, December 12, 1977.

4. Marty Robbins, International Festival of Country Music.

5. Marty Robbins, interview with Bob Allen, Nashville, February 12, 1981.

6. Bill Martinez, telephone interview with author, March 19, 2008.

7. Okie Jones, telephone interview with author, May 25, 2007.

8. Martinez, telephone interview.

9. Marty Robbins, interview with Bob Allen, Nashville, March 6, 1981.

10. Martinez, telephone interview, March 19, 2008, email to author, January 10, 2010.

11. Okie Jones, "Marty Robbins 75th Birthday Tribute," hosted by Eddie Stubbs, WSM Radio, Nashville, September 26, 2000, telephone interview with author, May 25, 2007.

12. Martinez, telephone interview, March 19, 2008, and email to author, January 8, 2010.

13. Delamont, telephone interview.

14. Marty Robbins, interview with Bob Allen, February 12, 1981.

15. Wayne Jackson, telephone interview with author, October 31, 2006.

16. Rex Allen Jr., telephone interview with author, June 24, 2008; Smoky Smith, telephone interview with author, January 30, 2008.

17. Marty Robbins, interview with Bob Allen.

18. Rex Allen Jr., telephone interview.

19. Smoky Smith, telephone interview.

20. Jeff Chandler, telephone interview with author, January 3, 2010.

21. Marty Robbins, interview with Bob Allen.

22. Wayne Jackson, email to author, November 2, 2006.

23. Conrad Noddin, telephone interview with author, December 29, 2009; Martinez, telephone interview, March 19, 2008.

24. Noddin, telephone interview.

25. Chandler, telephone interview.

26. Marty Robbins, International Festival of Country Music.

27. George Jones, interview with Ralph Emery, *Emery's Memories,* CD collection, 2006.

28. Tony Lioce, "Marty Robbins Presents Half a Program," *Providence Journal,* October 12, 1975; Jerry Hicks, "Marty Robbins Overdoes the Showbiz Sillies," *Louisville Times,* September 19, 1979; Gary Rice, "Robbins' Jokes Lack Rhythm," *Kansas City Star,* December 5, 1979.

29. Marty Robbins, interview with Bob Allen, February 12, 1981.

30. Marc Zakem, "Marty Robbins Did His Best to Fill in for Merle Haggard Despite Hecklers," *Louisville Courier Journal,* November 12, 1978.

31. Janet Robinson, telephone interview with author, February 7, 2010; Marizona Robinson, "Marty Robbins 75th Birthday Tribute," WSM Radio, September 26, 2000.

32. Noddin, telephone interview; Chandler, telephone interview.

33. Marty Robbins, *The Ralph Emery Show,* December 17, 1979, June 18, 1982.

Chapter 21. Into the '80s

1. Marty Robbins, interview with Bob Allen, Nashville, February 12, 1981.

2. Ronny Robbins, Marty Robbins band reunion, Nashville, July 18, 2009.

3. Marty Robbins, *The Ralph Emery Show,* WSM Radio, August 15, 1980.

4. Frank Sutherland, "Spring Construction Set on Music Row," *Tennessean,* October 18, 1968; Lucy Coldsnow Smith, telephone interview with author, November 12,

2009, email to author, December 31, 2009; Susan Scott, "Marty Robbins & His Hobby Cars," *Stock Car Racing*, September 1975, 15.

5. Mayf Nutter, telephone interview with author, October 19, 2006.

6. Ralph Emery, with Patsi Bale Cox, *The View from Nashville* (New York: William Morrow, 1998), 21; and Lucy Coldsnow Smith, telephone interview.

7. Jeanne Pruett, "Marty Robbins 75th Birthday Tribute," hosted by Eddie Stubbs, WSM Radio, Nashville, September 26, 2000; Steve DellaVecchia, telephone interview with author, April 7, 2010.

8. Okie Jones, telephone interview with author, May 25, 2007.

9. Jeff Chandler, telephone interview with author, January 3, 2010.

10. Marty Robbins, interview with Bob Allen, February 12, 1981.

11. Norman Wade, telephone interview with author, January 25, 2007.

12. Marty Robbins, *The Ralph Emery Show*, December 17, 1979, August 12, 1980.

13. Marty Robbins, interview with Bob Allen, February 12, 1981; Marty Robbins, *The Ralph Emery Show*, August 12, 1980.

14. Marty Robbins, *The Ralph Emery Show*, December 12, 1977, December 18, 1979.

15. "Celebrities Join in Festival Marking Reagan's Birthday," *Washington Post*, February 4, 1980; Conrad Noddin, telephone interview with author, December 29, 2009.

16. Laura Eipper, "Fans Favor Marty Robbins For Nine 'Cover' Awards, *Tennessean*, April 30, 1980.

17. Laura Eipper and Graeme Browning, "Fans Cite Stars At Awards," *Tennessean*, June 10, 1980; Bill Hance, "Marty's The Music Man According To His Fans," *Nashville Banner*, June 10, 1980.

18. Marty Robbins, *Miller and Company*, with host Dan Miller, TNN, early 1981; Jim Booth and Jim Albrecht, "Marty Robbins: Angry Patriot," *CountryStyle*, December 1980, 20.

19. Chandler, telephone interview.

20. Booth and Albrecht, "Marty Robbins: Angry Patriot," 19.

21. Marty Robbins band reunion.

22. Marty Robbins, interviews with Bob Allen, February 12, March 6, 1981.

23. Marty Robbins, *The Ralph Emery Show*, August 11, 1980.

24. Noddin, telephone interview.

25. Marty Robbins, *The Ralph Emery Show*, August 11, 1980.

26. Linda Cornett, "Marty Robbins: Something Unique in Country," *The Record Delta*, June 4, 1980.

27. Marty Robbins, *The Ralph Emery Show*, December 17, 1979; Carol Hutson Smith, email to author, March 25, 2010.

28. Carol Hutson Smith, email.

29. Marty Robbins, *The Ralph Emery Show,* December 21, 1979.

Chapter 22. NASCAR—Phase Two

1. Susan Scott, "Marty Robbins Gives Up Racing!" *Country Song Roundup,* November 1975, 10.
2. Bob Myers, "Marty's Magnum," *Circle Track,* January 1985, 64–65.
3. Marty Robbins, *The Ralph Emery Show,* WSM Radio, September 16, 1976.
4. Al Stilley, "The Indianapolis 500: Marty at the Helm," *Stock Car Racing,* October 1976, 28–30.
5. UltimateRacingHistory.com, http://www.ultimateracinghistory.com/racelist2 .php?uniqid=4889; "Manning Qualifies For Dixie 500," *Washington Post,* November 7, 1976.
6. Marty Robbins, *The Ralph Emery Show,* December 16, 1977.
7. UltimateRacingHistory.com; Myers, "Marty's Magnum," 64.
8. Marty Robbins, *The Ralph Emery Show,* December 17, 1979.
9. UltimateRacingHistory.com; Richard Petty, with William Neely, *King Richard I: The Autobiography of America's Greatest Auto Racer* (New York: MacMillan Publishing: 1986), 237.
10. UltimateRacingHistory.com; Marty Robbins, *The Ralph Emery Show,* August 12–13, 1980.
11. UltimateRacingHistory.com; Cotton Owens, telephone interview with author, December 7, 2006; Marty Robbins, interview with Bob Allen, Nashville, February 12, 1981.

Chapter 23. Super Legend

1. Marty Robbins, *Miller and Company,* with host Dan Miller, TNN, 1981.
2. Marty Robbins, *The Ralph Emery Show,* WSM Radio, October 26, 1981; Marty Robbins, telephone interview with Ralph Emery, WSM Radio, January 15, 1981; Marty Robbins, *Miller and Company.*
3. Laura Eipper Hill, "Marty Robbins In High Spirits Despite Heart Attack," *Tennessean,* January 8, 1981.
4. Marty Robbins, telephone interview with Emery.
5. Marty Robbins, *The Ralph Emery Show,* October 26, 1981.
6. Marty Robbins, telephone interview with Emery; "Marty's Mending," *Tennessean,* January 24, 1981.
7. Marty Robbins, telephone interview with Emery; Marty Robbins, *The Ralph Emery Show,* October 28, 1981.

8. Marty Robbins, telephone interview with Emery.

9. "A Robbins' Return," photo caption, *Nashville Banner,* January 17, 1981; "Marty's Mending," *Tennessean,* January 24, 1981; Marty Robbins, *Miller and Company.*

10. Marty Robbins, telephone interview with Emery.

11. Marty Robbins, interview with Bob Allen, Nashville, February 12, 1981; Eddie Kilroy, telephone interview with author, July 27, 2008.

12. Marty Robbins, interview with Bob Allen, February 12, 1981; Marty Robbins, *Miller and Company.*

13. Jeff Chandler, telephone interview with author, January 3, 2010; Bill Martinez, telephone interview with author, March 19, 2008.

14. Marty Robbins, interview with Bob Allen, February 12, 1981.

15. Bob Allen, "Marty Robbins: A Country Singer's Battle to Survive," *Hustler,* January 1982, 62.

16. Marty Robbins, interview with Bob Allen, February 12, 1981.

17. Marty Robbins, live performance at International Festival of Country Music, Wembley, England, April 18, 1981.

18. Marty Robbins, *Miller and Company.*

19. Chandler, telephone interview; Marty Robbins band reunion, Nashville, July 18, 2009.

20. Marty Robbins, *Miller and Company.*

21. Marty Robbins, interview with Bob Allen, February 12, 1981.

22. Marty Robbins, *Miller and Company.*

23. Marty Robbins, *The Ralph Emery Show,* October 26, 1981, June 18, 1982.

24. Stacy Harris, email to author, December 6, 2006.

25. Stacy Harris, "Marty Robbins: The Gunfighter Shoots Straight," *Country Song Roundup,* October 1981, 10.

26. Stacy Harris, "Marty Robbins, *Inside Country Music,* date unknown, 60.

27. Marty Robbins, *The Ralph Emery Show,* October 26, 1981.

28. Lynn Williams, "It's Hats Off to Marty Robbins," *Beaumont Enterprise,* October 19, 1981.

29. Marty Robbins, *The Ralph Emery Show,* October 28, 1981.

Chapter 24. No Plans of Quitting Any Time Soon

1. Wayne Jackson, telephone interview with author, October 31, 2006.

2. Marty Robbins, *Miller and Company,* with host Dan Miller, TNN, 1981; Marty Robbins, guest of Bill Mack, WBAP Radio, Fort Worth, TX, February 11, 1982.

3. Marty Robbins, *Miller and Company.*

4. Jim Hannaford, telephone interview with author, August 30, 2008, email to author, February 4, 2010.

5. Wayne Hobbs, telephone interview with author, October 24, 2006.

6. Marty Robbins, live performance at Silk Cut Festival, Wembley, England, April 14, 1982.

7. Jeff Chandler, telephone interview with author, January 3, 2010.

8. Conrad Noddin, telephone interview with author, December 29, 2009; Hannaford, telephone interview.

9. Chuck Morgan, telephone interview with author, July 11, 2008.

10. Marty Robbins, *The Ralph Emery Show*, WSM Radio, June 14–17, 1982.

11. Barbara Mandrell, *Marty Robbins: Super Legend*, VHS, Marty Robbins, Inc., 1989.

12. Marty Robbins, *The Ralph Emery Show*, June 15–18, 1982; Janet Robinson, telephone interview with author, February 7, 2010.

13. Marty Robbins, *The Ralph Emery Show*, June 18, 1982.

14. Joe Edwards, "Finalists Selected For 'Hall,'" *Tennessean*, July 3, 1982; Marty Robbins, interview with Ruud Hermans, *KRO Countrytime*, October 1982.

15. Cotton Owens, telephone interview with author, December 7, 2006; "His Anthem: Roar of the Engines Provides a Backup for Marty Robbins," *Detroit Free Press*, August 21, 1982; UltimateRacingHistory.com, http://www .ultimateracinghistory.com/racelist2.php?uniqid=4889; "Rising NASCAR Star Takes Pole," *Detroit Free Press*, August 22, 1982.

16. Marty Robbins, *The Ralph Emery Show*, June 17, 1982.

17. Marty Robbins, *Talking Country*, with host Charlie Cooke, KLAC Radio, Los Angeles, November 18, 1982.

18. Marty Robbins, *The Ralph Emery Show*, June 14–15, 1982.

19. Larry Jordan, email to author, May 28, 2007.

20. Gary Adams, telephone interview with author, September 2, 2008; Hobbs, telephone interview; Bill Martinez, telephone interview with author, March 19, 2008.

21. Mike Cutright, telephone interview with author, August 27, 2008.

22. Adams, telephone interview.

23. Hobbs, telephone interview.

24. Adams, telephone interview.

25. Hannaford, telephone interview.

26. Country Music Association awards show, October 11, 1982, video excerpt shown in *Marty Robbins: Super Legend* (1989).

27. Marty Robbins, interview with Hermans.

28. Marty Robbins, *Talking Country*.

29. Morgan, telephone interview.

30. Doug Green, telephone interview with author, June 4, 2007.

31. Marty Robbins, interview with Rodger Beard, Gibson County (Indiana) Fairgrounds, July 1982.

32. Cutright, telephone interview.

33. Bob Myers, "Marty's Magnum," *Circle Track,* January 1985, 65.

34. Marty Robbins, *Talking Country.*

35. Marty Robbins, *Talking Country.*

Chapter 25. "I'll Be Drifting Home"

1. Sandy Neese, "Producer Remembers Last Days With Marty," *Tennessean,* December 11, 1982.

2. Mike Cutright, telephone interview with author, August 27, 2008; and Gary Adams, telephone interview with author, September 2, 2008.

3. Jack Pruett, telephone interview with author, November 5, 2006.

4. Wayne Hobbs, telephone interview with author, October 24, 2006.

5. Adams, telephone interview; Cutright, telephone interview; Hobbs, telephone interview.

6. Cotton Owens, telephone interview with author, December 7, 2006; Bob Myers, "Marty's Magnum," *Circle Track,* January 1985, 64–65.

7. Ronny Robbins, telephone interview with author, February 11, 2010, email to author, January 13, 2010.

8. Bill Snyder and Red O'Donnell, "Marty Robbins Critical After 2nd Heart Operation," *Nashville Banner,* December 3, 1982; Ronny Robbins, telephone interview.

9. Snyder and O'Donnell, "Marty Robbins Critical After 2nd Heart Operation."

10. Hobbs, telephone interview.

11. Bill Snyder, "Pump Aids Marty Robbins' Heart," *Nashville Banner,* December 6, 1982; "Marty Robbins' Condition Drops," *Tennessean,* December 5, 1982.

12. "Marty Robbins Reported Still in Critical Condition," *Tennessean,* December 6, 1982; Bill Snyder, "Doctor: Odds Against Marty Robbins' Recovery," *Nashville Banner,* December 6, 1982.

13. Janet Robinson, telephone interview with author, February 7, 2010.

14. Sandy Daens, telephone interview with author, May 20, 2008.

15. Joe Vaughn, reporting for ABC Informational News, *Burrelle's Radio Clips,* December 7, 1982, 12:05 AM MST.

16. Bill Snyder, "Robbins' Condition Worsens Overnight," *Nashville Banner,* December 7, 1982; Lamar F. Jackson, Jr., Director of Public Affairs, Saint Thomas Hospital, letter to Carol Hutson, December 14, 1982.

17. Ronny Robbins, telephone interview.

18. Bill Snyder, "Robbins' Pump Rate to Be Cut," *Nashville Banner*, December 8, 1982; Cutright, telephone interview.

19. "Marty Robbins Has Many Local Friends," *Glendale News*, December 8, 1982; Snyder, "Robbins' Pump Rate to Be Cut"; Ronny Robbins, telephone interview.

20. Janet Robinson, telephone interview.

21. "Singer Marty Robbins Dies After Heart Attack," *Boston Globe*, December 9, 1982; Chuck Morgan, telephone interview with author, July 11, 2008; Cutright, telephone interview.

22. Jackson, letter to Carol Hutson.

23. Janet Robinson, telephone interview.

Chapter 26. Some Memories Just Won't Die

1. Frances Meeker, "Marty's Songs 'Touched Soul of America,'" *Nashville Banner*, December 11, 1982.

2. Janet Robinson, telephone interview with author, February 7, 2010.

3. Ronny Robbins, telephone interview with author, February 11, 2010.

4. Carol Hutson Smith, email to author, March 25, 2010.

5. Ronny Robbins, telephone interview; Bill Hudgins, "Loved Ones Pay Robbins Respects," *Nashville Banner*, December 10, 1982; Bill Snyder, "Scores File by Robbins' Casket Today," *Nashville Banner*, December 10, 1982; Meeker, "Marty's Songs 'Touched Soul of America.'"

6. Jeff Chandler, telephone interview with author, January 3, 2010.

7. Meeker, "Marty's Songs 'Touched Soul of America.'"

8. Sandy Daens, telephone interview with author, May 20, 2008.

9. John "Jay Dee" Hoag, telephone interview with author, December 28, 2009.

10. Doris Fjelstad, *Pen Friends*, Number 76, January 1983; "Marty Robbins Wins Music Awards," *Washington Post*, June 7, 1983.

11. Daens, telephone interview.

Index

Music in American Life

Diane Diekman, a retired U.S. Navy captain, is the author of *Live Fast, Love Hard: The Faron Young Story*; *Navy Greenshirt: A Leader Made, Not Born*; and *A Farm in the Hidewood: My South Dakota Home.*

The University of Illinois Press
is a founding member of the
Association of American University Presses.

University of Illinois Press
1325 South Oak Street
Champaign, IL 61820-6903
www.press.uillinois.edu